Adirondack Wildlife

DISCARD

Adirondack Wildlife

A FIELD GUIDE

James Ryan

UNIVERSITY OF NEW HAMPSHIRE PRESS

Durham, New Hampshire

Published by University Press of New England
Hanover and London

UNIVERSITY OF NEW HAMPSHIRE PRESS
Published by University Press of New England,
One Court Street, Lebanon, NH 03766
www.upne.com

Printed in the United States of America
5   4   3   2   1

Photo and illustration credits: The Adirondack fish illustrations were produced by Ellen Edmondson and Hugh Chrisp for the New York Biological Survey, 1927–1940. They were used by permission and are held in trust for the people of NY State by the New York State Archives, New York State Museum, and the New York State Department of Environmental Conservation. The bat illustrations were drawn by the author. The photographs of the water snake, timber rattlesnake, and red-backed salamander are courtesy of M. Pingleton. The star-nosed mole photograph is courtesy of K. Catania. The remaining photographs are from iStockphoto.com, BigStockPhoto.com, PhotoDisc, Fotolia.com, and Shutterstock.com.

LIBRARY OF CONGRESS CATALOGING-IN-PUBLICATION DATA

Ryan, James.
  Adirondack wildlife : a field guide / James Ryan.
    p.   cm.
Includes bibliographical references and index.
ISBN 978–1–58465–749–1 (pbk. : alk. paper)
  1. Animals — New York (State) — Adirondack Park. 2. Biotic communities — New York (State) — Adirondack Park. 3. Adirondack Park (N.Y.) I. Title.
  QL195.R93   2008
  591.9747'5 — dc22   2008038614

To my parents, Joyce and Bill, who allowed a boy
free rein to explore the woods and waters
of the Adirondacks.

Contents

Acknowledgments

I am indebted to the professionals and friends who were kind enough to review parts of the manuscript for this book. They include Stephanie Bishop and Professors Brooks McKinney and Elizabeth Newell from Hobart and William Smith Colleges. Fisheries biologist Doug Carlson provided many valuable comments on Adirondack fish species. Ed Woltmann and Doug Carlson of the New York State Department of Environmental Conservation were kind enough to guide me through the process of obtaining permission to reprint the beautiful illustrations of fish. The original color images of the fishes of New York were prepared by Ellen Edmondson and Hugh Chrisp as part of the New York Biological Survey conducted from 1927 to 1940. These images are held in trust for the people of the State of New York by the New York State Museum, New York State Archives, and the New York State Department of Environmental Conservation and may not be used in any fashion without permission of the aforementioned.

I am also grateful to Nathan Burch of the Finger Lakes Institute for preparing the beautiful Adirondack maps. His expertise in GIS software and his eye for detail was invaluable. In addition, I wish to thank Mike Pingleton for providing photographs of the timber rattlesnake, water snake, and red-backed salamander. Professor Ken Catania of Vanderbilt University kindly provided permission to reprint his photograph of the star-nosed mole.

I want to thank my editor Ellen Wicklum at University Press of New England for understanding my vision and for her enthusiastic support of the project. Finally, I wish to thank my family and friends for providing support and encouragement throughout the writing of this book. My wife Gillian and my daughter Kaylee, in particular, gave up many hours of family time to allow me to work on this book—your support is priceless.

1 A Brief History of the Adirondacks

GEOLOGIC HISTORY

The Adirondacks are curious mountains. On the one hand, they are built of rock that formed under tremendous heat and pressure some 1.1 billion years ago. On the other hand, like many younger mountain ranges, the Adirondacks are still rising at a rate of roughly 3 millimeters a year. Unlike most mountain ranges that form long chains of peaks, the Adirondacks form a nearly circular dome of peaks. Furthermore, huge boulders, called glacial erratics, lie strewn about the Adirondacks, suggesting that the entire region was once buried beneath a thick ice sheet. How can we reconcile these disparate facts?

The Adirondacks tell a fascinating geologic story that begins nearly 2 billion years ago. The rocks that now make up the Adirondacks had yet to be formed; in their place were thick coastal sediments of mud and sand. Over the course of hundreds of millions of years, these sediments created sedimentary rocks several miles thick. Fed by melting processes at great depths, a variety of magmas intruded into this pile of overlying sediments. Roughly 1.3 billion years ago, these rocks were involved in a collision with an adjacent continent. As the continents slammed together, they folded, distorted, buried, and cooked the sedimentary and intruded igneous rocks, creating metamorphic rocks with new mineral compositions and textures. These rocks belong to what is known as the Grenville Province. The collision forced these rocks upward into mountains, called the Grenville Mountains, which may have towered above today's Himalayas. Over the next 650 million years, the Grenville Mountains were eroded completely to a relatively flat band along what would become the east coast of North America. During this process, more than 12 miles (20 kilometers) of rock was eroded away, exposing the once deeply buried rocks beneath. At this point in time, the continents began to pull apart, forming a new ocean in between. During the Cambrian, some 570 million years ago, much of what is now New York State, including the eroded roots of the Grenville Mountains, was covered by a shallow coastal sea. Thick sediments buried the Grenville rocks. Over the next 300 million years or so, the continents reversed direction and closed in on one another several times, building mountains in the process. The Catskills and Appalachian Mountains were formed during these periods. In the last 60 million years, the Grenville-age rocks, along with an overlying blanket of sedimentary rocks, formed a dome as the Adirondack region was uplifted. The weaker sedimentary rocks on top were eroded away, exposing the Grenville-age rocks below; it is these ancient Grenville rocks that form the Adirondack Mountains. The present Adirondack Mountains form a shallow bulge roughly 150 miles across (see map 1.1). Thus, although the rocks that form the Adirondacks are very old, the mountains themselves are quite young and still growing. Furthermore, the Adirondacks form a unique range entirely separate from the Catskills and Appalachian Mountains.

The doming of the Adirondacks was not the only event to shape the mountains. Once formed, the Adirondacks were sculpted by Pleistocene ice sheets. Roughly a million years ago, the Earth entered a period of climatic oscillations, resulting in the repeated advance and retreat of several continental ice sheets. The last major ice sheet began its southward advance some 80,000 years ago. At this time, Earth's mean annual temperature was approximately 5°C (41°F) cooler than it is today. The resulting Wisconsin glacial period ended roughly 6,000 years ago. During this time, sea levels dropped, as more and more evaporated water

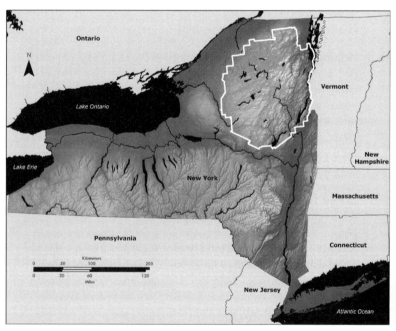

Map 1.1 *Shaded relief map of New York State showing the Adirondack Park boundary in white. The Adirondacks are a dome of mountains in the northeastern part of New York State. Higher elevations appears as lighter shades of gray.*

Introduction

The 6-million-acre Adirondack Park in Upstate New York is home to over 2,800 lakes and ponds, more than 30,000 miles of running water, and terrestrial communities ranging from lowland swamps to alpine meadows. The Adirondacks are also rich in wildlife. These mountains are home to countless insect species, from annoying black flies to spectacularly beautiful butterflies. Nineteen species of amphibians and another 16 reptile species inhabit the Adirondack Park. Some species occur throughout the park, while others, such as the timber rattlesnake, are restricted to isolated pockets of habitat. Both North America's smallest mammal, the tiny pygmy shrew (weighing as little as 3 grams), and one of its largest mammals, the moose, call the Adirondacks home. The most visible of Adirondack wildlife are its 220 bird species, some of which spend little time in the Adirondacks as they migrate through in spring and fall. Most are summer residents that return to court mates and raise young. A few bird species are year-round residents capable of surviving the harsh Adirondack winters.

Adirondack Wildlife is divided into two sections, plus an extensive glossary defining all the terms used. Part 1 introduces the history and habitats of the Adirondack Park. This section begins with a brief history of the Adirondack Park, covering both its geologic and political record. This section explains what geological forces drove the formation of the Adirondack Mountains, and the political realities that compelled the state to protect its northern forests. This chapter is not designed to cover all of the rich and fascinating history of the Adirondacks, but instead to whet your appetite to learn more.

The next two chapters take the reader on a journey through Adirondack habitats. Chapter 2 describes the forest communities, beginning above timberline and descending through the conifer and hardwood forests. Chapter 3 explores the park's streams, lakes, and wetlands. Along the way, you will discover what ecological processes shape and maintain each environment. The goal is to allow you to "read the land" and better understand why certain animals and plants are found within each habitat and not in others. The book does not cover individual plant species in detail; that would require a book in itself.

Part 2 introduces the wildlife of the Adirondack Park in an easy-to-understand series of species accounts. This section allows for quick and easy species identifications and provides a source of additional life history information. Chapters are organized by taxonomic group, beginning with the ubiquitous and often overlooked invertebrates. Chapter 4 describes only the most common invertebrate species, but should be enough to awaken the naturalist within. It will help you answer such questions as "What just bit me?" and "Why do only female mosquitoes feed on blood?"

The remaining four chapters cover the common vertebrates: fish, amphibians and reptiles, birds, and mammals. There are many North American field guides for each group; the goal here is to introduce the species present in the Adirondack region. On any given hike or paddle, you may want to identify one salamander, six birds, and one or two small mammals. Instead of having to refer to two or three different field guides, you can identify them all with this one guide. Each species, regardless of size or abundance, has a unique and fascinating story to tell. This guide is designed to introduce you to these stories by allowing you to identify the storyteller. Tuck it away in your daypack and carry it with you as you explore the trails and waterways of this spectacular park.

I · The History and Habitats

fell as snow that failed to melt and return the water to the oceans. Advancing glaciers joined together, forming a single massive ice sheet that covered all of Canada and extended southward into the midwestern and northeastern United States. Virtually all of New York State was buried beneath thousands of feet of ice and snow.

The advancing ice sheet captured loose rocks and soils and carried the accumulated debris hundreds of miles. In the process, the embedded boulders, rocks, and pebbles scoured away vegetation and soils and abraded the underlying bedrock. Because all the summits were covered in ice, even the rugged Adirondack peaks were rounded over in the process. As the millennia passed, temperatures gradually warmed and the vast ice sheets began to retreat northward. At the southern edge of the retreating ice sheet, melting ice formed huge lakes and dumped enormous piles of accumulated gravel and sand. At higher elevations in the Adirondacks, hundreds of smaller glaciers remained in the valleys as the ice sheet broke up. These local glaciers continued to erode the valley walls, until, eventually, they also melted away.

Evidence of Pleistocene glaciation is abundant in the Adirondacks. Huge boulders, bearing no resemblance to local rocks, were dropped as the glaciers carrying them disappeared. These glacial "erratics" can be seen throughout the Adirondacks, even on the summits of several high peaks. In addition, prominent scratches and gouges in the bedrock bear testament to the abrasive power of glaciers. The smaller valley glaciers also worked the underlying bedrock into U-shaped valleys with cirques (steep-walled bowls) at the head of the valley. The west-facing valley of Giant Mountain is a classic example of a glacially carved cirque that continues to erode as massive rock slides expose the steep walls.

Lakes and ponds also provide evidence for the Adirondacks' glacial past. Glaciers transport rocks and debris from the head of the valley to its base. Here, at the nose of the glacier, the debris is released to form terminal moraines. Terminal moraines may create natural dams that capture meltwater and form lakes. Lake Placid is one example of a lake formed by a moraine at its southwestern end. Just north of Glens Falls, a glacial moraine impounded the waters of Lake George. Star Lake in the western Adirondacks illustrates a different type of glacial deposit; a pair of eskers. Eskers are long, sinuous mounds of sand and pebbles that form when streams of meltwater tunnel through a glacier. Like most streams, they carry sand and other debris with them as they flow downslope. As the glacier retreats, the debris remains, forming low mounds that mark the path of the former stream channel. Star Lake is nearly split in two by an esker that forms a long, narrow peninsula extending northward from the south shore of the lake. A second, smaller esker forms an island in the eastern section of the lake. Both eskers are now forested, but evidence of a glacial past is found in their sandy sediments. Finally, kettle hole lakes are among the most interesting of glacial formations. As the ice sheet broke up and retreated northward, massive ice blocks were left behind in depressions at the face of the glacier. These stranded icebergs were then buried by glacial debris carried over them by glacial streams. Over time, these entombed icebergs slowly melted and the overlying sediments sank to the bottom of the depression, forming a kettle hole. Kettle hole ponds and lakes are oval or circular in shape, lack an obvious inlet and outlet stream, and, instead, are fed by rainwater, snowmelt, and a high water table. Ice House Pond and Helldiver Pond in the Moose River Recreation Area are among the many examples of Adirondack kettle hole ponds.

It is important to remember that only 10,000 years ago there was no Adirondack flora or fauna. The Adirondack region was buried beneath thousands of feet of ice. When the ice finally retreated, only barren rock, cold mountain streams, and sterile lakes and ponds remained. Thus, the plants and animals that inhabit the Adirondack wilderness today are relatively recent colonists.

The rebirth of the Adirondack forests was a slow process. Winds blowing across the barren landscape dropped soil particles into rocky crevices, which, over time, created the first patches of soil. With time, lichens colonized the exposed rocks and the seeds of cold-tolerant pioneer plants became established in the thin soil among the rocks. With each season, more and more organic matter was added until the soils were thick and nutrient-rich enough to support a more diverse array of boreal plants. The reestablishment of diverse plant communities on once barren rock is called "primary succession," and it probably occurred several times in the Adirondacks as Pleistocene ice sheets advanced and retreated. Cold-adapted animals also followed the retreating ice sheets northward in search of food, new territories, and mates. Thus, today's plant and animal communities are a reflection of the geologic and climatic history of the Adirondack Mountains. No wonder naturalists refer to the Adirondacks as "young mountains from old rocks."

HUMAN HISTORY

The Pleistocene epoch brought more than freezing temperatures and thick ice sheets. It also brought humans to North America. As temperatures plummeted, ice sheets formed, locking up much of the available water as ice. The result was that sea levels dropped some 300 feet, exposing vast areas of sea floor and creating new coastlines. Nowhere was this more important than in the Bering Sea between Alaska and eastern Siberia. The growing ice sheets and falling sea levels created a land bridge that united Siberia and Alaska. Over subsequent millennia, small bands of humans followed herds of large mammals across this land bridge from Asia to North America. These "First Americans" dispersed widely across the continent over several millennia.

Long before Europeans arrived in the region, several tribes belonging to the Iroquois language family settled in and around the Adirondacks. Foremost among them were the Mohawks, who seasonally inhabited much of the central Adirondacks. The Oneidas inhabited the western Adirondacks, including the Tug Hill plateau. Several other groups, belonging to the Algonquin language family, lived along the St. Lawrence River valley, the western shore of Lake Champlain, and in the Hudson River valley below Lake George.

Among the first Europeans to visit the region was Samuel de Champlain, a Frenchman, who explored the St. Lawrence River region in the early 1600s. In 1609, he mapped Lake Champlain with the aid of a large contingent of Native Americans, including the Wyandot (the French called them Hurons) and members of several Algonquin-speaking tribes. Champlain was instrumental in establishing a foothold for the French in what is now Quebec. He also brought the fur trade to the Adirondack Mountains.

By 1750, the French colony of New France extended from Newfoundland to Louisiana and included western New York and the northwestern half of the Adirondacks. The British claimed New England, the southeastern part of New York State, and most of the Atlantic states as far south as Georgia. Both France and England ignored native land claims as each sought to expand its fur-trading empire. Ultimately, their competition escalated into the French and Indian War. From 1754 to 1763, the French and their Huron and Algonquin-speaking allies fought running battles against the British, who were allied with the Iroquois Confederacy. In 1760, after several early victories, the French surrendered to the British. However, British control over the region was short-lived. In 1775, the colonists, tired of British rule, revolted, starting the American Revolutionary War.

The period following the Revolutionary War was one of exploration and expansion. The fur trade already had brought trappers and hunters to the Adirondacks, but now loggers and farmers began to settle in the mountains. Shortly thereafter, miners arrived, as iron ore deposits were discovered in Tahawas and the Champlain Valley. Land was cleared to create farmlands, iron mines, and the railroads. The rich forests of the Adirondacks, however, faced the greatest threat from loggers. By the late 1800s, loggers had pushed deep into the interior of the Adirondacks in search of timber. Many of the larger rivers were choked with millions of logs floating downstream toward the many sawmills that appeared around the margins of the mountains.

Despite the rapid extraction of minerals, timber, and furs from the Adirondacks, the region had yet to be surveyed or mapped. In 1872, Verplank Colvin, an Albany lawyer and engineer, received a commission from the New York State government to map the Adirondack wilderness. By the end of 1873, he and his survey teams had mapped much of the region and established the altitudes of many of the High Peaks. In his influential report to the New York State legislature, he argued forcefully that the Adirondack Mountains needed protection in order to preserve the watersheds that supplied water to the Erie Canal, a vital trade route at the time. Colvin continued his surveys, often at his own expense, for over a decade. He also tirelessly lobbied the state legislatures for protection of these important wilderness areas. Finally, in 1885, New York State amended the constitution to establish the Adirondack Forest Preserve. The amendment, under Article 14, reads in part, "The lands of the State, now owned or hereafter acquired, constituting the Forest Preserve as now fixed by law, shall be forever kept as wild forest lands. They shall not be leased, sold or exchanged, or be taken by any corporation, public or private, nor shall the timber thereon be sold, removed, or destroyed." Now known as the "Forever Wild" amendment (or Article 14), the Adirondack Forest Preserve Act of 1885 established constitutional protection for state lands in the Adirondacks.

Although Article 14 established protection for the Adirondack wilderness, it did not effectively define the limits of the Forest Preserve. It wasn't until 1892 that the State established the Adirondack Park boundary. The original park encompassed 2.8 million acres in the central and western Adirondacks, but excluded the more heavily populated agricultural and mining areas along the eastern Adirondacks (see map 1.2). The "Blue Line," as it came to be known from the color of the boundary line on maps, has changed considerably since that time. By 1931, the "Blue Line" included another 1.5 million acres to the north and east to the shore of Lake Champlain. Today, the Adirondack Park contains 6.1 million acres of state and private lands, making it the largest park in the continental United States.

Administration and management of state lands within the Adirondack Park fell to the Department of Environmental Conservation

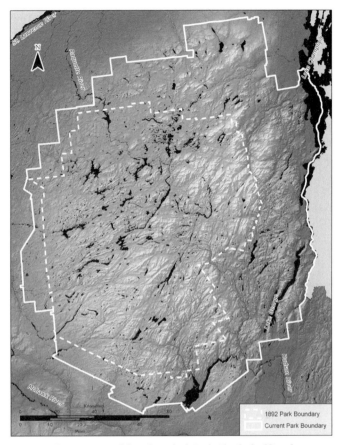

Map 1.2 *Elevation map of the Adirondack Park. The dashed line denotes the original 1892 park boundary. The solid line represents the park boundary today.*

(DEC), while private lands were administered by local towns or lacked management entirely. Thus land use policies, rules, and enforcement varied dramatically across the region. Finally, in the 1970s, a temporary commission was established to create a unified master plan for the Adirondack Park. The commission recommended, among other things, the establishment of an independent Adirondack Park Agency (APA) to oversee both state and private lands within the park. The APA, established in 1971, subsequently created nine land classifications based on degree of recreational use, human impact, and other practical considerations. The result was that large tracts were set aside as wilderness, wild forests, or primitive areas, each with strict rules of use. APA's subsequent strict enforcement of these rules led to considerable discontent among many Adirondack residents who felt their property and livelihoods were in jeopardy. The 11-member board of the APA remains unpopular among some Adirondack residents, but it continues to play an important role in designing long-range plans, reviewing permits, and enforcing laws for lands within the park.

THE ADIRONDACK PARK

At 6.1 million acres (9,531 square miles), the Adirondack Park is the size of New Hampshire and larger than the states of New Jersey, Connecticut, Delaware, and Rhode Island. By contrast, the 2.2-million-acre Yellowstone National Park is only one-third the size of the Adirondack Park. Approximately 42 percent, or 2.8 million acres, are public lands owned and managed by New York State. The Adirondack Master Plan divided these lands into seven land classifications: wilderness, primitive, wild forest, canoe area, intensive use area, historic area, and State administrative areas.

"Wilderness" areas are those that exhibit little or no human impact and are of sufficient size, usually greater than 10,000 acres, to maintain their natural state. No motor vehicles or powered equipment are permitted in wilderness areas. Recreational activities are limited to hiking, camping, and other low-impact activities. Nearly 1.1 million acres of the park are designated as wilderness areas.

"Primitive" areas are relatively pristine forests that do not meet the wilderness classification because they contain human structures, are smaller than 10,000 acres, or are adjacent to villages or other private lands. Less than 2 percent (45,670 acres) of state lands within the park are classified as primitive areas. "Wild Forest" areas, by contrast, are those with a larger human footprint. These forests may have been logged or may be used heavily for recreational activities such as snowmobiling, cross-country skiing, and hiking. Wild Forests constitute 46 percent of the state lands within the park. "Canoe Areas," comprising some 17,600 acres, include waterways and surrounding forests where lakes, ponds, and rivers permit significant canoe routes through relatively pristine wilderness (see map 1.3).

The state also manages 45 campgrounds and several day-use areas in the Adirondack Park, along with two large ski areas at Gore Mountain and Whiteface Mountain. These areas have parking lots, public restrooms, beaches, and other infastructure that supports a high degree of human activity. Such "Intensive Use" areas constitute less than 1 percent of public lands. The remaining 37,000 acres are "His-

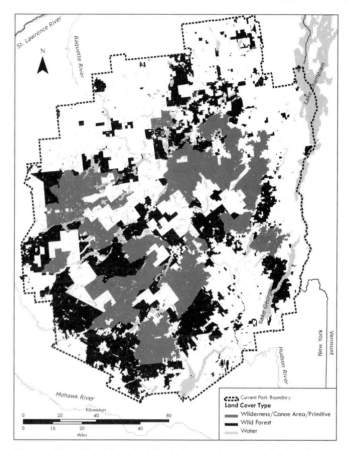

Map 1.3 *Map of the Adirondack Park showing the patchwork of public and private lands. Public lands are grouped here into two categories: Wild Forest Lands; and a combination of Wilderness Areas, Primitive Areas, and Canoe Areas.*

toric Areas," such as state-owned great camps and fire towers; "State Administrative Areas," which include prisons, fish hatcheries, and state-owned research facilities; or are areas that are currently pending classification.

The 2.8 million acres of public lands are woven together with over 3 million acres of privately held land. The largest private holdings include vast tracts of forests owned by pulp and timber companies, such as Finch Pruyn and International Paper. Private clubs, universities, and conservation organizations also own substantial tracts within the park. Finally, some 130,000 permanent residents and another 110,000 seasonal residents own property, houses, and businesses in the 105 towns inside the Blue Line.

Today's Adirondack Park remains a work in progress. The present Blue Line is unlikely to change in the future, but the percentage of public lands within the park continues to increase as New York State, with help from conservation organizations, acquires important parcels of wilderness. For example, New York State purchased the Whitney Tract near Tupper Lake in 1997. In 2003, The Open Space Institute acquired the 10,000-acre Tahawus Tract near Newcomb. Another 161,000 acres of forest, largely between Long Lake and Schroon Lake, was acquired recently from Fynch Pruyn by The Nature Conservancy.

The Adirondack Park, with its 6.1 million acres of gentle hills, 46 High Peaks, 2,800 lakes and ponds, and over 30,000 miles of rivers and streams, will continue to evolve as a natural area.

SOURCES AND ADDITIONAL READING

Isachsen, Y. W. 2000. *Geology of New York: A Simplified Account*, 2nd edition. Albany, NY: New York State Museum, No. 28.

Jaffe, H., and E. Jaffe. 1986. *Geology of the Adirondack High Peaks Region: A Hiker's Guide*. Glens Falls, NY: The Adirondack Mountain Club.

Jenkins, J. C., and A. Keal. 2004. *The Adirondack Atlas: A Geographic Portrait of the Adirondack Park*. Syracuse, NY: Syracuse University Press.

Schneider, P. 1998. *The Adirondacks: A History of America's First Wilderness*. New York: Henry Holt and Company.

Terrie, P. G. 1999. *Contested Terrain: A New History of Nature and People in the Adirondacks*. Syracuse, NY: Syracuse University Press.

Van Diver, B. 1985. *Roadside Geology of New York*. Missoula: Mountain Press Publishing Company.

2 Forest Communities

Hikers ascending Algonquin Peak or Mount Marcy pass through several ecological communities in relatively quick succession. At about 2,500 feet in elevation, they reach the spruce-fir zone. Here, red spruce and balsam fir create almost pure stands. Continuing up to approximately 3,200 feet, hikers emerge from the spruce-fir forest into a transition zone that consists of gnarled, stunted trees and is called the sub-alpine zone. Finally, the summit comes into view at the timberline. Timberline, the elevation above which trees cannot survive, occurs at approximately 4,000 feet in the Adirondacks. The remainder of the hike is through the alpine zone, where there is no cover from the sun, wind, or rain.

THE ALPINE ZONE

On a clear day, the view from the summit of Mount Marcy, New York's highest peak, is stunning. To the east, the peaks of Haystack, Saddleback, and Basin loom into view. To the north are Phelps, Tabletop, and Big Slide mountains. Wright, Algonquin, Colden, Iroquois, and Marshall frame the western skyline. To the south, Skylight looks deceptively close. In fact, when the weather permits, one can see nearly all of the 46 Adirondack High Peaks from the summit of Mount Marcy. Unfortunately, on many days the summit is buried in clouds and mist, and the only view is of the spectacular and unique alpine community at your feet.

Alpine communities are the tundra of the continental United States. Tundra refers to both an ecosystem and a type of vegetation. As an ecosystem, tundra can be either arctic or alpine. Either way, tundra is characterized by low temperatures, a short growing season, low rainfall, and constant winds. Alpine tundra is a zone of sparse ground cover interspersed with patches of bare rock above the timberline. Alpine tundra is rare east of the Rocky Mountains; it is found in isolated patches on a handful of the Adirondack High Peaks, Mount Mansfield in Vermont, the Presidential Range in New Hampshire, and Maine's Mount Katahdin. Of the more than 6 million acres comprising the Adirondack Park, only about 40 acres on ten summits are considered alpine tundra (see Table 2.1).

Timberline is not a simple matter of elevation. After all, timberline is nearly 12,000 feet above sea level in the Colorado Rockies but drops to about 4,000 feet in the Mackenzie Mountains in Canada's

Table 2.1 The number of acres of alpine plants on ten Adirondack summits

Mountain	Elevation	Acres of Alpine Plants
Marcy	5,344	6.6
Algonquin	5,114	14.4
Boundary	4,840	2.0
Haystack	4,960	7.4
Skylight	4,926	1.9
Iroquois	4,840	2.6
Basin	4,827	0.6
Gothics	4,736	0.8
Colden	4,714	0.9
Wright	4,580	2.9
Total		40.1

Source: Data are from the New York State Department of Environmental Conservation's 1999 High Peaks Unit Management Plan.

Yukon Territory. Even elevation and latitude together do not tell the whole story. Timberline is about 5,000 feet in the Olympic Mountains of Washington State, but at the same latitude (47.5° N) in Montana's Glacier National Park, timberline is over 8,000 feet. Furthermore, timberline on a given mountain is substantially lower on the cooler, north-facing slope than on the sun-exposed, southern slope.

Timberline is determined by a combination of conditions, such as low temperatures, frequent frosts, high winds, heavy snow pack, in-adequate precipitation during the short growing season, poor soils, and lower seed production and viability. In fact, the timberline is rarely a line at all. Rather, it is an irregular zone where the subalpine forest transitions into treeless alpine tundra. Boulders, cliffs, and fissures, coupled with the uneven distribution of snow, provide modest areas of protection from the scouring winds. Small clusters of stunted trees form tree islands, and where branches are exposed to the brutal winds, only the leeward branches survive, forming a "flag tree." In more exposed areas, natural forces may shape a forest of dwarf spruce and fir trees that hug the ground in prostrate mats. This is called the krummholz zone (see figure 2.1). Krummholz grows only as tall as the insulating snow layer permits. Above the krummholz zone, environmental conditions are so severe that trees cannot survive.

Summertime temperatures at the summit of Mount Marcy are often 30°F (17°C) cooler than in the valleys below. At higher elevations,

Figure 2.1 *View from the summit of East Dix Mountain. Note the clusters of dwarf conifers called krummholz in the foreground.*

the atmospheric pressure is lower, and the expanding air cools rapidly as it ascends; on average, temperatures drop 3°F with each increase of 1,000 feet. In the winter, summit temperatures below –60°F combined with howling winds produce a murderous environment for all but the best-adapted plants.

Where trees are unable to grow, life still survives because alpine plants have adapted themselves to the harsh conditions near the summit. Adirondack alpine communities include a variety of lichens, mosses, sedges, grasses, alpine wildflowers, and stunted shrubs (heathers and heaths). The High Peaks Unit Management Plan developed by the state Department of Environmental Conservation in 1999 lists ten peaks with alpine communities comprising a total of only 40.1 acres (see table 2.1). Alpine and subalpine plants live on other peaks over 4,500 feet in the Adirondacks but do not form complete alpine communities.

Wind-battered and buried under snow for up to nine months of the year, these alpine plants make the most of the short growing season. As soon as temperatures nudge above freezing, many alpine plants begin absorbing nutrients and water from their roots and are able to carry out photosynthesis; some species begin photosynthesis while still covered with a blanket of snow. This early growth is made possible by reserves of starch and sugars stored in the roots during the long winter months. As growth begins again in the spring, these reserves are converted rapidly into new tissue for growth, flower production, and seed formation. A few species get a head start by forming flower buds during the previous summer, protecting the buds over winter, and flowering quickly during snowmelt.

The most obvious adaptation of alpine plants is their tiny size. Hugging the ground keeps them out of the wind and their small size requires less energy for new growth. Although the entire plant may be no larger than a penny, the flowers remain of normal size. Low-growth forms and streamlined shapes are common in the windswept alpine zone. These shapes allow wind to pass harmlessly over the surface of the plant and at the same time expose the maximum leaf surface area to the sun. The protected inner region is often several degrees warmer than the air above the plant, which warms the roots and allows an earlier start. In addition, the inner parts are also shielded from the drying winds.

Unlike annuals, which need to grow, flower, and set seed all in one growing season, alpine plants tend to be perennials and simply build on the existing parts. In particularly bad years, alpine perennials may not produce any flowers. They can afford to wait until next year, whereas annuals cannot. Indeed, some alpine plants may be ten years old before they have the energy reserves to produce their first flowers. Other plants, such as mountain sandwort (*Minuartia groenlandica*), tend to form spreading mats that are able to root vegetatively. Branches at the outer edge of the mat touch the ground and are anchored in place by roots that are produced by the branch itself.

Other strategies for alpine survival are less common. Labrador tea (*Ledum groenlandica*), for example, feels wooly to the touch because its leaves are covered with tiny hair-like structures that provide a measure of insulation while also reducing evaporation. One plant, the viviparous alpine bistort (*Bistorta vivipara*), builds a stalk of tiny white flowers with bulbets below. The tiny bulbets fall to the ground and sprout into new plants just like a tulip bulb planted in the garden. In another strange twist, some alpine plants produce large quantities of a red pigment called anthocyanin (they also produce the green pigment chlorophyll) that is capable of using light to produce small amounts of heat to warm the plant.

The Adirondack alpine zone is a montage of grasses, wildflowers, heaths, and dwarf trees. The distribution of the various plants is patchy. Some of the plants prefer the shelter of the subalpine forest and only sneak into the alpine zone in protected locations. Wildflowers, such as false hellebore, goldthread, bunchberry, starflower, and narrow-leaved gentians, are not truly alpine plants, but do spread into the alpine zone at selected sites.

Mosses and heaths are typical lowland bog species that also make a home in the alpine zone because many of the environmental conditions are the same. Both alpine and bog soils are highly acidic and often water-saturated. In both habitats, sphagnum moss, which further acidifies the soils, is an abundant ground cover. For these reasons, alpine communities are often called elevated bogs. Many species of heath, including Labrador tea, bog laurel, leatherleaf, and small cranberry, among others, are bog-loving species that also grow above timberline in the Adirondacks. Other species are true alpine plants; they do not occur at lower elevations but often occur in more northern latitudes. True alpine plants find themselves at the extreme southern edge of their geographic range where there are few sites with appropriate, tundra-like conditions, except on a couple of Adirondack summits. Consequently, many of these species are among the most threatened or endangered plants in New York State.

Mountains, by their very nature, are rocky places. This is especially so above the tree line, where harsh alpine conditions produce thin soils and few plants to hide the stony surface. A closer look at these rock surfaces, however, reveals that they are varnished with another alpine inhabitant: lichens.

Lichens are neither animals nor plants. They are not even single organisms. Rather, they are communities consisting of a fungus and a photosynthetic algae, or cyanobacteria (formerly blue-green algae). Together, these completely unrelated organisms form a single lichen body (called a thallus). Scientists have long believed that the relationship between the fungus and the alga was one of mutual benefit or symbiosis. According to this view, the fungus provides shelter and protection for the algae enclosed within, while the algae in return manufacture carbohydrates for the fungus. While the benefit to the fungus is obvious, it is less clear how the alga profits from the relationship. Many researchers now believe that the "symbiotic relationship" in lichens is really one of "controlled parasitism." In this view, the photosynthetic alga or cyanobacteria is more a slave than a partner, producing food for its fungal jailor. While the extent of the "partnership" is debatable, one clear benefit accrues to both partners: together they are able to colonize places that neither organism could inhabit alone.

Lichens thrive in extreme environments. They live on desert rocks hot enough to fry an egg and in the severe cold of the Arctic. Indeed, lichens are prototypical pioneer species in many habitats because they are the first to colonize newly exposed rock surfaces. Once established on these barren facades, lichens dissolve minerals from the

LICHENS AS POLLUTION INDICATORS

Botanists began to notice a decline in lichens in and around urban areas as early as the mid-1800s. Over the next 20 years, scientists and amateur naturalists were able to link the disappearance of urban lichen species with declining air quality. During the industrial revolution in Europe, pollution emitted from coal-burning furnaces was gradually causing the eradication of lichen populations in urban areas (and areas downwind of cities).

Although many lichens are supremely adapted to harsh environments, most species are very sensitive to air pollution. Sulfur dioxide (SO_2), one of several molecules that contribute to air pollution, is known to damage plants. Lichens lack roots and must obtain water and nutrients by absorption of rainwater across their surfaces. Like tiny sponges, they soak up the pollutant-laden rainwater and because they have no way to rid themselves of pollutants like SO_2, the sulfur accumulates in the tissues. Eventually, the accumulating sulfur begins to break down vital chlorophyll molecules, which are responsible for photosynthesis in the algae. Without photosynthesis, the algae will die. Without the algae to generate energy and food for the fungi, the fungus is doomed as well.

A few lichen species, however, can survive in areas with high pollution levels; several other species can tolerate moderate levels of air pollution. By knowing which species are most sensitive to air pollution and documenting their abundance and distribution, scientists can use lichens as air-quality monitors. Lichens act as living biomonitors to record historical changes. As the air quality improves at a particular site, lichens reinvade in a slow process of recovery. Scientists also regularly collect small samples of lichen tissue, which can be analyzed chemically in the laboratory. These data allow scientists to monitor changes in pollutants over time and predict future trends in air quality.

rock, helping to form new soils on which other plants can take root. At lower elevations, lichens also grow on soils, tree bark, tree leaves, and other lichens.

Lichens have no roots, stems, or leaves and must receive all of their nutrients from rainfall. Rainwater, light, and carbon dioxide are the raw materials used by the photosynthetic alga to manufacture carbohydrates for itself and its fungal companion, which cannot manufacture carbohydrates on its own. In turn, some species of fungus use these sugars, along with minerals dissolved from the substrate, to make natural toxins that protect both partners from herbivores. Whatever the nature of the relationship that keeps them alive, lichens are extremely successful. Somewhere between 13,000 and 30,000 species occur worldwide, and many remain unknown to science. In New York alone, several hundred different species of lichens have been identified.

Alpine communities live on the edge, and as a result they tend to be fragile. Many alpine plants are considered threatened or endangered species and several, including glaucous rattlesnake-root (*Prenanthes racemosa*), have been lost entirely. Hikers are encouraged to:

- Walk on the trail and solid rock surfaces
- Leave the endangered plants in place (do not pick them)
- Avoid walking on bare dirt or gravel where plants can grow
- Keep dogs leashed above timberline
- Share the summit steward message with others

SPRUCE-FIR FORESTS

As hikers descend below treeline to altitudes of roughly 3,000 feet, they enter a forest community dominated by red spruce and balsam fir. Adirondack spruce-fir forests are restricted to the upper elevations of the High Peaks region. Here, balsam fir (*Abies balsamea*) is the dominant tree. Large numbers of red spruce (*Picea rubens*) also occur at these altitudes, along with the occasional mountain ash (*Sorbus americana*), mountain paper birch (*Betula cordifolia*) and hemlock (*Tsuga canadensis*). These tree species form thick stands with a closed canopy, where little light reaches the forest floor. Consequently, the shrub layer is sparse. Ground cover includes dense mats of pine needles and mosses, a variety of fern species, and isolated carpets of diminutive ground pines (Lycopodiaceae). Ground pines resemble conifer seedlings, but are actually clubmosses that are more closely related to ferns.

Balsam fir grows to 60 feet, but, at higher elevations, the poor soils and short summers restrict their growth to less than 30 feet. Balsam fir are easy to distinguish from other Adirondack conifers. Their dark-green needles are flattened and 1 to 2 inches in length. The underside of each needle is pale green due to the presence of stomates (openings that regulate gas and water exchange within the needle). The base of the needle is twisted and needles appear to be arranged in rows along the twig. The bark of older trees is reddish brown and scaly. Young balsam fir have thin, gray bark punctuated with resin blisters. When ruptured, they exude a thick, sticky resin that runs down the trunk. The dark-purple to brown cones stand upright on the upper branches.

Red spruce is the other dominant tree in this community. Like balsam fir, it is also shade-tolerant and can grow on the thin soils in the High Peaks. Unlike balsams, the needles are pointed and prickly to the touch. Spruce needles are four-sided in cross section, roughly half an inch in length, and yellowish green in color. Spruce cones have stiff scales and hang beneath the branch, as opposed to the upright cones of the balsam fir.

The needles and cones of balsam fir and red spruce provide food for red squirrels, spruce grouse, porcupines, and a variety of insects. The spruce budworm, for example, is a moth caterpillar that feeds on conifer needles. Outbreaks of these insects can devastate conifer stands. Both spruce and balsam fir are harvested for pulpwood. Red spruce is also used in the manufacture of guitars and violins. In addition, both species are prized Christmas trees, because they hold their needles well and have an aromatic scent.

MIXED CONIFER-HARDWOOD FORESTS

Descending below roughly 3,000 feet in elevation, hikers encounter a transition zone consisting of a mixture of conifer and deciduous hardwood species. Eastern hemlock replaces balsam fir in this zone. Red spruce and white pine (*Pinus strobus*) are present, along with a mixture of hardwoods, including sugar maple (*Acer saccharum*) and American beech (*Fagus grandifolia*). These hardwood-conifer forests are most extensive on steep, north-facing slopes or ravines.

Eastern hemlock is similar in appearance to balsam fir. Hemlocks have ¼- to 1-inch-long needles that decrease in size toward the tip of the branch. Like balsam firs, hemlock needles are flattened, dark green above, and have two lighter-colored stripes of stomates on the underside of the needle. Hemlock cones are oval and considerably smaller than those of balsam fir, usually less than 1 inch in length. Hemlock trees grow slowly, eventually reaching heights of 90 to 100 feet. Their dense crowns provide a great deal of shade in the summer, and hold or deflect much of the snowfall in the winter. White-tailed deer take advantage of the reduced snow depth beneath hemlock stands by gathering in "yards" to feed and save energy during the cold winter months.

Scan a nearby ridgeline and you are likely to see one or more trees that tower above the rest of the forest. These are invariably eastern white pines. White pines have long, flexible needles grouped into clusters of five needles per sheath. The sheath at the base is deciduous, resulting in the cluster being shed after roughly 18 months. Consequently, thick red-orange mats of dead needles carpet the forest floor under white pines. White pines produce slender cones up to 6 inches in length. In June, when new cones are produced, the cone scales are purplish, but as they mature over the next 18 months, the cones become greenish-brown. At maturity, the cone scales open and strong winds disperse the seeds.

Although white pine forests once covered much of the Adirondacks, very few virgin stands of white pines survived the extensive logging that occurred in the 1800s. However, small groups of old-growth white pines did survive on sites too difficult to log. Trees missed by loggers now reach heights of 160 feet, and may be over 4,000 years old. Today, most white pines are second-growth trees that rarely exceed 100 feet. Nevertheless, white pines are an important component of the mixed conifer-hardwood forests. They are fire-tolerant and often are among the first trees to colonize areas destroyed by forest fires. They provide nest sites for hawks, as well as food for squirrels, voles, pine siskins, migratory warblers, and many species of insects. In the summer months, fly agaric mushrooms (*Amanita muscaria*) appear among the carpet of needles at the base of white pines. These mushrooms have a red cap covered with white or yellow blisters. They benefit the pines by converting nitrogen in the soil to a form that white pines can use. While they benefit the pines, these colorful mushrooms contain several toxic and hallucinogenic compounds; they should not be eaten.

BEECH-MAPLE FORESTS

At lower elevations, hikers enter forests dominated by deciduous hardwood trees. American beech (*Fagus grandifolia*) and sugar maple (*Acer saccharum*) are the dominant species in most of the Adirondacks. This upland forest community occurs in areas with moist (mesic), somewhat acidic soils. Beech-maple forests are also characterized by a dense, relatively closed canopy (upper branches of adjacent trees overlap), a sparse shrub layer, and a relatively well-developed herbaceous ground layer. Hemlock, red spruce, yellow birch, white ash, basswood, and black cherry trees also may occur in smaller proportions in this forest community.

American beech trees grow to 90 feet or more. Because they are highly shade tolerant, they grow well in the understory of closed-canopy forests. American beech have smooth, silvery bark, and dark-green, oblong leaves that are coarsely serrated. Separate male and female flowers occur on the same tree during the spring months. The wind-pollinated flowers yield small nuts encased in a bristly, four-sided capsule or husk. In autumn, the husk splits open, releasing two triangular nuts. Every three to five years, an exceptionally large volume of nuts is produced; ecologists refer to this as a mast year. These nuts nourish a variety of forest birds and mammals. Blue jays, ruffed grouse, wood ducks, and rose-breasted grosbeaks all take advantage of the fall mast crop. White-tailed deer and black bear feed extensively on beech nuts in preparation for the lean winter months to come.

Chipmunks, red squirrels, and other small mammals also eat or cache beech nuts, and porcupine feed on the thin bark of the tree itself. Beech trees are attacked by a number of insect and fungus species. Notable among them is the artist's bracket fungus (*Ganoderma applanatum*). These large, semi-circular shelf fungi prey on the inner heartwood. The fungus is visible on the outside of the tree as a hard shelf with a light brown to white undersurface. Some artists etch the white undersurface to produce intricate wildlife portraits or landscapes.

Co-dominant with American beech are sugar maples, one of North America's most beautiful hardwood trees. Generally shorter than beech trees, mature sugar maples reach heights of 50 to 80 feet. Sugar maples have distinctive, deeply notched, five-lobed leaves. Young twigs are reddish, but turn gray as they mature. The bark is gray, becoming darker and more deeply furrowed with age. Sugar maples produce small clusters of yellowish flowers in early spring. In early fall, fruits (called samara) appear as paired winged seeds. These seeds are initially green, but turn light brown. Mature seeds fall to the ground in a helicopter-like fashion that may carry them well away from the parent tree. By germinating farther away, the seedlings do not compete with the parent tree for resources.

Sugar maples are probably best known for their dramatic fall colors. During the summer months, sugar maple leaves appear green due to an abundant green pigment called chlorophyll in the leaf's cells. Chlorophyll absorbs light energy and, with the help of other photosynthetic molecules, converts that light energy into chemical energy in the form of carbohydrates. In photosynthesis, the light energy is used to break up carbon dioxide (CO_2) and water (H_2O) molecules and rearrange the carbon, hydrogen, and oxygen into carbohydrates (sugars and starch), and in the process oxygen is released. The newly formed carbohydrates are transported throughout the plant and may be stored in roots or used immediately for new growth.

The chlorophyll in the leaves absorbs mostly red and blue wavelengths of light and reflects the green wavelengths; it is those reflected green wavelengths that enter our eyes and that we perceive as green. Other pigment molecules are also present in the leaf, including carotene and several types of anthocyanins. These accessory pigments absorb blue and green light, and reflect the red and yellow wavelengths.

Chlorophyll is the dominant pigment during the summer months, However, chlorophyll is not very stable and it is constantly being degraded, but as long as temperatures stay warm, it is replenished. In the fall, days shorten and temperatures drop, resulting in a loss of chlorophyll in the leaves. Carotene is not as temperature sensitive. As chlorophyll gradually disappears, and carotene becomes the dominant pigment, and the once-green leaves make their annual color change to bright reds, oranges, and yellows. As winter approaches, temperatures continue to fall and sugar maples (and other deciduous trees) shed their leaves.

Sugar maples stop growing in the fall and begin storing excess starch in specialized ray cells in the sapwood (a zone beneath the bark). As temperatures climb in late February and early March to roughly 40°F (4.5°C), enzymes convert the stored starch to the sugar sucrose. The cold nights and warm days induce the sugar-rich sap to flow. Any wounds, or tapholes, on the trunk or branches will cause the sap to leak out of the tree. Squirrels take advantage of this energy-rich resource by gnawing small holes in the bark and licking up the sap that runs out. Native Americans also took advantage of spring sap flows to harvest the sweet sap. They used it for food and bartered it for trade goods with European settlers. By the 1900s, millions of sugar maples were tapped for the commercial production of maple syrup in the northeastern United States and Canada. The sap leaving the tree is only 2 to 6 percent sugar. To make maple syrup, it must be concentrated further until it contains about 66 percent sugars. Maple syrup producers achieve this by heating the sap and evaporating off the excess water. Because sap is mostly water, it takes roughly 40 gallons of sap to make 1 gallon of maple syrup. No wonder maple syrup costs nearly $40 per gallon.

Despite their ecological and commercial importance, sugar maples are in decline across the northeast. Sugar maples' sensitivity to low-pH soils resulting from acid rain is one of the main reasons for the decline in the Adirondacks. Increased development and the forest fragmentation expose beech-maple forests to disease and increased competition from Norway maple and other disturbance-tolerant species. Maintaining large healthy tracts of beech-maple forests is vital, as many species of plants and animals rely of these forests for survival. Barred owls, woodpeckers, thrushes, and many other forest birds forage and nest in these forests. Red-backed salamanders, shrews, mice, chipmunks, fox, deer, and black bears also utilize the services these forests provide.

WINTER TREE SURVIVAL

Trees survive here only because they are adapted to the severe environmental conditions. All Adirondack trees face extreme cold and desiccation during the long winter months. Unlike animals, trees cannot migrate, hibernate, or seek shelter during winter. Instead, they stand exposed to winter storms and must endure long periods when temperatures remain below freezing. To survive, they must modify their internal physiology in ways that conserve energy, prevent water loss, inhibit the formation of ice crystals in cells, and minimize snow and ice loads.

Trees are in danger of freezing in winter because they are exposed constantly to subfreezing temperatures and they are not capable of generating their own heat. Plants, however, gradually become resistant to freezing in a process called hardening. Hardening takes place over several weeks in late fall. Light-sensitive pigments in the leaves, called phytochromes, detect the shortening days and signal genetic and cellular changes that lead to hardening. During the early stages, plant hormones cause growth to slow and eventually stop. At this stage, trees can tolerate temperatures slightly below freezing, such as those that occur during nighttime frosts. Later, water leaks out of the plant cells into the surrounding spaces between cells. Ice crystals may form outside the plant cells, but the increased concentration of sugars and other materials that remain within the cells reduces their freezing point and protects cells from deadly ice crystals. Trees are now able to tolerate temperatures as low as −20°F (−29°C). Some tree species have the ability to harden even further before reaching their killing temperature, the temperature at which ice crystals form inside plant cells causing them to rupture and die. Hardening is a gradual process and abrupt frosts early in the fall may kill plants that have not completed the early stages of hardening. Likewise, prolonged warm spells during the middle of winter can deharden trees, leading to dead branches or worse.

Annual snow accumulations of over 160 inches are not uncommon in the Adirondacks. On the summits, however, winds remove the protective snow pack in some areas and deposit it in massive mounds in other areas. Trees buried under the snowpack are insulated from the extreme cold and drying winds above. Branches that peek above the surface are often killed by a combination of winter drought and constant ice blasting. Heavy blankets of snow may cause branches to break, and snow slides or avalanches can shear off trees at the trunk. The late-lying snowpacks of spring occasionally provide optimum conditions for snow-mold fungus, resulting in matted, black conifer boughs. By itself, snow does not profoundly influence tree growth at timberline; it can be both beneficial and detrimental, depending on the quantity and duration. But in combination with drying winds, snow can shape the alpine environment dramatically.

Constant winds are thought to be one of the main causes of krummholz formation. Wind speeds on Adirondack summits average more than 30 miles per hour (mph) in the winter, with sustained winds of 40 to 60 mph commonplace. The highest wind velocity ever recorded, 231 mph, occurred on the summit of Mount Washington in New Hampshire. Alpine trees are not only battered and broken by hurricane force gusts, they also are blasted by ice pellets. Finally, sustained high winds are responsible for a unique mortality pattern called "fir waves." Fir waves are distinct, alternating bands of living and dead trees running in horizontal contours in the subalpine fir zone. The tallest trees in each wave are killed by wind and ice buildup on the exposed foliage, leaving the shorter, leeward trees protected. As these shorter trees grow up, they in turn are killed to form the next wave.

Perhaps the most important role that wind plays in shaping timberline communities is in causing water loss. Surprisingly, water is often in short supply in the alpine zone. Much of the moisture generated by melting spring snows is lost quickly to runoff on the steep slopes; the thin soils quickly become saturated and are unable to retain the excess. What moisture there is in the thin soils and plant tissues eventually evaporates under the constant, desiccating winds. In winter, winds draw moisture from the plant at a time when it cannot take up moisture from the frozen soil.

Like all trees, those living in the alpine zone transport water from the soil, up the trunk and branches, and use it for photosynthesis in the leaves or needles. The plant, however, faces a dilemma. It needs to conserve water in the spaces within the leaf or needle, but it must acquire CO_2 as a source of carbon and release excess O_2, a byproduct of photosynthesis. Normally, plants exchange these gases with the environment through small openings in the leaf or needle called stomates. The stomates can be opened or closed depending on the needs of the plant at the time. The problem is that in order to move the gases in and out in order for photosynthesis to occur, the stomates must be open. Open stomates allow the precious water to evaporate, a process called evapotranspiration. On a warm sunny day, for example, a large maple tree can lose over 160 gallons of water by evapotranspiration.

To prevent excess water loss during the dry winter months to come, deciduous trees drop their leaves in autumn. Leaf drop occurs because the shorter days of fall alter the production of certain plant compounds, including abscisic acid, ethylene, and auxin. Abscisic acid levels increase in the roots in response to water stress, and it is later transported to the leaves where, along with ethylene, it activates the process of leaf fall (called abscission). An abscission zone forms at the base of the leaf petiole (stem). Here, in response to plant hormones, cells swell at different rates and are simultaneously attacked by enzymes, resulting in fractures between adjacent cells. Wind and gravity expand these fractures until the leaf falls from the tree. The open wound left behind is covered by lignin and other protective compounds that prevent disease and water loss.

Conifers also shed their needle-like leaves, but not all at once. A typical conifer needle remains attached for two to three years before being shed. Needles are constantly shed and replaced so conifers appear "evergreen" despite needle loss. This leaf-retention strategy serves conifers well in northern boreal forests. Conifers conserve a great deal of energy by not having to replace all their needles each year. In addition, the needles themselves have a number of adaptations that enhance winter survival. As well as being small and slim, each needle has a waxy outer coating, and the stomata can be closed tightly to minimize water loss in winter. There is at least one exception to the needle-retention strategy of Adirondack conifers: tamaracks (also called larch) (*Larix decidua*) have spiral clusters of 20 to 40 short needles that turn yellow and drop in the fall like deciduous hardwood trees.

Even with these formidable winter adaptations, trees are subjected to fierce winter storms that may cause damage to limbs. Conifer's needle-retention strategy may conserve energy, but it also allows heavy snow loads to accumulate on branches. The weight of the snow may cause branches to snap. To minimize snow loads, conifers evolved a conical shape that sheds snow more easily. As snow accumulates, the flexible branches of conifers bend downward to dump snow.

Fierce winds, especially on exposed ridges or at higher altitudes, also pose serious problems for conifers. Snow-laden branches can be broken by gusts approaching hurricane force. Winter winds also blast the trees with ice chips. Isolated trees or those exposed on the outside of conifer stands are more prone to wind damage. As a result, such trees often display "flagging," where the upper branches are reduced or absent from the windward side of the tree. High winds and heavy snows are the principal agents stunting the trees in the krummholtz zone near timberline.

Beyond the severe weather, winter brings other hardships to trees. As more-nutritious foods disappear in early winter, trees, especially conifers, become fare for hungry animals. Moose and white-tailed deer browse on conifer needles, while porcupines, snowshoe hares, and mice gnaw away the outer bark to expose the inner cambium layers. Some tree species are able to defend themselves partially by either removing nutrients from the needles and outer shoots, or producing compounds that are distasteful or toxic. Nevertheless, high herbivore densities and long winters can reduce conifer survival significantly.

SOURCES AND ADDITIONAL READING

Arno, S. F., and R. P. Hammerly. 1984. *Timberline: Mountain and Arctic Forest Frontiers*. Seattle: The Mountaineers.

Chapman, W. K., and A. E. Bessette. 1990. *Trees and Shrubs of the Adirondacks: A Field Guide*. Utica, NY: North Country Books.

DeGraaf, R. M., and P. E. Sendak. 2006. *Native and Naturalized Trees of New England and Adjacent Canada: A Field Guide*. Hanover, NH: University Press of New England.

Dwelley, M. J. 2000. *Trees and Shrubs of New England*. Camden, ME: Down East Books.

Halfpenny, J. C., and R. D. Ozanne. 1989. *Winter: An Ecological Handbook*. Boulder, CO: Johnson Books.

Kricher, J., and G. Morrison. 1988. *A Field Guide to the Eastern Forests*. Peterson Field Guides. New York: Houghton Mifflin Company.

Purvis, W. 2000. *Lichens*. Washington, DC: Smithsonian Institution Press.

Steele, F. L. 1982. *At Timberline: A Nature Guide to the Mountains of the Northeast*. Boston: Appalachian Mountain Club.

Walker, L. C. 1990. *Forests: A Naturalist's Guide to Trees and Forest Ecology*. New York: John Wiley and Sons.

3 Adirondack Waters

Every drop of freshwater is precious. At first this may seem odd. After all, 70 percent of the Earth is covered by water; it's called the "Blue Planet" for a reason. However, the vast majority of this water, over 97 percent, is saltwater. Freshwater accounts for only 3 percent of the world's water resources, and the majority of that is locked up in glaciers, ice caps, and groundwater. Less than 1 percent of the world's freshwater is found on the surface in the form of lakes, ponds, marshes, rivers, and streams. Fortunately, water is recycled constantly through a process known as the global hydrologic cycle, a process powered by solar energy. In its simplest form, the hydrologic cycle is the movement of water, however slow, between the oceans, land, and atmosphere via the processes of evaporation, precipitation, runoff, and storage.

A single drop of rain may contain water molecules that originated in the Pacific Ocean or the Great Lakes or that were once part of the Antarctic ice sheet. In fact, some water molecules may have taken thousands of years to make the trip from an ice crystal buried in an Alaskan glacier, to meltwater reaching the ocean, and finally into the atmosphere to help form a rain cloud. Powering this water-transport cycle is radiant energy provided by the Sun. When the Sun warms surface water, some of that water evaporates, moving from a liquid to a gaseous state. Likewise, when the summer Sun warms the leaves of a maple tree, water is lost from the leaves to the atmosphere via a process called evapotranspiration. A mature maple tree may lose 160 gallons on a hot summer day, an amount that must be replaced by water uptake at the roots.

Once in the atmosphere, the warm, water-laden air rises until the water vapor cools enough to condense, forming clouds. As the clouds travel on the prevailing winds, they accumulate additional water vapor from surface waters or from plants. Eventually, the load becomes too great and the water vapor forms water droplets or ice crystals that fall back to the surface as precipitation.

Back on the surface, droplets of rainwater may join together and trickle downhill, forming a small rivulet. Further downslope, the rivulets coalesce forming small streams, and eventually this surface runoff enters a pond, lake, or a permanent stream channel. On Mount Marcy, a drop of rainwater may find its way into a tiny, shallow pond called Lake Tear of the Clouds, the source of the mighty Hudson River. Alternatively, the rainwater may soak into the thin Adirondack soils and travel downslope as groundwater flow. If the groundwater is not removed first by thirsty plants, it also may end up in a lake or stream, or it may percolate downward to recharge underground aquifers.

Water may be stored temporarily in lakes or ponds, may evaporate back into the atmosphere, or may continue its journey to the ocean. Regardless of the path, the hydrologic cycle continues to move water from one site to another across the globe, and in the process it erodes landscapes, creates weather, and sustains life.

WATERSHEDS

Depending on its location, an Adirondack cloudburst may contribute water to one of five major watersheds (see map 3.1). The entire region that contributes water to a river or stream is called its "watershed"

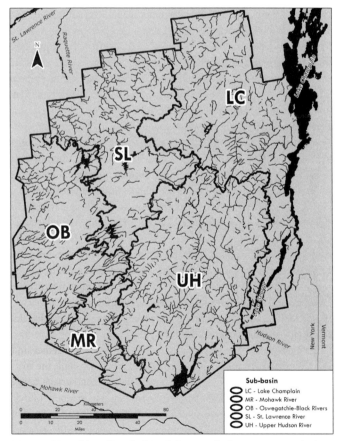

Map 3.1 *Map of the Adirondack Park showing the five major watersheds.*

(the terms "catchment" and "drainage basin" are also used). Boundaries between adjacent watersheds represent topographic high points, such as ridgelines or summits. Rain falling on the southwest side of Mount Marcy, for example, would drain into Lake Tear of the Clouds or into Feldspar Brook, travel downstream to join Opalescent River, and empty into Lake Colden. Here it would be stored temporarily until it either evaporates or leaves via Calamity Brook to wind its way downhill into the uppermost reaches of the Hudson River. Indeed, hundreds of springs, small brooks, streams, and rivers capture water that forms the Hudson River Watershed that exits into the Atlantic Ocean at New York City. In contrast, rain falling on the north side of Mount Marcy creates runoff that makes its way into the Ausable/Boquet Watershed and ultimately finds its way to the Atlantic Ocean via the St. Lawrence Seaway in Canada.

The Adirondack Mountains are essentially an upland dome, and water drains to the periphery like the spokes of a wheel. The Ausable, Saranac, and Boquet rivers flow eastward toward Lake Champlain. The St. Lawrence River captures the north-flowing Salmon, St. Regis, Raquette, Grass, and Oswegatchie rivers, while the Black River flows west to Lake Ontario. Along the southern border, East and West Canada creeks contribute to the Mohawk River before it joints the Hudson River north of Troy. An estimated 32,000 miles of streams and rivers pour through the Adirondack Park. Along the way, they nourish forests and offer habitat for aquatic organisms.

Surface runoff and streams coursing through the Adirondacks often are impounded temporarily in ponds, lakes, and marshes. Except for glacially formed kettle ponds, which have no outlet, most of the water captured by ponds and lakes eventually will exit via a stream or river and continue toward the sea. Not surprisingly, the Adirondacks are riddled with lakes and ponds. There are an estimated 3,000 lakes and ponds in the Adirondack Park. Many of them have glacial origins. As the Adirondack dome was thrust upward, it fractured in many places. These fault lines created deep valleys, which were then scoured by glaciers and, eventually, filled with water, forming lakes. Interestingly, most Adirondack faults run diagonally from the southwest to the northeast. Consequently, many of the larger lakes also follow this diagonal trend (see map 3.1).

RUNNING WATER

The diversity and composition of aquatic communities varies dramatically along a river's course. The upper reaches, or headwaters, are typically narrow, steep channels with high-velocity flow and cold waters. On the floodplains, at lower elevations, the river is broad and meandering, with warmer, silt-laden waters. At the watershed scale, each tributary contributes to the size and discharge of the next stream segment downstream. First-order streams are unbranched segments at the uppermost reaches of the watershed. When two first-order streams join, their combined flow forms a second-order stream. Third-order streams form from the combination of two second-order streams and so on.

Mountainous headwater streams cascade steeply down narrow V-shaped channels that follow the topography, carrying away all but the heaviest cobbles and boulders. In the steepest reaches, water tumbles over short waterfalls into small pools. Downslope, stretches of rapids alternate with deeper, quieter pools. Pool-riffle sequences create a mosaic of microhabitats for aquatic organisms. Air and water mix freely in the turbulent riffles, creating oxygen-saturated regions of high velocity. In quieter pools, or in the dead zones behind large boulders, velocity slows enough to deposit the leaves and other organic material carried by the stream. Here, organic material collects and begins to decompose, recycling important nutrients and consuming oxygen in the process. Eventually, riffles and pools give way to slow, meandering rivers as they exit the mountains. Although the surface is generally smooth, the current velocity is often quite high, owing to the greater volume of water being transported in these larger rivers. In many cases, the water is turbid and the substrate consists of fine particles of sand or silt. These conditions result in less oxygen and less light for photosynthetic plants and algae. In addition, the bottom is unstable and easily removed during floods, only to be deposited again as the flood recedes. The physical changes in river structure create new and different habitats for aquatic organisms, each adapted to a unique set of physical, chemical, and biological environments.

STILL WATERS

If streams and rivers are characterized largely by their current velocity, then lakes and ponds are at the opposite end of the continuum. Lakes, ponds, and wetlands are defined as open bodies of water surrounded by land, in which the water flows very slowly or not at all. Wetlands, including marshes, swamps, and bogs, are transitional areas where the terrestrial and aquatic environments intermingle. Ponds generally are considered to be smaller, shallower lakes, but the distinction between large ponds and small lakes is murky. For example, South Lake, east of the town of Speculator, is smaller and shallower (89 acres of open water and a maximum depth of 33 feet) than South Pond (426

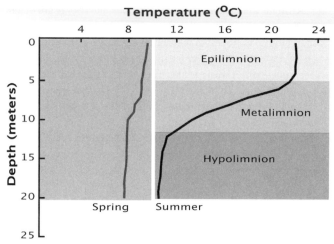

Figure 3.1 *A typical temperature profile for a lake in the early spring and late summer. In the early spring the lake is well mixed, with a temperature between 8 and 10 degrees C from top to bottom. As the Sun warms the lake into late summer, the lake becomes stratified into distinct temperature layers. The upper 5 meters (epilimnion) is roughly 22 degrees C. There is a middle layer of rapidly changing temperature with increasing depth (metalimnion). The deepest layer (hypolimnion) also has a relatively uniform, but much colder, temperature.*

acres and 54 feet deep) near Long Lake. Names aside, ponds and lakes reflect the size and topography of their watersheds, the character of their geology and soils, as well as the composition of the surrounding vegetation and land-use patterns.

Water enters lakes via precipitation, groundwater seepage, and runoff from the watershed, which is collected and transported by streams. Water exits the lake via surface evaporation, stream and river outflows, and, in many cases, pumping for human uses. Thus, lakes are not static pools of water. Instead, water is constantly on the move, but at a very slow rate relative to rivers and streams. Furthermore, lakes are not homogeneous below the surface; they vary in depth from shallow shorelines to deep open-water zones. Light availability, temperature, nutrient composition, substrate type, and diversity of aquatic life all vary widely from one location to another across a lake.

Despite this variability, lakes have order similar to that found in terrestrial ecosystems. For example, because cold water is denser than warm water, lakes develop ordered layers of temperature called thermoclines, with the coldest layers at the bottom (see figure 3.1). During the warm summer months, solar radiation heats the surface waters,

creating three distinct temperature zones. The upper layer, or epilimnion, is warmer and contains more dissolved oxygen because it is
mixed by wind and waves. The layer below, called the metalimnion, is
a zone where temperatures decline sharply with depth. At some depth,
water temperature remains constant all the way to the bottom. This is
the hypolimnion, the coldest and deepest zone. These three temperature strata are maintained as long as the warmer summer days keep
the epilimnion relatively warm.

As autumn approaches, surface-water temperatures cool. The den-
sity of these cooler surface waters also increases, resulting in an increase in the thickness of the epiliminion. Cooler, denser waters also
hold more dissolved oxygen, which is then mixed to greater depths by
fall winds. Eventually, surface temperatures equal those at the bottom
of the lake and the thermocline disappears. At such times, the entire
lake is mixed, bringing much-needed dissolved oxygen from the surface to the lake floor.

Early winter brings colder weather and surface waters continue to
cool until they freeze over. Ice is less dense than water, resulting in
a layer of ice at the surface. Except for a narrow zone of water just
beneath the ice, most of the lake's water is now 39°F (4°C). This thin
thermocline near the surface remains as long as the ice prevents winds
from stirring the surface waters. In the spring, as surface temperatures
warm again, the mixing process is repeated until surface temperatures
warm enough to reform the three temperature strata. Obviously, shallow lakes and ponds may not stratify at all because the Sun warms the
water all the way to the bottom. Most Adirondack lakes greater than
30 feet deep and with sufficient surface area for winds to create waves
exhibit seasonal stratification and mixing. Without seasonal mixing,
oxygen levels at the bottom become depleted and bottom-dwelling organisms (benthos) suffer.

Sunlight not only warms surface waters and contributes to seasonal turnover, it also controls photosynthesis and nutrient content.
The amount of light available varies with season and local weather
patterns. Some of the light striking the water surface is reflected. The
remainder penetrates the water surface, where it is largely absorbed
by water or suspended particles and converted to heat, creating the
epilimnion. Light intensity is strongest near the surface and decreases
sharply with depth (called attenuation). Therefore, light-dependent
photosynthesis is restricted to the upper reaches of the water column,
where more light is available. How far down light penetrates depends
on how much light-absorbing material is present in the water. The
more dissolved nutrients, suspended soil particles, and photosynthetic

organisms in the water, the less light penetrates to reach greater depths. In addition, water does not absorb all wavelengths of visible light equally. Rather, pure water absorbs red wavelengths best and transmits blue wavelengths to greater depths. Photosynthetic organisms, such as phytoplankton, contain a pigment called chlorophyll a, which is used to absorb light during photosynthesis. Chlorophyll a absorbs blue and red wavelengths of light and transmits more green wavelengths. Thus, clear, nutrient-poor lakes appear blue, while lakes with abundant phytoplankton often appear more greenish.

Various types of algae are the primary photosynthetic organisms in lakes and ponds. Free-floating algae are called phytoplankton, while algae attached to rocks or other surfaces are called periphyton. It is the thick mats of periphyton that make submerged rocks so slippery. In addition to algae, rooted aquatic plants (called macrophytes) also contribute to photosynthesis, especially along the shorelines. Light attenuation determines the maximum depth that can support photosynthetic macrophytes and algae. Above this depth is the highly productive euphotic zone, and below is the unproductive aphotic zone. The euphotic zone is important for two main reasons. First, the process of photosynthesis uses light energy to build organic compounds from available nutrients and, in turn, it releases oxygen into the water. Secondly, the organic compounds produced by photosynthesis become the food that supports the remainder of the aquatic food web (discussed below).

Scientists use nutrient levels and degree of photosynthesis to further classify lakes. Oligotrophic lakes are nutrient poor, have little photosynthesis, and are generally clear to greater depths. Lakes with good clarity and average nutrient loads are called mesotrophic lakes. Nutrient-rich lakes are said to be eutrophic and exhibit abundant algal and plant growth and poor water clarity. Humans often contribute to lake eutrophication. For example, leaking sewage systems and overuse of fertilizers add nutrients to lakes and ponds.

On a human timescale, lakes and ponds appear to change little or not at all. Yet on much longer timescales, most lakes and ponds are slowly disappearing. Rivers and streams continue to bring in sediments that are deposited on the lakebed. Aquatic plants fill in the shorelines and, when they die, contribute to these sediments. Eventually, the shallower sections, especially those near a stream mouth, become wetlands. If the lake is shallow, has a mostly muddy bottom, and little wave action, the process occurs more rapidly than in larger, rocky-bottomed lakes. Nevertheless, on geologic timescales, most lakes gradually fill in and close over with vegetation.

Rivers also may form wetlands in areas where water flow slows to a crawl. Whether formed along rivers or at the margins of lakes and ponds, marshes tend to have more open water than other types of wetlands. Sedges, reeds, cattails, and other semi-aquatic plants emerge above the waterline. Marshes can be 5 or 6 feet deep in spots and cover extensive areas. Swamps are similar to marshes in the extent of open water, but are dominated by alders, tamaracks, and other woody shrubs and trees instead of grasses. In the later stages, all that remains of a lake may be a shallow peat bog. Bogs are characterized by floating mats of sphagnum moss and other plants that surround a small area of open water. Bog soils are acidic and support a variety of unique plants such as rare orchids and the carnivorous plants. Spring Pond Bog, in the town of Altmont, is one of the largest peat bogs in the Adirondacks. It is home to carnivorous pitcher plants that survive by digesting insects that fall into the water at the base of the vase-like plant. Finally, vegetation blankets the entire area and the lake disappears.

AQUATIC LIFE

Healthy streams, rivers, ponds, lakes, and wetlands host an incredible diversity of aquatic life. From microscopic bacteria and algae to 30-pound northern pike, aquatic communities are structured into intricately woven food webs (figure 3.2). At the base of the food web are the organisms that produce the energy that supports the remaining organisms. These so-called primary producers, including rooted aquatic plants and free-floating phytoplankton, use light energy along with carbon dioxide, water, and various dissolved minerals to build organic compounds, such as the sugar glucose, and use those compounds for their own growth and reproduction. The carbon dioxide present in the water comes from three possible sources: the atmosphere, the slow weathering of limestones and other carbonate rocks, and from other aquatic organisms via respiration (the byproduct of respiration is CO_2). Dissolved nutrients, such as nitrogen, phosphorus, and calcium, enter from the atmosphere or via runoff from the watershed. Although essential for life, most of these nutrients are needed in tiny quantities, so sufficient nutrients are almost always available.

The energy available in the tissues of primary producers is consumed by a variety of organisms at the next level in the food web, the primary consumers. For example, photosynthetic plankton are consumed by tiny zooplankton floating in the water column. Algal mats attached to rocks are eaten by a number of aquatic insect larvae, and aquatic plants are eaten by turtles. The primary consumers are the vegetarians of the aquatic world; they cannot manufacture their own

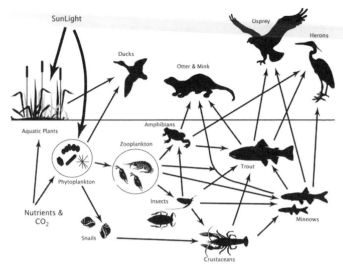

Figure 3.2 *A typical aquatic food web. The Sun's energy, along with CO_2 and other dissolved nutrients, is used for photosynthesis by phytoplankton and aquatic plants at the base of the food web. Tiny zooplankton, macro-invertebrates, and small fish form the next level in the web. In turn, they are consumed by other invertebrates and fish. Note that organisms feed on or are eaten by several different groups of organisms, creating a complex web of interactions.*

energy from light, so they harvest those who can. Zooplankton and other primary consumers use the organic compounds already present in the tissues of primary producers for their own growth, and use the oxygen released by producers for respiration.

Many primary consumers are highly adapted for feeding on specific types of producers. Black fly larvae, for example, live attached to rocks on the streambed. Here they cast their feathery fans (which are actually modified mouthparts) up into the flowing water to capture tiny organic particles that drift by. Snails and certain species of caddisfly larvae harvest producers by scraping them from rocks. Mussels pump food-rich water into their bodies through a siphon, filter out the food items, and pump out the inedible debris. The result is that consumers are specialized into feeding guilds; some species are specialized grazers, others are shredders, collectors, or predators. In all cases, consumers must eat vast quantities of producers to survive. As a result, there are fewer consumers than producers in any food web.

The third trophic level in the web consists of secondary consumers, so called because they eat the primary consumers. Stonefly larvae patrol the streambed for herbivorous insect larvae. Predaceous diving beetles ambush prey as large as small frogs. Many larval fish survive on a diet of zooplankton before they reach adulthood. These predators become prey as even larger fish, loons, ospreys, otters, and humans serve as tertiary or quaternary consumers at the highest levels in the food web.

Needless to say, food webs can be extremely complex. In part, the complexity is due to the fact that most organisms feed at multiple levels. A minnow may eat a combination of phytoplankton and zoo-plankton and therefore act as both a primary and secondary consumer. In fact, many species are omnivores in different seasons or life stages. Complexity is increased further because most aquatic food webs have hundreds or thousands of species at the lower levels, each with links to dozens of species at other levels. The result is that energy from the Sun and nutrients from the water move through the aquatic commu-nity as organisms consume each other. At some point, these nutrients are recycled back to the bottom by the decomposers.

Decomposers are an important and often overlooked component of aquatic and terrestrial food webs. In a typical stream or lake, the volume of dead plant and animal matter is greater than the volume of living organisms. The organic compounds in the tissues of these dead plants and animals still contain nutrients and energy. Because energy and nutrients remain, they attract scavengers and detritivores. Scav-engers feed on animal corpses, while detritivores consume dead plant material. However, scavengers and detritivores are not 100 percent efficient. They also leave behind energy and nutrients in the form of indigestible materials and feces. It is the true decomposers, primarily bacteria, who complete the process of recycling the remaining energy and nutrients.

When plants and animals are consumed, some of the undigested energy ends up as feces, which slowly falls to the bottom of the lake. On rare occasions, an entire organism may arrive at the lakebed. Here, decomposers slowly take apart the organic compounds, converting them back to basic nutrients, and making them available to primary producers again.

IMPACTS OF ACID RAIN

Aquatic ecosystems contain diverse communities of plants and an-imals, and efficiently recycle energy and nutrients, but they are not immune from human impacts. Lakes and rivers get most of their in-puts from the atmosphere or from runoff from their watersheds. Deforestation, lakeshore development, and application of excess fertilizer and pesticides all alter the quantity and/or quality of runoff. Likewise, pollutants carried on the winds from distant factories contribute unwanted atmospheric compounds to surface waters. Sadly, the Adirondacks have become a case study for the negative effects of acid rain, more accurately called acid deposition.

Nearly half a century ago, scientists conducted the first studies to measure the pH, or acidity, of rain and snow near the nation's industrial centers in the Midwest. Those studies demonstrated that smokestack emissions were responsible for increased soil acidity in regions immediately downwind from industrial smokestacks. In response, industries raised smokestack heights to carry emissions farther from urban and industrial neighborhoods. By the 1970s, scientists in New York State began to detect declines in the soil and water pH in the Adirondack and Catskill Mountains.

Utilities and industrial factories burn fossil fuels, which release sulfur dioxide (SO_2) and various nitrogen oxides into the lower atmosphere. In the atmosphere, as they are carried downwind, these compounds are transformed into sulfuric and nitric acid, respectively. Prevailing winds carry these acids eastward until they encounter mountains, where they condense and fall back to the ground as rain, snow, and fog. At high elevations, the acidic water vapor in clouds may bathe mountain top forests for days at a time.

Rainwater is naturally slightly acidic (pH of 5 to 7) because it contains carbon dioxide (CO_2) that dissolves in water vapor to form a weak carbonic acid. Carbonic acid contributes to the slow weathering of rocks, but it is a relatively weak acid compared to sulfuric and nitric acid. The addition of these two strong acids substantially lowers the pH of rainwater. Acidity is measured on a logarithmic pH scale from pH 1 to 14, with seven considered a neutral pH (figure 3.3). Because the scale is logarithmic, pH 4 is ten times more acidic than pH 5 and 100 times more acidic than pH 6. Furthermore, the myriad chemical reactions that occur constantly within living cells operate best within a relatively narrow pH range. Consequently, small changes in pH can have profound effects on living organisms.

In the 1970s, scientists began to document significant changes in red spruce forests in the Adirondacks Mountains. The crowns (upper third) of many spruce trees were dead or dying. Further research showed that spruce tree growth rates were declining and tree mortality was on the rise. By the 1990s, large patches of high-elevation spruce trees were dead. Ultimately, scientists were able to link the spruce die-off to acid rain.

Clouds, laden with acidic water vapor, sweep into the Adirondacks,

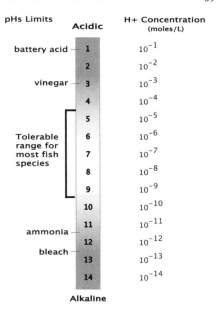

Figure 3.3 *The shaded bar in the middle represents a typical pH scale from extremely acidic (1) to extremely basic (14). To the left are pH values for familiar substances. Note that fish do not tolerate pHs much below 4.5 or above 9.5. On the right are hydrogen ion concentrations (a measure of acidity) in moles per liter. Note that for a one unit change in pH (from 6 to 5), there is a ten-fold increase in H+ ion concentration. Thus, small changes in pH have large consequences for aquatic organisms.*

blanketing mountaintops and bathing the spruce forests in an acidic mist. The low pH of the mist and rain leaches calcium out of the needles and reduces the needle's ability to tolerate freezing temperatures. The result is that many red spruce trees at higher elevations are dead or dying. Further injury results from acid rain's ability to reduce calcium and mobilize aluminum in soils. These changes alter soil fertility, and interfere with the tree's ability to acquire nutrients from the thin Adirondack soils. The combination of nutrient stress and reduced freeze tolerance is thought to be responsible for the loss of roughly half of the high-altitude spruce forests in the Adirondacks.

In addition to lowering the pH, acid rain indirectly contributes toxins to Adirondack waters. Aluminum, for example, is mobilized from the soil by acid rain and travels in runoff and groundwater to lakes and streams, where high concentrations are toxic to fish and other aquatic organisms. Mercury is also released by combustion of fossil fuels and enters the ecosystem via rainwater. In the soils, mercury can be transformed into a much more deadly form called methyl mercury. Methyl mercury also enters lakes and rivers, where it can accumulate in sediments and be picked up by aquatic organisms. When a crayfish, or some other aquatic organism, consumes methyl mercury, it is absorbed, transported freely throughout the body, and stored in its body tissues. Each time a fish eats a mercury-laden crayfish, it also stores the mercury, eventually accumulating high levels of toxic methyl mercury in its own tissue (this process is called bioaccumulation). The higher up the food web, the greater the potential mercury exposure. Consequently, fish-consumption warnings often are issued for lakes containing significant levels of mercury. Acid rain, therefore, brings both lower pHs and increased levels of toxic compounds to aquatic ecosystems.

All aquatic organisms tolerate a range of pHs, and, for most species, the acceptable range falls between pH 4.0 and pH 6.0. Organisms living in acidified waters at or near pH 4.0 face both physiological and reproductive stress. Low pH alters the proper function of many internal organs, impairing respiration, water balance, and nutrient absorption. Such chronic stress leads to poor health and reduced body weight, and makes individuals more susceptible to predation and disease. Increasing acidity and exposure to toxic metals such as mercury and aluminum also reduce reproductive success. Under such conditions, adults produce fewer eggs, fewer eggs hatch, and fewer young reach adulthood. Eventually, populations decline, resulting in a chain of events that may disrupt the entire food web. For example, acid-sensitive species of plankton, mayflies, and crayfish are typically among the first to disappear from acidified waters. With their main food sources dwindling, fish populations begin to suffer, which in turn affects larger fish, loons, herons, otters, and other fish-eating animals. In addition, acid-tolerant species, such as blackfly larvae, midges, and algae, now have fewer predators and their populations explode. The end result is a less-diverse ecosystem.

In 2005, the Adirondack Lakes Survey Corporation released a comprehensive report titled *Acid Rain and the Adirondacks: A Research Summary* (available on the Web at www.adirondacklakessurvey.org). This report details the results of several regional lake surveys conducted in the 1980s and 1990s. Among the major findings are that:

- Acidic lakes tend to be located in the western Adirondacks where rainfall is highest.
- Weakly acidic lakes typically suffer from the loss of one or more species from the food web, but strongly acidic lakes suffer the loss of entire feeding guilds, which drastically alters the entire food web.
- 10 to 25 percent of Adirondack lakes have pHs below 5.0 and another 20 to 40 percent of lakes have pHs less than 5.5.
- Lake sediments dating back to preindustrial times showed normal pH ranges, suggesting that lake acidification has occurred within the last century.

- Episodic release of acid and metals occurs during spring snowmelts and can harm fish populations.

Legislation aimed at reducing sulfur emissions, including the Clean Air Act Amendments and the New York State Acid Deposition Control Act, are having a positive affect on Adirondack lakes. Over the last thirty years, mandated cuts have led to a 38 percent reduction in sulfur emissions, and a slow, but encouraging, turnaround in the pH of precipitation. Results from long-term monitoring studies on Adirondack lakes are also encouraging. Both pH levels and acid neutralizing capacity (the ability of the water to buffer low pHs) are on the rise in many of the lakes studied. However, the recovery is likely to be slow. Scientists estimate that it may take fifty years or more for some lakes to recover. Further recovery may be impossible without additional cuts in sulfur and nitrogen emissions, because most of the emission reductions mandated by the Clean Air Act already have occurred. In the meantime, lake monitoring continues and scientists are guardedly optimistic about the health of Adirondack waterways.

SOURCES AND ADDITIONAL READING

Barnes, R. S. K., and K. H. Mann. 1991. *Fundamentals of Aquatic Ecology*. London: Blackwell Science Publishing.

Caduto, M. J. 1990. *Pond and Brook: A Guide to Nature in Freshwater Environments*. Hanover, NH: University Press of New England.

Cushing, C. E., and J. D. Allen. 2001. *Streams, Their Ecology and Life*. San Diego, CA: Academic Press.

Jenkins, J., K. Roy, C. Driscoll, and C. Buerkett. 2005. *Acid Rain and the Adirondacks: A Research Summary*. Adirondack Lakes Survey Corporation. (Available at www.adirondacklakessurvey.org/sosindex.htm).

II · The Wildlife

4 Common Invertebrates

The Adirondack Mountains are home to myriad species of invertebrates. Essentially, every animal that lacks a spinal cord surrounded by vertebrae is an invertebrate. Thus, invertebrates include some 30 animal groups, including sponges, flatworms, insects, spiders, crabs, and mollusks. Most go unseen, but some, like black flies and mosquitoes, are impossible to ignore.

The largest group of invertebrates, by far, is the arthropods. The name "arthropod" derives from the Greek words *arthros* for "jointed" and *poda* for "foot." Arthropods have a body divided into several segments, along with several pairs of jointed legs. Insects, for example, have three pairs of legs and three body segments: a head, thorax, and abdomen. Spiders and their relatives (called arachnids) have eight legs and only two body segments: a cephalothorax and an abdomen. Crustaceans, such as crayfish, also have a head, thorax, and abdomen, but the thorax and/or abdomen bear gills and they are further distinguished from the other groups by having two pairs of antennae and a number of other technical characteristics.

All arthropods, however, are covered by an outer exoskeleton that must be shed periodically in order to grow (a process called moulting). The exoskeleton is constructed from the polysaccharide chitin embedded in a matrix of proteins. This combination provides protection and prevents desiccation of the soft body parts within. Because this exoskeleton must be shed at regular intervals, arthropods undergo a series of moults as they grow. Blackflies, for example, begin growth within the egg, hatch into a larvae (or maggot), which continues to feed and grow, before forming an immobile pupae, where they complete development and emerge as an adult fly. Other species, such as dragonflies and many aquatic insects, hatch from the egg into an immature nymph. The nymph undergoes as many as 15 moults before forming an adult (there is no pupal stage in this case.)

Arthropods, and insects in particular, are an extremely successful group. Over one million arthropod species have been described so far. They occur in virtually every environment and on every continent and ocean. Some species are carnivorous, others feed on nectar, and a few are parasitic. They range in size from microscopic mites and zooplankton to yard-long marine crabs. Many species of insects have wings, and some species, such as the monarch butterfly, migrate thousands of miles each year. A few species of arthropods are economically important. Lobsters, crabs, crayfish, and some mollusks are consumed as food. Honeybees are managed for the honey they produce and for their role as pollinators of most of the food crops we eat. Others are economically important for the damage they cause: Certain beetles can damage crops or forest trees, deer ticks may carry Lyme disease (a debilitating illness), and black flies may reduce tourism in the spring months.

The invertebrate accounts that follow are by no means comprehensive. Rather, they include species or groups that are likely to be encountered on the trail, at the lakeshore, or at camp.

COMMON FLIES

Flies belong to the Order Diptera. Adults typically have a single pair of wings, with the hind wings modified into tiny, club-shaped structures called halteres that help maintain balance during flight. Over 124,000 named species belong in this group, including the familiar black flies, mosquitoes, and midges. While flies are often considered pests, it is important to remember that many species play important roles as scavengers, pollinators, and food sources for birds and other vertebrates.

Black Fly (Family Simuliidae)
Description: Roughly ⅛ inch or less in length, black flies are dark brown to black in color with a distinctly humped back. They have short legs and transparent wings that are slightly iridescent in the right light.
Behavior: Spring visitors to the Adirondacks are introduced quickly to swarms of biting black flies. The greatest densities occur in wooded areas near streams. Females require a protein-rich blood meal from a mammalian host in order to form eggs. Males apparently feed on nectar. Black flies are not known to transmit diseases to humans, but their bites can leave large, painful welts. Mating occurs in the summer, after which females lay their eggs on the surface of fast-flowing streams or attach them to submerged rocks. After the eggs hatch, the larvae remain attached to the rock and filter plankton from the fast-flowing waters. Later, they build small "cocoons" and enter the pupal stage for roughly five days before emerging and floating to the surface as adult black flies.

Deer Fly (Family Tabanidae)
Description: Deer flies are roughly ⅜ inch long, with black and yellow bodies. Their eyes are metallic green and yellow. The wings have a distinctive smoky brownish black pattern.

Behavior: Deer flies prefer to remain near a water source; they frequent deciduous and mixed conifer forests, grassy meadows, and roadsides. Female deer flies pester hikers by rapidly circling the head before landing for a painful bite. Deer flies locate their victims by sight and by following invisible plumes of carbon dioxide given off during breathing. Males feed on nectar. After mating, females deposit several masses of shiny black eggs on vegetation adjacent to a stream or pool. The larvae are aquatic and spend the remainder of the year feeding on tiny aquatic insects. Larvae pupate and adults emerge in May through July.

Horsefly (Family Tabanidae)

Description: Horseflies are closely related to deer flies, but are larger and more robust. Horseflies can reach 1 inch in length. They have black bodies and smoky black wings.

Behavior: Like deer flies, horseflies circle their victims before landing. Females feed on mammal blood by cutting into the skin using two serrated, blade-like mandibles and lapping the blood that pools in the cut. The bites can be exceedingly painful. As is typical for many flies, males feed on pollen and nectar. Horseflies are found in wooded or open areas, but are less common than deer flies. Eggs are laid on plants over a water source. The worm-like larvae are over 1 inch long and drop into the water to feed. The larvae overwinter in the mud before pupating into adult horseflies in the late spring and summer.

Punkies, No-see-ums (Family Ceratopogonidae)

Description: Also known as biting midges, these flies are a diminutive $\frac{1}{10}$ to $\frac{1}{20}$ of an inch long. Adults have black or dark gray bodies, dark wings, and long feathery antennae.

Behavior: Another unpleasant inhabitant of the Adirondacks, punkies are small enough to pass through window screens. They swarm in large numbers, especially at dawn and dusk. Punkies usually emerge later in the season than black flies. Females lay strings of eggs in ponds or pools of standing water. The larvae feed on plankton and other tiny aquatic animals before pupating into adults.

Mosquitoes (Family Culicidae)

Description: Mosquitoes are delicately built flies roughly $\frac{1}{8}$ to $\frac{1}{4}$ inches in length. The wings and abdomen are brownish gray and quite slender. The abdomens often have faint brown bands. The legs are long and delicate.

Behavior: Mosquitoes are found in virtually all Adirondack habitats, but favor areas near stagnant water. At dawn and dusk, clouds of mosquitoes emerge to forage for food. High-pitched humming, produced by wings that beat at nearly 600 beats per second, signals the presence of nearby mosquitoes. Females have a long, syringe-like proboscis that is used to penetrate the skin and suck the blood from mammalian hosts, including humans. The blood meal is used to aid the development of the ovaries and the formation of eggs. Male mosquitoes feed only on nectar, but they join the evening swarms in search for mates. Females lay clusters of eggs on the surface of virtually any stagnant water source, no matter how small. The eggs hatch in a day or two. The larvae feed just below the water surface for a week or so before pupating. Because the life cycle is short, there are many generations per year.

Hover Fly or Flower Fly (Family Syrphidae)   PLATE 1
Description: Hover flies are ⅜ inch in length with stout, banded yellow and black abdomens. They resemble small bees. The wings are transparent and beat at frequencies high enough to allow them to hover for long periods.
Behavior: Hover flies, also known as flower flies, are important pollinators because adults feed exclusively on nectar. Consequently, they are often found in meadows, marshes, and other areas where flowers are abundant. After mating, females deposit single eggs on plants

infested with aphids. The maggot-like larvae prey on the aphids until they drop to the ground and pupate in the leaf litter. Hover flies are beneficial insects, serving as pollinators for many flowering plants, while simultaneously ridding them of harmful aphids.

Crane Fly (Family Tipulidae)
Description: Adult crane flies resemble giant mosquitoes. They have slender bodies, thin legs that are twice the body length, and wingspans of nearly 3 inches.
Behavior: Crane flies are slow, somewhat clumsy fliers that typically are found near streams, ponds, or marshes. In some species, adults feed on nectar, but most species do not eat as adults. Rather, adults form small swarm clouds above vegetation or near lights as they seek mates. After mating, females lay several hundred eggs in moist soil. The resulting lar-

vae feed on rotting vegetation. A few weeks later, the larvae form pupae and either transform into adults, or overwinter in the mud as pupae.

Midges (Family Chironomidae)
Description: Midges are often mistaken for mosquitoes. Midges, however, do not bite. Unlike mosquitoes, resting midges hold their wings out to the sides. Midges also have feathery antennae.
Behavior: Adults form dense clouds near water sources during the spring and summer mating season. Eggs are laid in the water and hatch into larvae in a few days. These larvae may feed for several months before pupating into adults. The larvae of certain species are reddish in color because they contain red hemoglobin, which is visible through their transparent bodies. Midge larvae are an important source of food for fish. The adults are food for swallows and bats.

BEES, WASPS, AND ANTS

Bees, wasps, sawflies, and ants are all members of the Order Hymenoptera. This group is characterized by the presence of four transparent wings on those members of the colony that have wings. Females in this group have an egg-laying structure called an ovipositor that often is modified for stinging. Another interesting feature of the Hymenoptera is the formation of large colonies that include a fertile queen, sterile females, and fertile male drones.

Bald-faced Hornet or White-faced Hornet
(Family Vespidae, *Dolichovespula* species)
Description: Bald-faced hornets are not hornets; rather they are large black-and-ivory-colored yellowjackets. They are roughly 1 inch in length, with distinctive black and white markings on the head. The abdomen is black with white on the posterior tip.
Behavior: Bald-faced hornets are common throughout the Northeast. Each spring, as the weather warms, a queen begins the construction of a new nest. Nests are built from small strips of bark to which the queen adds saliva to form a small, smooth, paper container where she deposits her eggs. These eggs hatch into larvae, which are fed by the queen until they pupate into workers. These workers now expand the size of the nest, defend the growing colony, and forage for food, while the queen lays more eggs. The nests can reach 12 inches or more across by the fall and contain colonies of several hundred hornets. Disturbing such nests often results in painful stings as the aggressive workers attempt to defend the nest.

Eastern Yellowjacket (Family Vespidae, *Vespula* species)   PLATE 2

Description: Yellowjackets are roughly ½ inch long, with stout bodies and alternating bands of black and yellow on the abdomen. Many species have yellow patches on the head and face.

Behavior: Like other social insects, yellowjackets live in colonies con-

sisting of a single queen and many workers and males. In spring, a fertile queen emerges from her winter home and seeks out a suitable place to build a nest. Nests are typically constructed underground or in stumps or logs; buildings are also used as nest sites. The queen lays eggs in the new nest and feeds the brood once they hatch. This brood of workers soon assumes the job of expanding the nest, defending the col-

ony, and foraging for food. The queen remains inside laying eggs until she dies in the fall. During the summer, the colony expands to several thousand wasps. Late in the summer, the queen lays eggs destined to become males and new queens. The adult males and potential queens leave the nest to mate; shortly after mating, the males die, while the mated queens seek shelter for the winter. Adult yellowjackets feed on fruits, nectar, and other sugar-rich foods, but the larvae eat protein fed to them by workers returning with insects or meat. Yellowjackets are persistent pests at picnics because, like us, their diet includes fruits, sodas, and meats. Foraging workers rarely attack humans, but they sting repeatedly if the colony is threatened or disturbed.

Bumblebee (Family Apidae, *Bombus* species)

Description: Bumblebees are ½ to 1 inch in length, with thick, hairy bodies. They typically have black heads with yellow on the thorax and

alternating bands of yellow and black on the abdomen. The wings are smoky gray and relatively small for such a large-bodied insect.

Behavior: Bumblebees live near clearings and meadows where summer flowers are abundant. Bumblebees are social and form small colonies of roughly 50 to 100 bees. Colonies are typically at or below ground level. The queen populates the colony by laying eggs that hatch into

workers. Adult workers forage for nectar that they extract from flowers with their long tongues. During foraging, bumblebees are dusted with pollen from the flowers, which is transferred to other flowers or groomed by the bee into "pollen baskets" on the legs. Harvested nectar and pollen is returned to the colony and deposited into waxy cells for storage. Unlike honeybees, bumblebees store the food for a few days and do not process it into honey. Bumblebees are not aggressive and sting only when directly threatened.

Honeybee (Family Apidae, *Apis* species)

Description: Honeybees vary in size depending on the caste; the queen is the largest at ¾ inch, male drones are ⅝ inch, and the sterile female workers are the smallest at roughly ½ inch in length. Honeybees are typically reddish brown to nearly black on the head and thorax, with yellowish bands on the abdomen. They are less densely haired and less stocky than bumblebees.

Behavior: Honeybees are not native to North America, but instead were introduced here in 1622 by colonists. Like other bees, colonies contain one queen, several thousand males (called drones), and a variable population of sterile female workers. Workers construct a waxy honeycomb consisting of tubes, into which the queen lays a single egg. Once hatched, the larvae are fed by workers until they pupate into adults. Newly hatched workers remain in the hive feeding larvae and cleaning the honeycomb. As they mature  they leave the hive as foragers. Honeybees communicate the location of food sources to the remainder of the colony by an elaborate "waggle dance" that conveys information on the distance and direction from the hive. Honeybees are not particularly aggressive, but will sting to defend the colony. Unlike wasps and hornets, the honeybee stinger is barbed and lodges in the skin of the victim. Consequently, each bee is capable of stinging only once. New colonies are founded by a queen and several hundred to a thousand workers, who leave the existing colony as a large "swarm." Wild colonies are found in hollow trees; beekeepers build special hive boxes to house and transport the colonies more efficiently. Honeybees are pollinators of many important agricultural crops.

Mud Dauber Wasp (Family Sphecidae, *Sceliphron* species)

Description: Mud dauber wasps are 1 inch or more in length, with slender bodies and a thin "waist" between the thorax and abdomen. The body is generally black or brown with some yellow on the thorax and legs. The related blue mud dauber has a steel-blue body with no traces of yellow.

Behavior: Mud daubers are solitary and build small mud nests in shaded areas, such as under bridges, near window ledges, or under roof eaves.

Female mud daubers make repeated visits to puddles or shorelines to collect mud, which they roll into a ball and carry back to the nest. Once a cell of the nest is constructed, the female lays a single egg inside the cell, provisions it with paralyzed spiders or insects, seals the cell with mud, and begins construction of the next cell. Although adult wasps feed on nectar, the larvae are carnivorous. Once the larvae have reached sufficient size, they pupate within the cell and chew their way out. Mud daubers rarely use their venom to sting humans.

Paper Wasp (Family Vespidae, *Polistes* species)

Description: Paper wasps are up to 1 inch in length, with slender bodies that superficially resemble yellowjackets (to which they are closely related). Paper wasps have a narrow "waist" between thorax and abdomen. They are reddish brown to black with thin yellow rings around each segment of the abdomen. The wings are reddish brown.

Behavior: Paper wasps gather plant fibers, which they mix with saliva, to construct nests that appear to be made of gray paper. The nests are umbrella shaped, with the cells opening downward and a thin stalk anchoring the nest. Paper wasps prefer open areas and frequently attach their nests to buildings. Unlike yellowjackets and hornets, paper wasps are generally not aggressive, but can inflict a painful sting if provoked. Adult paper wasps feed on nectar and rotting fruit. Larvae are fed a diet of insects, including caterpillars, flies, and beetle larvae. Consequently, gardeners consider paper wasps to be beneficial.

Ants (Family Formicidae)

Description: Ants come in a wide variety of shapes, colors, and sizes and are difficult to tell apart. Ants are distinguished from other insects by their bent antennae and a constricted second abdominal segment that forms a distinct "waist." They have strong mandibles (jaws) used for defense and for carrying food back to the colony. A sharp claw at the end of each leg allows them to climb vertical surfaces.

Behavior: Ants are social insects related to wasps and bees; both groups belong to the Order Hymenoptera. They live in highly organized underground colonies consisting of thousands of individuals. Colonies typically include a fertile queen, sterile female workers, and fertile males called drones. In fall or early spring, hundreds of winged drones swarm around winged queens during a brief mating period. After mating, the queen and males lose their wings and the queen builds an underground nest and lays eggs. The eggs hatch into the workers and males that will form the residents of the new colony. The workers remain in the nest, tending the queen and developing larvae, while drones forage for food above ground along trails marked with chemical signals called pheromones.

TERRESTRIAL BEETLES AND BUGS

There are more species of beetles than any other group of insects. They differ from other insects in possessing hard, shield-like forewings, which are folded over the true wings when not in flight. The forewings (called elytra) are elevated to expose the second pair of wings (true wings) during flight. Upon landing, the beetle folds its wings and stores them beneath the protective elytra. In ground beetles, which have lost the ability to fly, the elytra are fused into a solid shield over the abdomen.

The word "bug" is used by many people to refer to any unidentified insect, but, to scientists, it refers to the Order Hemiptera. Although they may resemble beetles or other insects, true bugs have several unique characteristics. For example, unlike beetles, their forewings are only hard at the base. In addition, hemipterans have elongated mouth parts used to puncture leaves or stems and suck out the plant fluids within. Hemiptera include aphids, leafhoppers, stinkbugs, and cicadas.

Firefly or Lightning Bug (Family Lampyridae)

Description: Fireflies are actually beetles with long, somewhat flattened bodies up to ¾ inch in length. The head often has a dull yellowish color with a central band of black or red. The elytra, or wing covers, are brown with yellow streaks. Both sexes produce flashing green or yellow light from their abdomens.

Behavior: Fireflies live in meadows and other open areas, where they hunt for insects, slugs, mites, and other small invertebrates. Adults emit flashes of light from special glands in the abdomen as a means of attracting mates. Because the light is produced by chemical reactions involving the enzyme luciferase, it is referred to as bioluminescence. Some species are cannibalistic; females use these light flashes to lure males to their deaths. Eggs are laid in the leaf litter or in rotting logs, where they hatch into luminscent larvae call "glow-worms." The larvae overwinter in the soil and pupate in the spring. Adults emerge in the summer.

Ground Beetle (Family Carabidae)

Description: Over 2,000 species of ground beetles have been identified in North America. They range in size from ⅛ inch to over 1 inch long. Most species are shiny black, but others are iridescent green or some combination of other bright colors. They have small heads, prominent thoraxes, and relatively long legs.

Behavior: Ground beetles are diverse. Some species of ground beetles, including tiger beetles, are carnivorous and hunt during the day. Others are nocturnal and eat pollen, berries, and other plant parts. Most species are restricted to the ground and are often found under rocks or logs.

Click Beetle (Family Elateridae)

Description: These beetles range in size from ⅒ inch to well over 1 inch in length. They are brown or gray over the entire body. The body is long and flattened, with a relatively large thorax.

Behavior: Click beetles produce a sharp clicking sound when an over-turned beetle flips itself upright. This flip is accomplished by arching the body, which forces a spine of the front segment of the thorax to snap into a groove in the middle thorax. This mechanism flips the beetle into the air. Adults of some species eat leaves and decayed wood, but larvae live in the soil, where they eat the roots and seeds of economically important crops such as wheat, corn, and cotton.

Carrion Beetle or Burying Beetle

(Family Silphidae, *Nicrophorus* species)

Description: These black and orange beetles reach 1½ inches in length. The elytra (wing covers) have patches of bright orange or red on a field ot black. The head and thorax are generally black. The antennae end in a club, which may be orange in some species.

Behavior: Burying beetles feed on corpses of mice or songbirds. A pair of adults locates a carcass by scent. They may bury the carcass at the site or drag it several feet before burying it beneath loose dirt. Once buried, the pair scrapes off the fur or feathers, covers the flesh with antibacterial saliva, and forms it into a ball. The female lays her eggs nearby, and when they hatch, the larvae begin feeding on the carcass. Adults tend the developing larvae until they move up into the soil and pupate. Burying beetles are common in deciduous woodlands and old fields.

Ladybug or Ladybird Beetle (Family Coccinellidae)   PLATE 3

Description: Ladybugs are small, oval beetles approximately ¼ inch in length. The dome-shaped wing covers (elytra) have roughly a dozen black spots on bright orange or reddish brown backgrounds. The head is small and tucked under the first segment of the thorax.

Behavior: Ladybugs inhabit woodlands, meadows, and suburban flowerbeds. They feed on aphids and other small insects, and as a result are considered a beneficial insect. Females lay groups of 10 to 30 eggs on plants in the spring. The larvae feed primarily on aphids and insect eggs. Two weeks later, the larvae pupate into adults. The adults can form large swarms as they seek overwintering sites, which sometimes include houses. Overwintering beetles are sometimes collected and sold as a natural form of pest control.

Milkweed Bug (Family Lygaeidae, *Lygaeus* species)

Description: Milkweed bugs are true bugs (Hemiptera) roughly ⅜ inch long, with black and orange markings on the back. When the wings are

folded over the back, the wing covers form an orange X on a black background.

Behavior: As their name implies, these bugs live on milkweed plants in meadows and along roadsides. Their diet consists of milkweed seeds. They are able to digest the toxic compounds produced by the milkweed plants. In fact, these chemicals make the milkweed bug highly toxic to birds and other insect predators. Their bright orange and black colors signal their toxicity to would-be predators. Females lay eggs on the undersides of milkweed leaves. The eggs hatch into small nymphs, which look like tiny adults. The nymphs undergo a series of moults before reaching adulthood.

Annual Cicada (Family Cicadidae)

Description: Cicadas are 1 to 2 inches in length, with black or dark brown bodies and widely spaced, bulging eyes. The transparent wings, when folded, extend well beyond the tip of the abdomen. Cicadas are best known for the sounds they produce.

Behavior: Cicadas live in deciduous woodlands or mixed conifer forests, usually near meadows or pastures. Males produce one of the loudest sounds in the insect world with the help of special structures

in the abdomen called tymbales. Although both sexes have tymbales, only the males use them to attract females. Muscles in the abdomen vibrate the tymbal membranes, producing sounds as loud as 100 decibels. The sound is a raspy whine that rises and falls in pitch. After mating, female cicadas repeatedly cut a slit in tree bark and deposit several eggs inside each slit. The newly hatched nymphs fall to the ground, burrow into the soil, and suck the fluids from roots. Mature nymphs emerge from the ground, climb nearby vegetation, and moult into adults, leaving the old exoskeleton behind.

GRASSHOPPERS AND CRICKETS

Grasshoppers and crickets are members of the Orthoptera. They have two pairs of functional wings, with the hind wings broader than the forewings. The wings typically are folded against the abdomen at rest. Orthopterans also have large hind legs, which, in grasshoppers, are capable of producing extraordinary jumps. Some members of this group, notably crickets, are capable of making sounds by rubbing their wings together or against their legs. Nearby crickets detect these sounds with "ears" on their legs.

Field Cricket (Family Gryllidae)

Description: Field crickets are roughly 1 inch in length, brown in color, and have thick, cylindrical abdomens. Like their close relatives the grasshoppers, cricket hind legs are long and powerfully built. The antennae are longer than the body.

Behavior: Field crickets eat plant material as well as other insects; when starved, they sometimes resort to cannibalism. Eggs hatch in early spring and the nymphs feed voraciously before moulting into adults. Males begin chirping in summer to attract females. The chirp is produced by rubbing comb-like ridges on the wings together. The rate of chirping increases as temperatures warm. Females listen to the chirps with a special ear-like structure on

the leg and evaluate the quality of the male prior to choosing him as a mate.

Grasshopper (Family Acrididae)

Description: Up to 2 inches in length, grasshoppers have long, brown or green bodies with huge hind legs for jumping. The head is blunt and the antennae are generally shorter than the body.

Behavior: Grasshoppers live in fields and meadows, feeding on grasses and other plant material. Males rub their hind legs against their forewings to produce a characteristic sound. Males are typically smaller

than females and often ride piggyback on the female during mating. Females lay eggs in the ground or inside plant tissues. The eggs hatch into nymphs that resemble miniature adults. Some species in the family Acrididae form large swarms that can be very destructive to agricultural crops.

BUTTERFLIES AND MOTHS

Seventy-four species of butterflies, in six families, inhabit the Adirondacks along with an unknown number of moth species. Butterflies are active during the day, while moths are active primarily at night. Butterflies have thin antennae with a club-shaped tip. In contrast, moths (especially males) usually have feathery antennae, which increases the surface area for specialized receptors used to detect pheromones (chemical cues used to attract mates).

Tiger Swallowtail   PLATES 4A AND 4B
(Family Papilionidae, *Papilio glaucus*)

Description: Tiger swallowtails get their name from the prominent

black and yellow stripes across the wings. The outer margins of fore- and hind wings are black with a row of yellow spots. The hind wing has a long, tail-like extension. Both sexes have a band of blue on the hind wings, but the band is much larger in females. Tiger swallowtails are large butterflies with wingspans that reach 5 inches. Females come in two color morphs; the more common yellow morph is similar to that of males described above, but the dark morph has black wings with a broad zone of blue on the hind wings. Young caterpillars are rough in texture, brown over most of the body with a white patch in the middle, and resemble bird droppings. Older caterpillars are light brown or green with a pair of distinctive yellow and blue eyespots on one end.

Behavior: Tiger swallowtails favor open deciduous woodlands, orchards, roadsides, and other sunny areas. Adults forage for nectar in the late morning and afternoon and may form small groups. Eggs are laid on willows, cherry trees, birches, and other deciduous trees. The eggs hatch in roughly ten days into small caterpillars that mimic bird droppings. The caterpillars feed on the leaves of the host plant, completing several moults in the process. They pupate in a brownish chrysalis that resembles a dead leaf. If pupation takes place late in the season, they may overwinter in the chrysalis and emerge as adult butterflies in May or June.

Black Swallowtail (Family Papilionidae, *Papilio polyxenes*)   PLATE 5
Description: Black swallowtails have wingspans of 3 to 4 inches. The upper wing surface is black with two rows of large yellow spots toward the posterior edge of the wing. Where the two hind wings meet near the abdomen, there is a pair of large orange spots with a black spot in the center. Females have a band of iridescent blue on the hind wings. The undersurface of the wings have a band of blue sandwiched between two rows of large orange spots. Caterpillars are green with numerous black bands around the body and rows of small yellow spots on alternate bands.
Behavior: Black swallowtails prefer open meadows, grassy marshes, and roadsides. Adults feed on nectar from a variety of flowers, including those of the milkweed plant. After mating, females lay eggs on suitable host plants. Caterpillars feed until they reach lengths of nearly 2 inches. Mature caterpillars construct a chrysalis that stands upright on a twig. Pupation takes

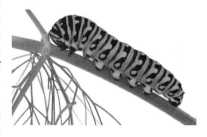

roughly nine or ten days; they may overwinter in the chrysalis if pupation occurs in the fall.

Clouded Sulphur (Family Pieridae, *Colias philodice*)
Description: These are small, yellow butterflies with wingspans of 2 to 2¾ inches. The upper wing surface is yellow with a black trim on the margins. The undersurface of the wing is yellow with one or two prominent silver spots trimmed with orange or pink. Females sometimes occur in a "white" morph that is pale green to white instead of yellow.
Behavior: Clouded sulphurs are common along roadsides and in open fields. Small groups are often seen at puddles along wet trails. Pale yellow eggs are laid on clover, alfalfa, or other host plants. In a few days,

the eggs hatch into slim, green caterpillars roughly 1 inch in length. Up to three generations are possible in a single year.

Monarch   PLATES 6A AND 6B
(Family Nymphalidae, *Danaus plexippus*)

Description: Monarchs are large, orange and black butterflies with wingspans of nearly 4 inches. The upper wing surface is orange with thick, black wing veins. Two or three rows of white spots extend around the otherwise black outer margins of the wings. The undersurface of the wings is a pale orange. Monarch caterpillars have many thin bands of white, black, and yellow around the body.

Behavior: Monarchs are unique among butterflies in making long-distance migrations. Adults begin their annual migration in the fall. Adirondack monarchs fly southwest and spend the winter in remote fir forests in the Sierra Madre of Mexico. Here they rest and feed until the spring, when they head northward. When they reach the Gulf Coast, they breed and lay eggs on milkweed plants. It is these offspring that continue the journey northward in the late spring and summer. By late June or early July, adult monarchs born in the southern United States have arrived in the Adirondacks. Here they feed on flower nectar and breed. Females lay several hundred eggs, one at a time, on the undersides of milkweed leaves. In 7 to 12 days, the eggs hatch into brightly colored caterpillars that feed exclusively on milkweed leaves. During feeding, they accumulate and store the toxic chemicals produced by milkweed plants in their bodies; their bright colors serve to warn predators that they are highly toxic. The caterpillars moult several times as they grow, eventually forming a hanging pupae called a chrysalis.

Within the jade-green chrysalis they undergo metamorphosis over a two-week period and emerge as an adult butterfly.

American Painted Lady   PLATE 7
(Family Nymphalidae, *Vanessa virginiensis*)

Description: Also known as "cosmopolites," painted ladies are among the most-common North American butterflies. The upper wing surface is primarily orange, with black patches on the forewings and a row of black-rimmed blue spots on the hind wings. The forewing tips are black with white spots. The undersurfaces of the wings are brown, black, and white with two large eye-spots on the hind wings and patches of rosy pink on the forewings. Wingspans are 2 to 2¼ inches. Caterpillars are just over 1 inch in length and vary greatly in color; most are black with purple and yellow spots and have numerous spiny hairs.

Behavior: Painted ladies prefer open meadows, forest edges, and mountaintops above treeline where alpine flowers are blooming. They do not overwinter in the Adirondacks. Instead, they recolonize the park each year from broods born in more southern states. Adults feed on nectar from a variety of flowers. Caterpillars are solitary and spend their time feeding on host plants inside a "tent" made of leaves bound together with silk.

Mourning Cloak (Family Nymphalidae, *Nymphalis antiopa*)
Description: Mourning cloaks are large butterflies with wingspans reaching 3½ inches. The upper wing surface is a dark brown with hints

of maroon iridescence. The outer wing margin is trimmed with yellow and just inside the yellow band is a row of bright blue spots. The undersurface of the wing is dark gray with a dusty cream-colored border. Caterpillars are black with many tiny white spots and a single row of large red spots on the back. They are covered with stiff black bristles and reach 2 inches in length.

Behavior: Mourning cloaks typically are found along waterways or in open areas such as roadsides, gardens, and meadows. With their wings closed over the back, mourning cloaks resemble a dead leaf. Adults feed on nectar and tree sap from willows, poplars, and birch trees. Females lay a cluster of eggs on a twig of a host tree. The caterpillars feed in groups before dispersing to pupate. Adults disperse to find new feeding sites prior to hibernating for the winter beneath loose bark. Because the adults hibernate, they often are the earliest butterfly seen in spring.

Red Admiral (Family Nymphalidae, *Vanessa atalanta*)   PLATE 8
   Description: The red admiral is a brightly colored butterfly of medium size; they have a wingspan of roughly 2 inches. The upper surface of the wing is brown or black with a thick orange to reddish bar across the forewings and a similar bar at the posterior margin of the hind wing. The tips of the forewings are covered with white spots. The undersides

of the wings are mottled brown with orange or pink bars and white or blue spots. Caterpillars are approximately 1 inch long, tan to nearly black in color, and have many spiny bristles.

Behavior: Red admirals disperse northward each spring to repopulate the Adirondacks from more southern populations. Migrating adults arrive in late spring, mate, and lay their eggs on nettles. The eggs hatch into caterpillars that enclose themselves in a tent made of a folded nettle leaf held shut by silken threads. Adults feed on flower nectar and are common around gardens, along roadsides, in old fields, and along open shorelines.

Gypsy Moth (Family Lymantriidae, *Lymantria dispar*)
Description: Males typically have wingspans of less than 1 inch, while the larger females can have wingspans of 2½ inches or more. Males have tan wings with irregular brown or gray lines or crescents in several rows across the wings. A band of dark brown covers the posterior margin of the wings. Males have feathery antennae and thin abdomens. Females are lighter and more yellowish in color, with a series of brown spots on the posterior wing margins and thicker abdomens. The caterpillars have long hairs covering their gray bodies. There are five pairs of bluish-gray warts and six pairs of brick red warts on their back.
Behavior: Gypsy moths are native to Europe and Asia, but were introduced to New England in 1869 by a scientist attempting to hybridize them with native silk-producing caterpillars. Since their arrival, they have spread rapidly, leaving millions of acres of denuded deciduous trees in their path. Females are poor fliers and stay close to the ground. They attract males by emitting a chemical pheromone that the male detects with his large antennae. After mating, females lay as many as 1,200 eggs on the branches or trunks of nearby trees. These eggs overwinter and hatch when the trees bud out in the spring. At night, the caterpillars crawl into the canopy of the tree to feed, often returning to the trunk at daybreak to rest. When populations are high, they feed constantly and easily strip a tree of all of its leaves.

Isabella Tiger Moth or Woolly Bear   PLATE 9
(Family Arctiidae, *Pyrrharctia isabella*)
Description: Isabella tiger moths have a wingspan of roughly 2 inches. The adult moth has yellowish or light-pink wings with small brown spots near the outer margins. The abdomen is furry and has one or more rows of black spots, one per segment, extending down the abdomen. The caterpillars commonly are called "woolly bears" because of their thickly haired bodies. They are black at both ends and reddish brown in the middle.

Behavior: Isabella tiger moths live in a variety of habitats, including fields, roadsides, and other open areas. The caterpillars often are encountered crossing roads and trails in the late summer and fall. There are typically two or three generations per year and those caterpillars seen in the late fall will overwinter and pupate in the spring. The caterpillars feed on a wide range of grasses as well as on the leaves of maples, birches, and other deciduous trees. An old folktale holds that the width of the caterpillar's brown band predicts how long the coming winter will last. There appears to be no truth to this myth, because the width of the band varies greatly even within a single brood and the brown band increases in length with each moult.

Eastern Tent Caterpillar Moth
(Family Lasiocampidae, *Malacosoma americanum*)

Description: Tent caterpillar moths are stocky, hairy moths, with tan or reddish wings. A pair of light lines often extends across the wings. The caterpillars are 1 to 3 inches in length, with long thin bodies covered with short hairs. They have a yellow stripe running the length of the back, and the flanks have a row of white or blue spots.

Behavior: Fertile females lay several hundred eggs on trees, including cherry and apple trees, in late spring. Newly hatched caterpillars build a silken tent in the crotch of several branches. Here, these highly social caterpillars rest before leaving on feeding bouts several times a day. Apparently, the caterpillars lay down silken trails to indicate where to feed and how to get back to the tent. Tents are expanded as the colony matures. Mature caterpillars disperse, construct silken cocoons, and pupate over several weeks into adult moths.

AQUATIC INSECTS

The insects described below are grouped together because they share a fully or semi-aquatic lifestyle, rather than because they represent a single taxonomic group. For example, water boatmen, water striders, and back swimmers are members of the Hemiptera (true bugs). Aquatic beetles include whirligig beetles and the predaceous diving beetles. Other aquatic insects, including the stoneflies and mayflies, spend most of their lives as aquatic nymphs. Thus, they form an important component of the food base for fish communities. Dragonflies and damselflies, on the other hand, spend their adult lives foraging near steams and ponds.

Water Boatman (Family Corixidae)

Description: Water boatmen are ½ to ¾ inch in length, dark gray or brown in color, and have long, oar-like hind legs. The front legs are small and modified for scraping, while the middle and hind legs are long, fringed with stiff hairs, and serve as oars to row the insect through the water.

Behavior: Water boatmen are found in ponds, lakes, and streams. Unlike backswimmers, water boatman swim beneath the surface in an upright position. They feed on algae attached to submerged surfaces by scraping the algae free with their front legs. In the summer, females cement eggs to submerged plants and rocks. The eggs hatch into nymphs in a week or two. Nymphs undergo five moults before becoming adults.

Water Strider (Family Gerridae)

Description: Water striders have long, somewhat flattened bodies roughly ½ inch in length. The front legs are short and used for grasping prey. The middle and hind legs are long and thin; the tips of these legs are covered with microscopic hairs, which prevent the leg from getting wet and allow the strider to skate across the water using surface tension.

Behavior: Water striders are common on the surface of ponds and other standing water. Adults feed at the surface on mosquito larvae and other insects. Mating occurs in the spring and summer. Females deposit rows of eggs on objects at the surface. The nymphs feed and mature over the next month, before moulting into adults. Adults are gregarious and may form large groups.

Backswimmer (Family Notonectidae)

Description: Backswimmers are roughly ½ inch in length. They swim on their backs using their long hind legs as oars. Their first two pairs of legs are used for grasping and holding prey. Backswimmers have large eyes and are generally black on the undersides. Their backs have ivory and reddish patches, but these are difficult to see when they are swimming.

Behavior: Backswimmers inhabit ponds and other slow-moving waters, where they prey on mosquito larvae and other aquatic insects. They can inflict a painful sting. Mating takes place under water in the spring. Females attach eggs to submerged plant stems. Two to three weeks later, the eggs hatch into predacious nymphs that resemble small adults.

Diving Beetle (Family Dystiscidae)

Description: Also known as predacious water beetles, these brown or black beetles have oval bodies that are 1 to 2 inches in length. The hind legs have a fringe of hairs that aid in swimming. The elytra (wing covers) are often grooved. Some species have a golden trim around the margins of the head, thorax, and abdomen.

Behavior: Both adults and larvae are carnivorous. They wait patiently until an aquatic insect, tadpole, or small fish comes within reach. Diving beetles live in ponds and quiet reaches of streams with ample vegetation and muddy bottoms. Mating occurs in early spring. The female inserts up to 50 eggs, one at a time, into a slit that she makes in a plant stem. The larvae hatch in roughly three weeks and spend the next month feeding, before pupating into adults.

Whirligig Beetle (Family Gyrinidae)

Description: These shiny black, oval-bodied beetles reach ½ inch in length. The front legs are longer and reach forward, while the middle and hind legs are tucked under the body. The wing covers (elytra) have many rows of tiny depressions.

Behavior: Whirligig beetles are found on the surface of ponds and quiet sections of streams. They swim erratically, often in circles, and may form large groups. Adults have divided eyes such that they can see above and below the surface simultaneously. They prey on aquatic insects. Female whirligig beetles lay eggs on submerged plants. The predaceous larvae hunt insects and mites before leaving the water to construct a gray cocoon, where they spend a month pupating.

Stoneflies (Order Plecoptera)

Description: Many species of stoneflies have been identified in North America. Adults have two pairs of transparent wings folded over the back, except in flight. Wingspans can reach 2 inches. The brownish body is long and somewhat compressed. The legs and antennae are relatively long. Two cerci (long thin projections) extend from the tip of the abdomen. The aquatic larvae are called naiads; they are similar to adults but lack wings.

Behavior: Adult stoneflies emerge in late spring and summer and rarely venture far from freshwater. Adults cling to vegetation and feed on lichens, decaying wood, and other vegetation prior to mating. Females fly over streams, dropping eggs into the water as they pass. The eggs sink to the bottom and hatch into larval stoneflies. Larvae are either predaceous, hunting other aquatic insect larvae among the gravel on the stream bottom, or herbivorous and feed on algae and detritus. Depending on the species, they may moult more than twelve times over the course of several years before emerging from the water as adults. Larval stoneflies require cool, clean water and are considered good indicators of water quality.

Mayflies (Order Ephemeroptera)

Description: Adult mayflies have two pairs of transparent wings. The front wings are much larger and are held vertically over the back. The antennae are short and 3 long, tail-like cerci extend from the tip of the abdomen. The aquatic nymphs are similar, but lack wings and typically have leaf-like gills on each abdominal segment.

Behavior: Over 600 species of North American mayflies have been identified. All have a very short adult lifespan; usually a few hours to a couple days in length. Adults emerge synchronously, forming massive mating swarms near lakes and streams. After mating, eggs are laid on the water surface and sink to the bottom. Depending on the species, aquatic nymphs forage near the bottom for algae, decaying leaves, or aquatic insect larvae. The nymphs undergo many moults over the course of a year before emerging as adults. Mayflies prefer cool, clear streams and are useful indicators of water quality.

Dragonflies (Order Odonata)

Description: Dragonflies are large insects with long, slender bodies roughly 2 to 4 inches in length. They have two pairs of transparent wings that are held horizontally at rest. Wingspan often exceeds body length. There may be markings on the wings in some species. The eyes are huge and bulge out from the head. Aquatic larvae have short, stout bodies and do not resemble adults.

Behavior: Adult dragonflies are voracious predators that consume large numbers of mosquitoes and flies. Dragonflies locate prey using their massive eyes; each eye contains tens of thousands of individual lenses. They are very efficient fliers and have been clocked as speeds of over 30 miles per hour. Mating typically takes place in flight, with the pair flying while coupled together. Depending on the species, mated females deposit eggs below the water surface or inside plant tissues. The eggs hatch into nymphs that feed on aquatic insects, tadpoles, and small fish. These nymphs use specialized mouthparts that dart outward and grasp any prey that comes within reach.

Damselflies (Order Odonata)

Description: Damselflies are similar to dragonflies in having long, thin bodies, two pairs of transparent wings, and large eyes. They differ in that damselflies hold their wings vertically when resting and the compound eyes are typically farther apart than in dragonflies. Damselflies are 1 to 2 inches in length and often have brightly colored bodies. The aquatic nymphs are long and slender, with a set of leaf-like gills at the tip of the abdomen.

Behavior: Like dragonflies, damselflies patrol ponds and marshes for mosquitoes and other insect prey. Mating occurs in flight and it is common to see a co-joined pair flying together during the mating season. Eggs are laid in water or inside a submerged plant. The nymphs feed on water fleas, mosquito larvae, and other small insects. The nymphs breathe using a set of fan-like gills that protrude from the tip of the abdomen. After

several moults, adults emerge at the water surface and begin their search for prey.

OTHER INVERTEBRATES

While insects are the most abundant and diverse of Adirondack invertebrates, several other groups deserve mention. Spiders, mites, and ticks have eight legs (four pairs) and belong to a group of arthropods called Arachnida. Members of this group are typically carnivorous or parasitic. Some construct elaborate silken webs from glands in their abdomens. Many use specialized venom glands to subdue their prey.

A few species are adapted for a parasitic life and must find a suitable host to complete their life cycle.

Crayfish are freshwater crustaceans that superficially resemble miniature lobsters. Crayfish have a cephalothorax that houses the gills and other organs, and a segmented abdomen. One pair of enlarged forelegs end in robust pinchers. These claws are used to capture or manipulate prey and for aggressive fights with other crayfish.

Aquatic leeches are not arthropods, but belong to a group called annelids, or segmented worms, a group that includes the familiar earthworms. The aquatic leeches most familiar to Adirondack residents are haemophagic, or blood feeders. They feed on the blood of fish, frogs, turtles, and mammals. In turn, leeches are preyed upon by crayfish, and many species of fish.

Wolf Spider (Family Lycosidae)

Description: Wolf spiders are typically less than ½ inch in length, with four pairs of slender legs and a tan or gray body. The body may have faint, light and dark stripes that aid in camouflage. Up close, one can see that these spiders are covered with tiny hairs.

Behavior: Wolf spiders occur in a wide range of habitats, including alpine meadows. They do not build webs, preferring to capture prey with a swift burst of speed.  The female prepares a silk cocoon, which she produces from a set of spinnerets on her abdomen. She carries her eggs in the cocoon until they hatch. The tiny spiderlings climb onto the mother's back and remain there for the next month. They are not considered dangerous, but they can give a painful bite if provoked.

Harvestman or Daddy Longlegs (Order Opiliones)

Description: Harvestmen have four pairs of extremely long, thin legs and a small oval body. The body retains the typical head, thorax, and abdomen configuration, but the thorax and abdomen appear to be a single unit. They are roughly ¼ inch in body length, but may be 3 inches between leg tips.

Behavior: Harvestmen do not build webs. Instead, they hunt tiny insects or feed on fungi and decaying plants. After mating in the fall,

females insert eggs deep into the soil, where they spend the winter. In the spring, the tiny harvestmen emerge to feed. They will undergo several moults before they reach adult size. Harvestmen do not produce venom and are of no threat to humans.

Deer Tick or Black-legged Tick (Family Ixodidae, *Ixodes scapularis*)

Description: The deer tick is an arachnid and, like a spider, has four pairs of legs. The family of hard ticks, to which the deer tick belongs, have a hard plate on top of the body. Adult deer ticks are dark brown with a reddish brown abdomen. Immature ticks are uniformly dark brown or tan in color. Adults are roughly ¼ inch in length, but nymphs can be tiny.

Behavior: Deer ticks feed on the blood of host animals, including white-tailed deer, mice, dogs, birds, and humans. Deer ticks detect a passing host by the carbon dioxide and heat they emit. Once a tick locates a suitable host, it climbs aboard, bites the host, and consumes the resulting blood meal. In the process, deer ticks may transmit a bacterial parasite to the host that is capable of causing debilitating Lyme disease. Symptoms of Lyme disease include an expanding reddish rash around the bite that may last for several weeks. Some people also

suffer muscle aches, joint pain, weakness, dizziness, and a variety of other symptoms. Lyme disease should be treated early or it may progress and become difficult to cure.

Crayfish (Order Decopoda)

Description: Several species of crayfish are found in Adirondack waters. They are 2 to 6 inches in length and look like small lobsters. They have two enlarged claws on the front legs and four pairs of walking legs. Crayfish have one long pair of antennae. The abdomen consists of a series of flexible segments with a fan-shaped tail at the end. Color ranges from tan to brown or olive green.

Behavior: Crayfish inhabit streams, rivers, lakes, and ponds. They spend most of the day under rocks and logs at the bottom. At night, they emerge to feed on both plant and animal material. Crayfish are territorial and use the enlarged foreclaws (called chelae) as weapons and to defend themselves. Not surprisingly, these powerful claws can give a painful pinch if the crayfish is mishandled. Mating generally takes place in the fall. Females store the sperm over the winter and fertilize the eggs in the spring. The female carries the eggs for a month or more, attached to the underside of her body. After hatching, the young undergo a series of moults as they grow to adulthood.

Freshwater Leeches (Class Hirundinea)
Description: Leeches, along with earthworms, belong to a group called annelids, or segmented worms. Leeches are 1 to 2 inches long, olive green to almost black in color, and have small sucker disks at each end of the body. They may have red and black spots on the dorsal surface.
Behavior: Leeches are found in lakes, ponds, swamps, and other slow-moving waters. They feed on vertebrate blood, often consuming twice their own body weight in host blood. Leeches swim toward movements in the water made by a potential host. They attach to the host with their sucker-shaped mouth and make a tiny Y-shaped incision in the skin. They secrete chemicals that act as anti-coagulants and anesthesia to keep the blood flowing and the host unaware. A single blood meal may last the leech for several months. Leeches are hermaphrodites; each individual has both male and female reproductive organs in its body. Two leeches come together and inseminate each other, and both lay fertilized eggs in the bottom sediments.

SOURCES AND ADDITIONAL READING

Dunkle, S. W. 2000. *Dragonflies through Binoculars: A Field Guide to Dragonflies of North America*. New York: Oxford University Press.

Glassberg, J. 1999. *Butterflies Through Binoculars: The East, A Field Guide to the Butterflies of Eastern North America*. New York: Oxford University Press.

Kaufman, K., and E. R. Eaton. 2007. *Kaufman Field Guide to Insects of North America*. Kaufmann Field Guide Series. Boston: Houghton Mifflin Company.

Marshall, S. A. 2006. *Insects: Their Natural History and Diversity: With a Photographic Guide to Insects of North America*. Richmond Hill, Ontario: Firefly Books.

Resh, V. H., and R. T. Carde. 2003. *Encyclopedia of Insects*. San Diego: Academic Press.

Voshell, J. R. 2002. *A Guide to Common Freshwater Invertebrates of North America*. Granville, OH: McDonald and Woodward Publishing Company.

5 Fish

Roughly the size of the state of Vermont, the 6.1-million-acre Adirondack Park is home to more than 3,000 lakes and ponds and over 30,000 miles of streams and rivers. The Adirondack Park now borders the western shoreline of Lake Champlain, and includes the 32-mile-long Lake George. Not surprisingly, these vast freshwater habitats are home to 86 different fish species. Some fish species occur in virtually all Adirondack waters, while others require special habitats, and are found in only a few locations within the park. Several species are not native to the higher elevations of the Adirondacks, but were introduced either intentionally as sport fish for anglers or accidentally as escaped baitfish. The consequences of accidental introductions are often dire and some native species have become locally extinct as a result.

Fish biologists generally group species into families based on shared characteristics. Thus, bullhead and catfish comprise the Family Ictaluridae, based in part on the presence of long, whisker-like barbels around the mouth. Pikes and pickerel (Family Esocidae) have long, thin bodies, with their dorsal fins located back near the tail. The species accounts that follow are grouped by family. They include only species that are relatively common within the park. A few species, including sea lamprey, brook lamprey, and brook silversides, are more typical of Lake Champlain and make short forays into the Adirondacks via tributaries. These and other species found only on the margins of the Adirondacks are not included in the accounts below.

BULLHEAD AND CATFISH (Family Ictaluridae)

Members of the family Ictaluridae have four pairs of long, whisker-like barbels on the head near the mouth. They use the taste receptors on their barbels to detect food as they scavenge along the murky bottom. They have a long anal fin on the belly in front of the tail and a small fleshy adipose fin on the back between the dorsal fin and the tail. The dorsal fin and the pectoral fins contain a bony spine.

Brown Bullhead (*Ameiurus nebulosus*)

Description: Brown bullhead are black to olive-brown above and pale yellow below. They have four pairs of sensory barbels surrounding the mouth. The barbels at the margin of the upper jaw are especially long. The pectoral fins contain a bony spine that can inflict puncture

wounds if an angler is not careful. Bullheads have a flattened head, thick body, and square tail fin. The average brown bullhead is roughly 6 to 12 inches in length and weighs less than 2 pounds.

Behavior: Brown bullhead are common in shallow areas of many Adirondack lakes and ponds. They prefer areas with aquatic vegetation and soft bottoms, but are less tolerant of murky waters than other bullhead species. Brown bullhead patrol the warmer, shallow waters at night and locate prey by using the taste receptors on their barbels. They feed on insect larvae, young crayfish, leeches, and a wide range of other invertebrates. Spawning takes place in late May or early June. Parents guard the young bullhead through the summer months until they reach about 2 inches in length.

SUCKERS (Family Catostomidae)

Suckers, family Catostomidae, include a variety of freshwater fish characterized by a mouth located under the head (subterminal position) and bordered by thick, fleshy lips that give the mouth a sucker-like appearance. They are primarily bottom feeders, eating a variety of plant and animal material.

Longnose Sucker (*Catostomus catostomus*)

Description: Longnose suckers are slender fish with a long snout and a downward-projecting, sucker-like mouth. The upper parts are dark gray or olive-brown in color and the underparts are pale yellow or whitish. During the breeding season, males may be black above with a red stripe along the side of the body. Adults are 12 to 18 inches in length and weigh up to 2 pounds.

Behavior: Longnose suckers are found in a few dozen Adirondack waters and appear to be declining in the region. They inhabit clear, cold streams and lakes. During the spring breeding season, they migrate up small streams to deposit their eggs. The eggs hatch after two weeks and the tiny suckers remain hidden in the gravel for another two weeks.

They reach adulthood in four years and may live more than 20 years in the wild. Like most suckers, longnose suckers are bottom feeders. Their diet includes algae scraped from rocks, insect larvae, copepods, and other invertebrates.

White Sucker (*Catostomus commersonii*)

Description: White suckers are slender and resemble the longnose sucker in coloration, but have a shorter snout. The upper body is olive-brown to black, shading to copper or brass on the sides and cream on the belly. The lips are thick and may have tiny wart-like tubercles, especially in breeding adults. White suckers are 6 to 20 inches in length and typically weigh under 4 pounds.

Behavior: White suckers live in virtually every aquatic habitat, from cool streams to warm, muddy ponds. Spawning occurs in April or May, when white suckers move into streams to deposit their eggs. A unique population of white suckers spawn in July and August and are thought to be a separate species called summer suckers. Young white suckers feed on protozoans and tiny invertebrates. As they mature, the diet shifts to aquatic insect larvae, snails, and other bottom-dwelling invertebrates.

MINNOWS (Family Cyprinidae)

The word "minnow" often is used to describe any small fish, but it actually refers to over 2,400 members of the family Cyprinidae, including carp and other large species. New York State is home to 48 species of Cyprinidae, but only the 15 species described below are common in the Adirondacks. These include various species of minnows, chubs, dace, and shiners. They mature rapidly, reaching adulthood as yearlings or two year olds and rarely live beyond three years of age in the wild.

Cutlips Minnow (*Exoglossum maxillingua*)

Description: These 3- to 6-inch-long minnows are a drab olive-gray color. Cutlips minnows can be identified by their distinctive mouths.

The lower jaw is divided into three lobes: two fleshy lateral lobes with a bony lobe in between.

Behavior: Cutlips minnows prefer clear streams with gravel or sandy bottoms. In spring, males build round, pebble nests up to 18 inches in diameter. Females approach the nest and mate with the resident male. Adults feed on algae and tiny mollusks scraped from rocks with their unique lips. They also eat mayflies and other bottom-dwelling aquatic insects. Cutlips minnows also have the unusual trait of plucking and eating the eyes of other fish species, especially when population densities are high.

Golden Shiner (*Notemigonus crysoleucas*)

Description: Adult golden shiners have flattened bodies and small, triangular heads. They are greenish gold on the upper back, fading to silver or light gold on the sides. The fins may be slightly orange-colored at their base. The dorsal fin is positioned behind the midpoint of the body. The lateral line forms a bow-shaped curve. Golden shiners range from 3 to 8 inches in length.

Behavior: Golden shiners prefer the still waters of ponds and the pools of slower-running streams and rivers, where aquatic vegetation is abundant. They feed primarily on zooplankton, aquatic insects, and occasionally small snails and algae. Golden shiners spawn in the late spring. Adults do not build nests or tend the eggs. Rather, the sticky eggs adhere to vegetation until they hatch.

Lake Chub (*Couesius plumbeus*)

Description: Lake chubs have long, streamlined bodies and relatively large eyes. They are a dull silver or olive-gray above and whitish on the belly. The scales of the lower flanks often are peppered with pigment granules. The fin bases may be reddish in males during the breeding season. A distinguishing feature of lake chubs is the presence of a bar-

bel (small fleshy bump) at the corner of the mouth. Adult lake chubs are roughly 2 to 5 inches in length.

Behavior: Lake chubs live in streams, ponds, and lakes. They move into streams to spawn in early spring. Eggs drop into crevices among the gravel, where they hatch in roughly ten days. The young fry feed on zooplankton, while older chubs also eat small aquatic insects and algae.

Eastern Blacknose Dace (*Rhinichthys atratulus*)

Description: Eastern blacknose dace are 2- to 4-inch-long minnows with dark olive-green to brown backs, light-colored bellies, and a wide band extending from the eye to the tail. A fleshy, tiny barbel is present at the corner of the mouth. A strip of skin called a frenum binds the upper lip to the snout. During the breeding season, the fins may be orange at the base and small tubercles form over the snout in males.

Behavior: Blacknose dace inhabit clear, small streams and are more widespread than any other stream minnow. Adults feed on diatoms, midges, and other small aquatic insects. They breed in late spring and early summer over gravel beds, where males establish small breeding territories.

Longnose Dace (*Rhinichthys cataractae*)

Description: Longnose dace are olive-green to brown above with cream-colored bellies. Patches of darker scales are present on the sides. The snout is longer than the blacknose dace and adults frequently have a dark stripe in front of the eye. Like the closely related blacknose dace, they have a frenum connecting the upper lip to the snout and small barbels at the corner of the mouth.

Behavior: Longnose dace prefer narrow, swiftly flowing streams or lake shores with gravel bottoms and frequent waves. They feed on aquatic insect larvae and algae. In spring, males defend small spawning beds used to attract females. The eggs are left undefended among the pebbles until they hatch several days later.

Creek Chub (*Semotilus atromaculatus*)   PLATE 10

Description: Creek chubs are relatively large minnows; they reach lengths of up to 10 inches. Adults are dark olive on the back and silvery white below, but may have a blue or purple sheen to the upper sides and back. Juveniles have a lateral band that extends from the head to the tail. During the spawning season, males become more reddish in color and develop prominent bumps or tubercles on the head (they are sometimes called horned dace). Adults are readily distinguished from other minnows by the mouth extending to the tip of the snout and by a dark patch at the base of the dorsal fin (absent in juveniles).

Behavior: Creek chubs are common in many Adirondack waters, including streams, rivers, and lakes. As they grow, their diet finally switches from tiny plankton to small fish. Spawning occurs in April or May. The male constructs pebble nests roughly a foot across, and, after spawning, he covers the eggs with gravel to protect them from predators.

Fallfish (*Semotilus corporalis*)

Description: Fallfish, New York's largest native minnow, reach lengths of up to 18 inches. They are silvery blue in color. The scales on the upper body are relatively large and have a small, dark crescent at the base of each scale. A small barbel is present at the corner of the mouth.

Behavior: Fallfish require clear streams and lakes. They are omnivorous as adults. They in turn fall prey to larger fish and ospreys, and are often caught by anglers. Spawning begins in April, when males begin building gravel nests 1 to 4 feet across. Several females may spawn over the same nest. The eggs hatch in five or six days.

Pearl Dace (*Margariscus margarita*)
Description: As their name implies, pearl dace are a pearl gray or silver color with hints of pink in males. Adults have irregularly shaped dark patches on the sides. Breeding males have orange-red sides.
Behavior: Pearl dace are found in clear, cool streams, tannin-stained bogs, and ponds. They feed on a variety of small aquatic invertebrates and occasionally algae. Spawning begins in spring; males establish small territories over the sandy bottom. Females mate many times and often with several males.

Brassy Minnow (*Hybognathus hankinsoni*)
Description: Brassy minnows rarely exceed 4 inches in length. They are olive-green above with brass-colored sides and white bellies. A faint side stripe may be present. The lower jaw is crescent shaped instead of U-shaped, like the jaws of shiners.
Behavior: Brassy minnows are uncommon in the Adirondacks. They favor slow currents, muddy bottoms, and the tannin-stained waters of bogs and marshes. The diet consists mainly of algae and an occasional copepod or fly larvae. Brassy minnows spawn in large schools during May through July.

Common Shiner (*Luxilus cornutus*) PLATE 11
Description: Common shiners are roughly 2 to 4 inches long. They are deeper-bodied than many minnows. They have silver bodies grading to white on the belly. Breeding males have red on the fins and sport many tubercles on the head.
Behavior: Widely distributed in Adirondack streams, common shiners tolerate a wide range of water temperatures. Spawning occurs in spring over gravel-bottomed riffles. They often spawn over nests constructed

by other minnows and chubs. After spawning, males defend the newly laid eggs from predation by other minnow species. Common shiners forage near the water surface for aquatic insects and other tiny prey.

Bridle Shiner　(*Notropis bifrenatus*)

Description: Bridle shiners have relatively large scales with dark halos, slender bodies, and a lateral stripe running from the snout to the tail. The body is sometimes yellowish above the stripe and white below. They rarely exceed 2 inches in length.

Behavior: Bridle shiners live in warmer, slow-moving streams as well as the quiet coves of ponds and lakes. They prefer muddy bottoms with some vegetation or debris for protection. They feed on insect larvae and other small invertebrates, but will take plant material as well. Spawning occurs between June and July in openings surrounded by vegetation. Females mate repeatedly during the day and release a few eggs at a time.

Northern Redbelly Dace　(*Phoxinus eos*)

Description: Northern redbelly dace are brown on the back, shading to cream or silver on the belly. There are two lateral stripes; the lower stripe extends from the snout to the tail, while the upper stripe is less distinct and often broken into patches. The flanks below the lower stripe are bright red or bright green in breeding males. The head is relatively small, but the eyes are large. This species is frequently confused with the closely related finescale dace.

Behavior: These native fish live in small, slow-moving streams and quiet ponds. They prefer areas with aquatic vegetation, including filamentous algae. They feed on diatoms, algae, zooplankton, and an assortment of aquatic insects. The first of two potential spawnings begins in late May. The fertilized eggs develop among the tangled strands of filamentous algae. The young fish reach sexual maturity after their second summer. Northern redbelly dace sometimes hybridize with the far less common finescale dace.

Bluntnose Minnow　(*Pimephales notatus*)

Description: Bluntnose minnows are 2 to 4 inches in length with triangular heads and blunt snouts. They are pale olive on the back and silvery on the sides and belly. A narrow lateral stripe extends from the snout to the tail, with a separate tail spot. Breeding males are much darker and have several rows of tubercles on the snout.

Behavior: Bluntnose minnows occupy a variety of habitats, from lakes and ponds to small streams. They spawn from late May through July.

Males use their tails to sweep out a nest cavity beneath a log or under a rock. Males mate with several females and guards the eggs until they hatch roughly one week later.

Fathead Minnow (*Pimephales promelas*)

Description: Fathead minnows have thick bodies and blunt heads. They are olive-gray above shading to white on the belly. Juveniles have a lateral stripe, but it is often lost in adulthood. Breeding males are dark with a lighter ring behind the head and numerous tubercles on the snout.

Behavior: Fathead minnows inhabit both ponds and slow streams. They appear to tolerate low oxygen levels and are found in warmer, more turbid waters. They are commonly used as baitfish and have become established in many waters outside their native range. Their diet includes algae, insect larvae, and zooplankton. Like the bluntnose minnow, fathead minnows build nests and attach clusters of eggs to the undersides of rocks or logs. Males tend the eggs until they hatch.

SALMON, TROUT, AND WHITEFISH (Family Salmonidae)

Salmonids are important sport fish in New York State. They include three salmon species, four trout species, and three species of whitefish. All salmonids have soft-rayed fins and a small, fleshy adipose fin between the dorsal fin and the tail. The whitefish, subfamily Coregoninae, have smaller mouths and more uniform color than salmon and trout. Adirondack populations of several salmonid species are maintained by supplemental stocking from hatchery populations.

Cisco (*Coregonus artedi*)

Description: Also known as lake herring, ciscoes are roughly 8 to 15 inches in length and have clear fins and streamlined bodies. They are bluish gray on the back, shading to silver on the sides and belly. The tail is forked and they have a small adipose fin on the back between the dorsal fin and the tail.

Behavior: Ciscoes live in the deep, cold waters of lakes. They feed on plankton and small fish throughout most of the year. In late fall, large schools of ciscoes move into the shallows to spawn. Males arrive first, followed by females. There is no parental care; the eggs fall to the bottom and hatch in the spring. Ciscoes are an important part of the aquatic food web; they are a staple in the diet of salmon, trout, and other game fish.

Lake Whitefish (*Coregonus clupeaformis*)

Description: Lake whitefish are 18 to 24 inches long and weigh between 2 and 5 pounds. They are silvery gray in color. The body is long and flattened, with a slight arch behind the small head. An adipose fin is present behind the dorsal fin and the tail is forked. The mouth is positioned under the snout.

Behavior: Lake whitefish have been introduced into several of the larger Adirondack lakes. They thrive in large, deep lakes. They feed near the bottom on amphipods, other invertebrates, and small fish. In late fall, they move into the shallows to spawn over gravel or sandy bottoms. Eggs settle into cervices in the bottom to continue their development through the winter. In spring, they hatch and the young move into deeper waters.

Round Whitefish (*Prosopium cylindraceum*)

Description: Round whitefish are long, slender, and somewhat round in cross section. They are roughly 8 to 20 inches long. The back is olive or bronze; they are sliver or white on the sides and belly. The fins may be amber or brownish in color.

Behavior: Round whitefish live in deep, cold waters at depths over 100 feet. Here they forage along the bottom for crustaceans, mollusks, and other invertebrates. They begin spawning in November as they move into gravelly shoals, often near the mouths of streams. They spawn over gravel in small groups or pairs.

Rainbow Trout (*Oncorhynchus mykiss*)

Description: Rainbow trout have long, streamlined bodies roughly 10 to 24 inches in length. They typically weigh 1 to 8 pounds. They are olive or bluish green on the back, shading to white or cream on the belly. Adults have a wide, pinkish band along the sides. They are covered with small dark spots on the back, sides, and tail. The adipose fin has a dark edge and the mouth is white. Rainbow trout that migrate to the ocean and back are called steelheads.

Behavior: Rainbow trout prefer cooler, well-oxygenated water, such as those in rivers and streams or in the turbulent waters below dams and waterfalls. They also are found in many Adirondack lakes and ponds, but typically require stocking to sustain their populations. Rainbow trout feed on crustaceans, leeches, insects, and small fish. In the early spring, they spawn over gravel beds in rivers and streams. Females construct nests with powerful sweeps of their tails. After mating, the females cover the fertilized eggs with loose gravel. Rainbow trout are reared in hatcheries and stocked into many lakes and ponds.

Atlantic Salmon (*Salmo salar*)

Description: Atlantic salmon were native to Lake Ontario, the Finger Lakes, and Lake Champlain, but were extirpated (became extinct in these waters). Now they are stocked in these waters plus several Adirondack lakes. They are olive brown above, bluish silver on the sides, and have silver bellies. The upper body is covered with small black spots that are often in the shape of an X or Y. The jaws do not extend behind the eye. Males may have reddish spots on the sides.

Behavior: Native Atlantic salmon are anadromous; they migrate to the sea after hatching and return to the rivers where they were born to spawn. A few landlocked populations are able to breed in the larger tributary rivers, but all Adirondack populations are maintained by stocking from hatchery populations. Atlantic salmon prey upon a wide range of invertebrates and smaller fish, such as ciscoes and smelt. They spawn in the fall. Females sweep depressions in the gravel beds with their tails. The eggs hatch in the spring and juveniles remain in the river for several years before migrating downstream to Lake Ontario or Lake Champlain.

Brown Trout (*Salmo trutta*)   PLATE 12

Description: Brown trout are not native to North America; they were introduced to New York in the 1880s from Europe. Naturalized populations now inhabit many cold streams and hatchery stocking maintains lake populations. Adults are roughly 12 to 24 inches in length and

weigh 2 to 10 pounds. Brown trout are olive-green on the back and sides, shading to cream color on the belly. Small black, yellow, and red spots, often with lighter halo, are scattered over the head and body.

Behavior: Brown trout are mainly found in rivers and streams, where they feed on a wide range of insects, crustaceans, and fish. When not actively feeding, they prefer the cover of large boulders, logs, and undercut banks. In late fall, females dig shallow nests with their tails. Mating occurs repeatedly over several days. The eggs remain buried in the gravel until they hatch in the spring.

Brook Trout (*Salvelinus fontinalis*)   PLATE 13

Description: Brook trout are beautifully colored. They are dark olive-green on the back, shading to white on the belly. Pale, wormlike lines cover the head and upper back and distinguish them from other trout species. These lines break into spots lower on the sides. Bright red spots, surrounded by light blue halos, dot the sides of the fish. The lower fins are white at the front edge followed by black and red behind. The Adirondacks are home to eight "heritage strains" of brook trout. These native strains are genetically and physically distinct from domesticated hatchery strains.

Behavior: Brook trout prefer the cooler, oxygen-rich waters of mountain streams and lakes. Adults eat insects, leeches, crayfish, tadpoles, and small fish. Spawning begins in October as they move onto their spawning beds. The female excavates shallow depressions in the gravel, which she and her partner defend from other trout. After re-

peated mating, the female brushes additional gravel over the eggs and departs. Brook trout and lake trout are related (both are members of the Char Family) and both spawn in the late fall. Hybrids, called splake, occasionally are produced. Hatchery reared splake have also been stocked into some Adirondack ponds.

Lake Trout (*Salvelinus namaycush*)

Description: Lake trout are dark, greenish gray on the back and sides with a white belly. They are covered with irregular, creamy white spots. The tail is more deeply forked than in other trout species. Most Adirondack lake trout are 15 to 26 inches in length and weigh 2 to 10 pounds, but they are long-lived and capable of reaching weights exceeding 30 pounds.

Behavior: Lake trout inhabit deep, cold-water lakes and ponds in the Adirondacks, but hatchery stocking is now required to maintain many of the populations. Young lake trout feed primarily on zooplankton and small crustaceans. Adults feed on bottom-dwelling crustaceans and a range of small fish, including smelt, ciscoes, yellow perch, sculpins, and minnows. Lake trout move into shallow, rocky-bottomed areas in the late fall to spawn. Females produce large numbers of eggs over several weeks, which fall into crevices among the rocks. Here the eggs develop slowly over the winter months and hatch in the spring.

SMELT (Family Osmeridae)

A single species inhabiting the Adirondacks, the rainbow smelt are small, slender fish with relatively large silvery scales, and a deeply forked tail. While most coastal populations are anadromous, landlocked populations occur in a few Adirondack lakes.

Rainbow Smelt (*Osmerus mordax*)

Description: Rainbow smelt are long, slim fish roughly 6 to 8 inches in length. They are silver on the sides, occasionally with a purplish iridescence, and white on the belly. They have prominent scales and an

adipose fin between the dorsal fin and the tail. Their large mouths enclose numerous sharp teeth.

Behavior: Most smelt are anadromous, living in the sea and spawning in freshwater streams, but landlocked populations are known in Adirondack lakes and are all from stocking efforts that took place long ago. Smelt form large schools in deeper waters, where they feed on crustaceans, aquatic insect larvae, and amphipods. They, in turn, are preyed upon by trout and salmon. In the spring, large numbers of smelt move up tributaries at night to spawn. During spawning runs, smelt are caught in dip nets by anglers, who consider them a delicacy.

MUDMINNOWS (Family Umbridae)

Two species of mudminnow live in New York State, but only one is commonly found in the Adirondacks. Mudminnows have short, stocky bodies, with both dorsal and anal fins placed near the rounded tail fin. Mudminnows are able to survive in warm, poorly oxygenated waters.

Central Mudminnow (*Umbra limi*)

Description: This small mudminnow is roughly 3 inches long, with a long, posteriorly positioned dorsal fin and rounded tail. They are dark brown with faint vertical bars on their sides. Although superficially resembling sculpins or killifish, they are more closely related to pike.

Behavior: Mudminnows inhabit the poorly oxygenated waters of shallow ponds, swamps, and marshes. They prefer muddy bottoms with dense vegetation, where they forage for tiny crustaceans, midges, and

other small aquatic insects. In April, pairs spawn in flooded areas. Females lay one or two eggs at a time, which stick to aquatic vegetation. After roughly one week, the eggs hatch and the young mudminnows remain among the weeds. Mudminnows swallow air at the surface to supplement their oxygen supply and are reported to aestivate (a type of hibernation in response to drought) by burrowing into the mud during droughts.

PIKE AND PICKEREL (Family Esocidae)

Members of the Esocidae are long, streamlined predators. They have large heads and jaws. The dorsal and anal fins are both located well back towards the tail. Only the northern pike and chain pickerel are common throughout the Adirondacks. Muskellunge are found in the larger rivers on the periphery of the Adirondack Park (for example, the Black River) and the tiger muskellunge (a hybrid between northern pike and muskellunge) has been stocked into several Adirondack waters.

Northern Pike (*Esox lucius*)

Description: Pike have long, slender bodies with the dorsal fin located back near the tail. They are dark green on the back and sides and white

or cream-colored on the belly. The back and sides are covered with large gold or cream-colored spots. The head is large, with the lower jaw protruding beyond the upper jaw. One of the largest Adirondack fish species, northern pike can exceed 3 feet in length and reach 30 pounds. Pike in the 2- to 3-foot range are more common.

Behavior: Northern pike live in large streams, rivers, weedy ponds, and lakes. They are most common in weedy or grassy areas among the shallows, but may move into deeper water in the heat of the summer. They are voracious predators that lie in wait for unsuspecting minnows, perch, frogs, crayfish, ducklings, or other small vertebrates that venture too close. They spawn in the spring shortly after ice melts from ponds and lakes. At this time, adults move into the shallows to mate. Eggs hatch in two weeks and the young remain in the weeds feeding on zooplankton and insect larvae. Tiger muskellunge, a hybrid between a muskellunge and a northern pike, are stocked in a few Adirondack lakes as a sport fish.

Chain Pickerel (*Esox niger*)

Description: Similar in body form to northern pike, the chain pickerel has a long body, protruding lower jaw, and a posteriorly placed dorsal fin. They have a dark green back and sides, a yellowish belly, and a series of gold or brass bars extending the length of the fish along the sides and back. These bars give them the characteristic chain-link pattern from which they get their name. There is a distinctive dark vertical line below the eye.

Behavior: Chain pickerel inhabit clear streams, rivers, ponds, and lakes. They prefer weedy areas where they can lie in wait for small fish. They also feed on crayfish, frogs, and juvenile pickerel if the opportunity arises. Chain pickerel spawn in the spring in quiet backwaters. They grow to 2 feet in length and weigh 3 to 4 pounds.

KILLIFISH (Family Fundulidae)

Killifish are small fish with upward pointing mouths and flat heads; both are adaptations to surface feeding. The tail fin is slightly rounded.

Banded Killifish (*Fundulus diaphanus*)

Description: Banded killifish are 2 to 4 inches long and have slender bodies, triangular heads, and small upward-pointing mouths. They are olive-green on the back, shading to cream on the belly; the sides have regularly spaced dark bars. Banded killifish also have large eyes and a dorsal fin positioned closer to the tail than the head.

Behavior: Banded killifish are found in quiet or slow-moving waters of lakes, ponds, rivers, and streams. Spawning begins in late May as males establish breeding territories and pursue females. Eggs are laid in weedy areas and hatch in four to eleven days, depending on water temperature. Adults form small schools and feed on insects and mollusks plucked from vegetation or from the water surface.

SUNFISH AND BASS (Family Centrarchidae)

Centrarchid family members have a minimum of three spines on the anal fin and from five to thirteen spines at the front of the dorsal fin. They are generally deep-bodied fish with thin profiles. Sunfish and bass are popular sport fish in New York State.

Rock Bass (*Ambloplites rupestris*)

Description: Rock bass are deep-bodied fish with red eyes and large mouths. They have five spines at the front of the anal fin. They vary in color from dark olive-green to dark bronze, with several rows of dark spots along the body below the lateral line. Adults may reach 6 to 12 inches in length.

Behavior: Rock bass inhabit rocky-bottomed streams with a moderate to strong current and the rocky ledges of lakes. The diet consists of a wide range of aquatic insects, crayfish, and minnows. Breeding takes place in the spring, when males move into the shallows and construct a circular depression in the gravel. Males defend these nests from other males and await the arrival of females. After spawning, males guard the eggs or young for two weeks.

Redbreast Sunfish (*Lepomis auritus*)

Description: Redbreast sunfish are dark olive-green above, shading to bluish bronze on the sides, and yellow, orange, or red on the belly. Unlike the rock bass, redbreast sunfish have only three spines in the anal fin. Redbreast sunfish are unique in having a long, ear-like, posterior projection of the operculum (gill cover) that is often black in color. These sunfish are 5 to 8 inches long as adults.

Behavior: Redbreast sunfish inhabit ponds, lakes, and slow-moving sections of streams. They frequent areas with sandy bottoms and abundant aquatic vegetation or areas with boulders and submerged logs for cover. They consume a wide variety of insect larvae, small snails, crayfish, and young fish. Breeding occurs from June through August.

Pumpkinseed (*Lepomis gibbosus*)   PLATE 14

Description: Pumpkinseeds are small, deep-bodied sunfish with three spines on the anal fin and a small mouth. Adults are dark green above and white or cream colored on the belly. The sides have irregular patches of brown. In adult males, the head and gill cover may have alternating reddish brown and blue stripes; a black spot paired with a smaller orange spot are present on the posterior margin of the gill cover. Pumpkinseeds are 4 to 8 inches in length and rarely weigh a pound.

Behavior: Pumpkinseed inhabit the weedy shorelines of ponds and lakes as well as the slower portions of streams and rivers. They feed voraciously on insect larvae, crustaceans, mollusks, worms, and minnows. Breeding begins when water temperatures warm.  Males build circular nests in the shallows. Several females contribute eggs to a nest, which the male defends for up to two weeks.

Smallmouth Bass (*Micropterus dolomieu*)

Description: Smallmouth bass reach lengths of up to 20 inches and can weigh 8 pounds, but weights of 2 to 4 pounds are more typical. They are olive-bronze in color. Several dark vertical bars are present along the sides with shorter dark patches on the upper sides. The mouth of the smallmouth bass extends to the middle of the eye (in largemouth bass, the mouth extends to the posterior margin of the eye).

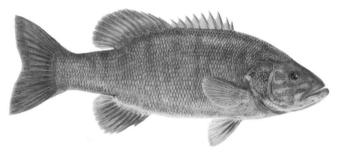

Behavior: Smallmouth bass remain in deeper waters of lakes and in streams and rivers with moderate currents and rocky bottoms. In lakes, they congregate around rocky ledges with large boulders for shelter. Adults prey on crayfish, minnows, yellow perch, insects, and crustaceans. Spawning begins in spring, when males construct circular depressions in the gravel bottom. Several females may deposit eggs in a single nest. Males guard these nests during and after spawning. Smallmouth bass are native to New York State, but were introduced into many Adirondack waters in the late 1800s. They have since become a prized sport fish.

Largemouth Bass (*Micropterus salmoides*)

Description: Largemouth bass are dark green in color with a wide, but broken dark stripe along sides. The jaw of the largemouth bass extends beyond the posterior margin of the eye. The dorsal fin is divided into two sections by a deep notch in the middle. Adult largemouth bass are typically 10 to 20 inches in length and weigh 1 to 6 pounds.

Behavior: Largemouth bass prefer warmer waters than smallmouth bass; they are found along the weedy shorelines of ponds and lakes, and in slow-moving sections of rivers. Although young largemouths feed mostly on zooplankton and tiny crustaceans, adults feed on small fish, crayfish, amphibians, and just about anything that falls into the water. Spawning begins in June. Males excavate shallow nests in which females deposit several thousand eggs. Males defend the eggs until shortly after they hatch. Largemouth bass reach sexual maturity after three to five years. The introduction of largemouth bass into Adirondack ponds has ruined many good brook trout fisheries.

PERCH, WALLEYE, AND DARTERS (Family Percidae)

Members of the perch family have dorsal fins divided into a front spiny section narrowly separated from a soft-rayed rear section. The anal fin has only two spines in front. They lack an adipose fin.

Tessellated Darter (*Etheostoma olmstedi*)

Description: Tessellated darters are 2 to 3 inches long. They are olive-brown above with five or six darker patches on the back. The sides have ten or eleven dark X- or Z-shaped patches, and the belly is whitish. They have large pectoral and dorsal fins with thin dark bands running across the fins. The head is blunt and the eyes sit high on the head. A close relative, the johnny darter, is found farther to the west.

Behavior: Tessellated darters inhabit slow-moving streams and quiet lake shores. They feed primarily on aquatic insects. These fish spawn in the spring. Males create a small nest cavity under a rock or log. Females adhere their sticky eggs to the underside of the rock. The male remains to guard the eggs until they hatch.

Yellow Perch (*Perca flavescens*)

Description: Yellow perch are olive-brown on the back, shading to yellow on the sides; there are six to eight dark, vertical bars extending down the sides and fading out at the white belly. Adults typically reach 6 to 12 inches and weigh roughly 1 pound.

Behavior: Yellow perch are common in the weedy sections of lakes, ponds, and rivers throughout the Adirondacks. Adults eat aquatic insects, crustaceans, and small fish. Spawning begins in early spring as males move into the shallows. Females arrive soon after and produce

a long ribbon of eggs that becomes tangled among the weeds. Small groups of males follow each female and fertilize the eggs. There is no parental care. The eggs hatch in a few weeks and the young form schools that feed on zooplankton in the weedy shallows. Young perch are important prey for many larger fish.

Walleye (*Sander vitreum*)

Description: Walleye resemble long, slender, yellow perch with vampire-like teeth. They are yellow-olive or brownish in color and lack obvious vertical bars. Walleye have a distinct dark spot on the back of the front dorsal fin. They have large canine-like teeth and their eyes have a cloudy appearance. Typical walleye are 2 to 5 pounds and 15 to 20 inches long, but individuals may reach 10 to 15 pounds on occasion.

Behavior: Walleye live in lakes and large rivers, where they frequent rocky shoals and bedrock areas. Adults feed on a wide range of fish, including minnows, small trout, perch, and sunfish. They also will take earthworms, leeches, and crayfish. Walleye breed in the early spring. Both sexes congregate in the shallows over gravel bars to spawn. There is no parental care; the eggs fall between gaps in the rocks and continue their development for two to four weeks, depending on water temperature. Young walleye feed on zooplankton and insect larvae for two months before switching to tiny fish.

SCULPINS (Family Cottidae)

Freshwater sculpins are small fish with large eyes located high on the head. They have rounded tail fins, a two-part dorsal fin, and enlarged pectoral fins just behind the gills.

Slimy Sculpin (*Cottus cognatus*)

Description: Slimy sculpin have wide, somewhat flattened heads with eyes that sit near the top of the head. There are two dorsal fins, with the front being the smaller of the two. The pectoral fins are large and fan-shaped. Slimy sculpins are mottled brown in color above and white below. There are dark bands on the pectoral fin. The front dorsal fin may have an orange trim in breeding males. Slimy sculpins are 3 to 4 inches in length.

Behavior: Slimy sculpins prefer clear, cold streams and gravel-bottomed lake shorelines. They spend the day hidden under rocks or logs and come out at night to feed on aquatic insects, crustaceans, fish eggs, and small fish. Slimy sculpins are spring spawners; males defend spawning sites under rocks, where females attach a mass of eggs to the ceiling of the nest site. Males guard the nest until the newly hatched sculpins are ready to leave in about four or five weeks.

SOURCES AND ADDITIONAL READING

Hubbs, C. L., and K. F. Lagler. 2004. *Fishes of the Great Lakes Region.* Ann Arbor, MI: University of Michigan Press.

Smith, C. L. 1985. *The Inland Fishes of New York State.* Albany: New York State Department of Environmental Conservation.

6 Amphibians and Reptiles

AMPHIBIANS

Adirondack amphibians include 10 salamander species and 9 frog species. Although very different in appearance, they share a number of important features, including moist, permeable skin, and gelatinous eggs that must be kept moist until they hatch. Consequently, amphibians are not fully terrestrial; at least part of their lives must be spent in freshwater or in an environment saturated with moisture. Typically, the eggs are laid in shallow water and begin their development within a jelly-like coating. The larval amphibians hatch as small tadpoles (pollywogs) with external gills. As development proceeds, these tadpoles undergo a transformation, called metamorphosis, into an adult frog or salamander capable of life on land. Metamorphosis is triggered by hormones and includes the formation of four legs for movement on land. In frogs, the external gills are replaced with lungs and the tail is gradually lost. In salamanders, the tail is retained, and, in lungless species, glands develop in the skin that keep it moist so that oxygen can be acquired directly across the skin surface without the aid of lungs. While this is the typical developmental pattern for amphibians, there are many interesting exceptions. The lungless salamanders (Family Plethodontidae), for example, may complete most of their metamorphosis inside the gelatinous egg, and hatch as miniature adults. Other species, like the red-spotted newt, hatch in freshwater, spend several years on land as juvenile salamanders (eft stage), and then return to ponds to transform into adult newts.

SALAMANDERS (Order Caudata)

Salamanders are amphibians with long, slender bodies, short legs, long tails, and moist skin. They live in or near water, or under leaf litter where the environment is moist. Moisture is essential for survival because salamanders lay gelatinous eggs that will quickly desiccate if not kept moist. In addition, terrestrial salamanders use their moist, capillary-rich skin as a respiratory surface, extracting precious oxygen directly across the skin surface. Some salamander species remain aquatic throughout their lives and use gills for respiration. Other species have a terrestrial stage and acquire oxygen from lungs and across their moist skin. Plethodontid salamanders are terrestrial as adults, but lack lungs and rely entirely on their skin for respiration (a process called cutaneous respiration). Adult salamanders forage among the leaf litter or at the waters edge for small invertebrates, which they capture by flipping their sticky tongue out of the mouth like a slingshot. Prey become stuck to the mucous covered tongue, and are drawn back into the mouth when the tongue is retracted. Because salamanders require water for survival, they are important indicators of water (and environmental) quality.

Northern Two-lined Salamander (*Eurycea bislineata*)

Description: Two-lined salamanders are one of the most common streamside salamanders in the Adirondacks. They are up to 4 inches long and have a wide yellow stripe on the back bordered on either side by a dark brown stripe. These stripes extend nearly the full length of the body; on the tail, the yellow stripe is often broken up as the two dark bands join near the tip. The tail is oval in cross-section, with 14 to 16 costal grooves along the abdomen.

Behavior: Two-lined salamanders inhabit wet deciduous or mixed conifer forests near springs, brooks, streams, rivers, and swamps. They prefer coarse gravel or rocky bottoms and often are found under stones along streams. They will move up to 100 yards into the forest after rains. Because they are tolerant of soils with low pH, they remain common in the Adirondacks even at high altitudes. Little is known about their breeding system, but they are thought to breed from September through May. Females attach strings of several dozen eggs underneath submerged rocks or woody debris in running water. The eggs are tended by a female and hatch a month or two later depending on the water temperature. The ½-inch-long larval salamanders have external gills and remain aquatic for two or three years, after which they undergo metamorphosis into the adult form. Adults feed on many types of aquatic and terrestrial insects. The larvae feed primarily on midge larvae, fly pupae and other small aquatic insects.

Red-backed Salamander (*Plethodon cinereus*)   PLATE 15

Description: This terrestrial salamander is 2 to 4 inches in length with a long, slender body and widely spaced legs. Red-backed salamanders occur in two color morphs. The more common red-backed morph has a broad red stripe running from the top of the head out onto the tail. The median red stripe is bordered by dark brown or black pigment along the sides. The lead-backed morph has a solid dark-gray or black body that is peppered with tiny white spots. The belly of both color morphs is speckled with black and white. There are 19 costal grooves between the front and back legs.

Behavior: Red-backed salamanders are cold tolerant and abundant in the Adirondacks. They inhabit the leaf litter of the forest floor. They often are found inside rotting stumps or logs and under mats of moist leaves. In the winter, they hibernate in crevices or loose soils. Breeding occurs in the spring and sometimes again in the late fall. Females lay clusters of up to 14 eggs in cavities in decaying logs or under rocks. Females remain with the eggs until they hatch roughly two months later. The larval stage occurs within the egg and they hatch looking like tiny adults. They forage in the leaf litter for small invertebrates such as earthworms, slugs, sow bugs, and soil mites.

Northern Dusky Salamander (*Desmognathus fuscus*)

Description: These salamanders are 2 to 5 inches in length and have 13 to 15 costal grooves. They have a keeled tail, which is thicker at the base and tapers to a thin edge at the top. The body coloration is tan to brown with broken stripes on the upper flanks that extend from the eye to the tail. The belly is a mottled gray or white. Juveniles have several pairs of yellow spots on the back.

Behavior: Northern dusky salamanders prefer wooded areas with abundant rocks, logs, and other debris not far from brooks or streams. They forage at night for a variety of aquatic and terrestrial invertebrates. Two breeding periods occur per year, one in late spring and another in September. Females lay clusters of up to 30 eggs beneath rocks or logs near a water source. After roughly eight weeks, the eggs hatch and the larval period begins. Metamorphosis into the adult form takes another eight to twelve months, and they become sexually active several years later.

Spring Salamander (*Gyrinophilus porphyriticus*)

Description: Spring salamanders are between 4 and 8 inches long as adults. Their coloration varies from salmon to dark reddish brown on the upper body to peach on the belly. Small dark spots cover much of the body and there is a faint line extending from the eye to the nostril. The tail is keeled and there are 17 to 19 costal grooves.

Behavior: Spring salamanders are semi-aquatic, remaining near springs, brooks, or other water sources. They require cold, well-oxygenated water because they lack lungs and respire entirely across their moist skin. Adults forage along stream banks and in the leaf litter for aquatic and terrestrial insects, earthworms, and other invertebrate prey. This species also preys on smaller salamanders and has been know to eat the larvae of its own species. Courtship and breeding take place in the late fall, but the eggs are not deposited until spring. Females may lay up to 100 eggs in cool, wet crevices or underwater. The eggs hatch in the early fall and the aquatic larval period may last up to four years.

Eastern Red-spotted Newt (*Notophthalmus viridescens*)   PLATE 16

Description: Red-spotted newts have both an aquatic and a terrestrial stage in the life cycle. Aquatic larval newts typically transform into the

terrestrial, or "eft," stage that is 1 to 3 inches in length with bright orange skin and two rows of black-rimmed spots on the back. After several years on land, the efts return to water and transform into aquatic adults. These fully aquatic adult newts are 3 to 5 inches long, with yellow to olive-brown coloring, and a series of orange spots with a black rim on the back. The tail, back, and belly are covered with tiny black spots. The tail is flattened and the costal grooves are indistinct.

Behavior: Red efts are found in the leaf litter of the forest floor, under logs and stones, where they hunt for soil mites, springtails, and other invertebrates. Their bright color serves to warn predators of their toxic skin secretions. Aquatic adults prefer ponds with abundant aquatic vegetation. Like the efts, they too produce toxins in the skin that protect them from most predators. Breeding takes place in ponds in the early spring. After mating, females lay several hundred eggs, which attach to submerged vegetation. Aquatic larvae with external gills hatch after nearly two months of incubation. The larvae feed on zooplankton, including water fleas, until they transform into either the terrestrial eft stage or directly into an aquatic adult. Adult newts are quick swimmers and feed on many invertebrates and sometimes on their own larvae.

Spotted Salamander (*Ambystoma maculatum*)   PLATE 17

Description: At 6 to 9 inches in length, the spotted salamander is the largest Adirondack salamander species. It is a thick-bodied, nearly black salamander with large, bright yellow spots on the head, back, and tail. The belly is blue-gray with 12 costal grooves.

Behavior: Spotted salamanders live in moist deciduous woodlands, temporary forest ponds, and floodplains. They spend most of the time under the forest litter foraging for earthworms, slugs, and beetles. Adults hibernate underground in winter. They are rarely seen on the surface except during nocturnal migrations to breeding ponds. In

March, adults migrate several hundred meters back to small, fish-free ponds to breed. A single female lays several clusters of up to 100 eggs on submerged vegetation. Approximately six weeks later, the half-inch larvae hatch. The larvae feed on zooplankton and small invertebrates for two to three months before transforming into terrestrial salamanders in mid summer. Under crowded conditions, larval mortality is high, but adult spotted salamanders are long-lived and may survive for 15 to 20 years in the wild.

TOADS AND FROGS (Order Anura)

Over 85 percent of living amphibian species are frogs or toads (order Anura). To herpetologists (scientists who study amphibians and reptiles), all species belonging to the order Anura are frogs. Residents of North America, however, tend to think of frogs as having moist skin and toads as having dry, leathery skin. While this distinction may be useful for the amateur naturalist, it is not used in taxonomy. For example, within certain anuran families there are both frogs and toads; only the family Bufonidae contains only toads. As adults, frogs and toads have long hind legs used for jumping or climbing, a thick body without a tail, and webbed toes. They lay their gelatinous eggs in water, where they eventually hatch into larvae called tadpoles or pollywogs. These larvae lack limbs and breath via gills as they forage for algae, plant material, and tiny invertebrates. As the tadpole stage ends, they undergo one of the most dramatic changes in the animal world. The tadpole transforms into a frog (or toad) in a process called metamorphosis. During metamorphosis the tadpole slowly replace gills with lungs, develops limbs, lose their tail, and transform their mouths and digestive system to one specialized for a diet of invertebrates. The resulting froglet continues its maturation into an adult frog.

American Toad (*Bufo americanus*)

Description: American toads have dry, rough skins covered in small, reddish-brown "warts." They are up to 4 inches in length and generally brown in color. These portly animals have a large parotoid gland behind the eye that secretes a toxin when they are handled roughly or attacked by predators.

Behavior: Toads should be handled with care because the toxins produced by the parotoid glands can cause inflammation and nausea, and can even kill cats and dogs. American toads are found in a wide variety of habitats, from moist forests to village lawns. They feed in the evening on insects and other invertebrates including sowbugs, spiders, and

earthworms. They burrow into the ground and hibernate through the winter months. Breeding begins in March or early April, when they return to shallow ponds or forest pools to lay their eggs. Females lay masses of up to 12,000 eggs in long spirals attached to aquatic plants. The gelatinous eggs hatch in a few days, after which the young remain as tadpoles for up to 10 weeks.

Gray Tree Frog (*Hyla versicolor*)

Description: This 1- to 2-inch frog resembles a small toad because of its rough skin. Tree frogs, however, are arboreal and use their long limbs and adhesive toe pads to climb among the branches. They are greenish brown to gray above with irregular patches of darker pigment on the back and legs. The belly and inner thighs are orange-yellow. A distinctive whitish spot below the eye is bordered by darker bands.

Behavior: Gray tree frogs inhabit areas near water with abundant shrubs and small trees. They are nocturnal and their calls, described as a slow trill, are heard on many spring and summer evenings. Breeding begins in early May. Adults gather near water and chorus to attract mates. Females lay clusters of 20 to 40 eggs in shallow water, but fe-

males may lay up to 2,000 eggs in a season. The eggs hatch in a few days, and the tadpoles remain in the water until they transform into frogs in mid- to late summer.

Spring Peeper (*Pseudacris crucifer*)

Description: Spring peepers are roughly 1 inch in length and tan to brown in color, with an X-shaped region of darker pigmentation on the back. Large adhesive pads on the toe tips aid in climbing.

Behavior: Spring peepers prefer wooded areas near permanent or temporary ponds or marshes. Their chorus of high-pitched whistles are familiar evening sounds in the spring and summer. Males call to attract mates as breeding begins in March through June. After mating, females retreat to nearby ponds and lay several hundred eggs attached to submerged vegetation. The eggs hatch after roughly ten days; the tadpoles transform into frogs after two to three months. Peepers are nocturnal and feed primarily on terrestrial insects. They hibernate under logs or buried in moss during the long winter months.

Bullfrog (*Rana catesbeiana*)

Description: The bullfrog is the largest Adirondack frog at up to 8 inches in length. They are green or olive-brown above with a whitish belly. They have a large, circular tympanum (ear region) behind the eye with a distinctive brown rim. The hind feet are fully webbed, but the fourth toe extends well beyond the webbing.

Behavior: Bullfrogs are often found along the shores of lakes and ponds. They leap into water or disappear below aquatic vegetation when

disturbed. Their diet consists of insects, crayfish, small minnows, tadpoles, and other available prey. In the Adirondacks, breeding begins in May and lasts through July. Females lay several thousand eggs that hatch four days later into small tadpoles. The aquatic tadpole stage may last up to three years before they transform into frogs. It may be another two or three years before these young frogs reach sexual maturity. Bullfrogs may live ten years in the wild; they survive the frozen winters by hibernating deep in the mud.

Green Frog (*Rana clamitans*)

Description: This 2- to 4-inch-long, greenish brown frog has irregular dark patches on the flanks and legs. Green frogs have a large tympanum (ear) behind the eye and distinct dark stripes extending from the tympanum almost to the hind legs.

Behavior: Green frogs are abundant near water sources such as ponds, swamps, vernal pools, and streams. They feed on a wide variety of invertebrates including insects, worms, and crayfish, and will also take small frogs, newts, and minnows. Breeding occurs between May and August. Females lay 3,000 to 4,000 eggs in several masses in shallow water. After a few days, the eggs hatch and the young remain in the tadpole stage for up to two years.

Wood Frog (*Rana sylvatica*)

Description: Wood frogs are medium-sized, tan to brown frogs with a distinctive dark-brown facemask that also includes the tympanum (ear). The belly is light with faint speckles.

Behavior: Wood frogs prefer woodland habitats and may be found far from water after temporary pools dry up. They breed in early spring, often when ice still partially covers the breeding ponds. Two thousand or more eggs may be laid in shallow water. Hatching takes roughly ten days because of the cold water temperatures. Tadpoles transform into frogs between three and four months later, depending on the water temperatures. During winter, wood frogs hibernate. These cold-tolerant frogs are found as far north as the Canadian tundra, further north than any other amphibian in North America

Northern Leopard Frog (*Rana pipiens*)

Description: Leopard frogs are green (occasionally brown) with numerous dark spots over the back, flanks, and legs. A thin, light line runs around the perimeter of each spot. The dorsolateral ridges (lines running along either side of the back) are light in color and extend all the way to the groin.

Behavior: Leopard frogs prefer wet fields, marshes, slow-moving streams, and weedy shorelines. They feed on a wide array of insects including grasshoppers, beetles, and ants, and they also take small crayfish. Breeding begins in March. Egg masses containing up to 5,000 eggs are laid in the vegetation at the waters edge. Hatching takes roughly 20 days, and they remain as tadpoles for up to 12 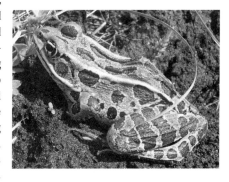 weeks before transforming into frogs in the fall. They hibernate buried in the mud at the bottom of ponds during the cold winter months.

Mink Frog (*Rana septentrionalis*)

Description: Mink frogs are roughly 3 inches in length, olive-brown in color, and strongly mottled or spotted on the backs and flanks. There is no light line around the spots as in leopard frogs. Dorsolateral ridges are less conspicuous and the belly is yellow. Mink frogs have a large tympanum (eardrum). They get their name from their musky odor.

Behavior: Mink frogs live in cold-water lakes, ponds, and streams where oxygen levels are high. They prefer shallow shorelines with lily pads and other emergent weeds. Mink frogs breed from June to August, when females lay several hundred eggs. The tadpole stage may last up to two years in some areas. Mink frogs are mostly nocturnal and spend evenings feeding on insects, leeches, and sometimes small minnows. They spend the winters hibernating deep in the muddy sediments at the pond bottom.

Pickerel Frog (*Rana palustris*)

Description: Pickerel frogs are between 2 and 3 inches in body length, tan to yellow in color, with two parallel rows of dark squares on the back. The dorsolateral folds and the belly are yellow.

Behavior: Pickerel frogs require clear, cold waters and typically are found near lakes, ponds, and streams. They hibernate buried in the muddy pond bottom and emerge to breed in March. Females lay several thousand eggs in round masses attached to aquatic vegetation. After two or three weeks, the eggs hatch into tadpoles; the tadpoles transform into frogs in early fall. Adults feed primarily at dawn and dusk on snails, crayfish, and other invertebrates. Pickerel frogs secrete a toxin from their skin glands that may protect them from certain predators.

REPTILES

Reptiles have thick, scaly skin, which is impermeable to water. Consequently, they do not rely on access to freshwater for reproduction. Instead, reptiles have evolved a series of extraembryonic membranes, including a leathery shell, that surround the developing embryo and protect it from desiccation. While several species of Adirondack turtles inhabit ponds and lakes as adults, they lay their eggs in dry, sandy soils on land. Snakes may lay eggs or they may give birth to live young. Adirondack reptiles include 5 turtle species and 10 species of snakes, including the venomous timber rattlesnake. The five-lined skink is the only lizard species known to occur within the park boundaries, but this species is restricted to the easternmost margins of the park. Only relatively common species or those that are distributed broadly within the park are described below.

TURTLES (Order Testudines)

Turtles are reptiles belonging to the Order Testudines. Turtles are easily identified by their dome-shaped upper shell (called a carapace) and their typically flat lower shell (plastron). The carapace is an expanded set of ribs and vertebrae covered by large scales called scutes (which form in the skin). Together with the plastron they form a protective case over the body. Turtles may spend considerable time in the water, but, like all reptiles, they have lungs and must surface to breath. They lay their eggs on land in sandy depressions dug by the female. She then buries several dozen leathery eggs and leaves them to continue their development underground. Eventually the young hatch and dig their way to the surface.

Wood Turtle (*Clemmys insculpta*)

Description: The upper shell, called the carapace, is brown and covered with large, rough scutes (scales). Each scute resembles a short pyramid with concentric rings radiating outward from the central peak. The lower shell (or plastron) is yellow with black splotches at the margins. Wood turtles have reddish orange skin on the chin, neck, and front legs.

Behavior: Wood turtles inhabit slow, meandering streams and rivers with sandy bottoms and abundant streamside vegetation. In the summer, they move into adjacent fields and woodlands. They are omnivorous and will feed on grasses and other vegetation as well as worms, slugs, insects, tadpoles, frogs, and minnows. Breeding begins in March or April. Females deposit up to 12 eggs in a shallow nest in May or June. In the Adirondacks, the eggs may overwinter in the nest, or they may hatch in the fall of the same year they were laid. Wood turtles are relatively long-lived and typically don't reach sexual maturity for seven to ten years.

Painted Turtle (*Chrysemys picta*)

Description: Painted turtles have a smooth, dark olive carapace (shell). The scutes on the carapace form rows and each scute has a yellowish margin. The scutes along the outer margin of the carapace are smaller and marked with yellow or red crescents. The plastron (shell over the belly) is yellow. There are yellow stripes on the head and throat and two yellow spots on either side of the head. The legs and tail also have red stripes.

Behavior: These turtles are mostly aquatic, preferring ponds, meandering streams, marshes, and other sites with standing water and muddy bottoms. Painted turtles are often seen basking in groups on exposed logs or rocks. They feed on a variety of invertebrates and small vertebrates, but at least half of their diet is plant material. The breeding period lasts from April to July. Females bury up to a dozen eggs in sandy soils near water. The eggs incubate in the nest for two months and hatch in late August or September. Females often lay two clutches per summer, with the last clutch overwintering in the nest.

Snapping Turtle (*Chelydra serpentina*)

Description: Snapping turtles are unmistakable; they have large heads with powerful, hooked jaws. They can grow to 30 pounds in the wild, with carapace diameters of up to 18 inches. The carapace is brown with three rows of keeled scutes. The plastron is small and yellowish in color. Snapping turtles have long tails covered with alligator-like keeled scales. Their powerful jaws can inflict a very serious bite.

Behavior: Snapping turtles are good swimmers. They feed on crayfish,

other aquatic invertebrates, fish, ducklings, and other vertebrate prey, which they ambush when prey ventures too close. They prefer shallow ponds, lakes, and rivers with soft bottoms and abundant vegetation. Snappers hibernate during the winter months. Breeding takes place from April through the fall. Females bury 25 to 50 eggs in a clutch. The hatchlings emerge after two to four months depending on the temperature. Later clutches may overwinter in the nest and emerge the following spring.

SNAKES (Order Squamata, Suborder Serpentes, Family Colubridae and Family Viperidae)

Snakes have long, thin bodies covered with scales. Living species lack limbs, and fossil evidence indicates that snakes probably evolved from limbless lizards. Further evidence comes from living pythons, which still retain the vestiges of a tiny pelvis deep within their otherwise limbless body. Snakes capture prey by stealth, and, once captured, swallow it whole. Snakes are able to swallow prey larger in diameter than their own heads because they are able to disarticulate their lower jaws and thus considerably widen the mouth opening. Members of two snake families are found in the Adirondacks: The Colubridae include several common species, such as garter snakes, milk snakes, and their allies. The family Viperidae is represented by a single venomous species, the timber rattlesnake.

Red-bellied Snake (*Storeria occipitomaculata*)

Description: Red-bellied snakes are small and slender, with dark brown or gray above and a red or orange belly. They often have a faint stripe down the back. There are three light spots just behind the head.

Behavior: Red-bellied snakes prefer moist woodlands, swamps, wet meadows, and bogs. These snakes emerge from hibernation in the spring and give birth to roughly a dozen live (viviparous) young in early fall. Adults feed on slugs, earthworms, small salamanders, and insects.

Brown Snake (*Storeria dekayi*)

Description: These small brown snakes have two rows of dark spots along the back. The belly is light yellow or pinkish and bordered with tiny black spots. There is often a dark, vertical band behind the eye.

Behavior: Brown snakes can be found in many habitats, from forests to rural lawns, and wet stream banks to dry fields. Large numbers of brown snakes hibernate together in underground dens until April, when they emerge to breed. After a three-and-a-half-month gestation period, the female gives birth to 10 to 15 live young. Adults prey on invertebrates such as slugs and earthworms, but also take small frogs and minnows on occasion.

Ringneck Snake (*Diadophis punctatus*)   PLATE 18

Description: The ringneck snake is a slender, darkly colored snake with a distinctive golden collar around the neck. The belly is orange to yellow and contrasts sharply with the dark gray or brown back.

Behavior: These snakes live in forested areas with abundant rocks or woody debris for cover. They emerge from hibernation in May. Females lay up to ten eggs under rotting logs or rock piles. The eggs hatch after roughly one month. Adults feed on a variety of insects, earthworms, and small vertebrates. Ringneck snakes are rarely encountered because they are largely nocturnal and tend to remain hidden during the day.

Common Garter Snake (*Thamnophis sirtalis*)

Description: The garter snake is one of the most common snakes in the Adirondacks. Color patterns vary, but they often have yellowish side stripes on a brown background. There are two rows of alternating dark spots between the lighter stripes. The belly is olive-green or yellow in color.

Behavior: Garter snakes are found in many terrestrial habitats, from marshes to forest edges. During the winter months, they hibernate in large colonies in rock crevices or under woody debris. They emerge from hibernation in March to mate. Females give birth to as many as 80 live young in late summer or early fall. The 4- to 5-inch young mature in two years and may live up to ten years in the wild. Garter snakes hunt for small frogs, salamanders, and young mice. When threatened, they are aggressive and release a musky odor.

Eastern Ribbon Snake (*Thamnophis sauritus*)

Description: Closely related to garter snakes, ribbon snakes are long and slim; adults are 12 to 26 inches in length. The back and sides are dark brown with three, sharply contrasting, light yellow stripes extending from head to tail tip. The belly is yellow or greenish, but otherwise unmarked.

Behavior: Ribbon snakes are semi-aquatic and seldom live far from water. Typical habitats include lake and pond shorelines, marshes, and slow-moving streams. Breeding begins shortly after they emerge from hibernation in March. Females give birth to as many as 20 live young in early fall. Adults feed almost exclusively on amphibians (including tadpoles) and small fish.

Milk Snake (*Lampropeltis triangulum*)

Description: One of the most distinctively patterned of Adirondack snakes, milk snakes have tan bodies covered with large, black-rimmed brown patches above. Toward the head, the dark patches become Y-shaped. There are smaller dark patches along the flanks. The belly has a checkerboard pattern of black and cream-colored patches. Young milk snakes have reddish patches instead of brown. These snakes are relatively large at body lengths of 24 to 36 inches.

Behavior: They are found in many habitats, including deciduous woodlands, grassy meadows, and pine forests. They frequent barns and other outbuildings in search of mice and other small mammals. They hibernate from October to April. Females lay up to two dozen eggs in loose soil during early summer. The eggs hatch in early fall. Unfortunately, milk snakes often are killed because they resemble the venomous cottonmouth.

Smooth Green Snake (*Opheodrys vernalis*)

Description: This unmistakable snake is bright green above and white below. Adults are 12 to 24 inches in length with long tails.

Behavior: Their coloration provides camouflage, as green snakes hunt in grassy fields for insects, spiders, ants, and other small invertebrates. Breeding occurs from late spring to late summer. Females lay up to a dozen eggs in late summer or early fall and may share nest sites with other females.

Northern Water Snake (*Nerodia sipedon*)

Description: There is considerable variation in the coloration of northern water snakes; background color ranges from reddish brown to black. There are dark bands across the neck and irregularly shaped dark patches over the remainder of the back and tail. The belly is white or cream-colored and may have crescent-shaped spots scattered along the bell. Adults are 24 to 36 inches in body length.

Behavior: Northern water snakes are semi-aquatic and are never found far from water. They prefer lake shores, swamps, marshes, streams, and rivers. They are active at all times of the day and night. Their diet consists largely of fish, but they also prey on frogs, salamanders, crayfish, and the occasional mouse or vole. In April or early May, water snakes emerge from hibernation to mate. Females give birth to 10 to 40 live young in the fall. Water snakes are aggressive and bite repeatedly when threatened.

Timber Rattlesnake (*Crotalus horridus*)

Description: Timber rattlesnakes are restricted to a few isolated rocky areas near Lake George. At 36 to 72 inches in length, they are New York's largest venomous snake. There are two color phases; the yellow phase has dark blotches over a yellow or light brown background color, while the dark phase can be nearly solid black. Like all rattlesnakes, the tail terminates in a rattle that makes a buzzing sound when vibrated. The

head is triangular and there is a pit or opening on the side of the face below the eye that is used to sense body temperature of their warm-blooded prey.

Behavior: *Timber rattlesnakes are venomous and should never be handled; they have hollow fangs that inject venom into the wound as they bite. They are aggressive only when threatened, and use the "buzz" of the tail rattle as a warning.*

Timber rattlesnakes are listed as "Threatened species" by the New York State Department of Environmental Conservation. They survive in a few isolated populations in rugged, rocky terrain. They overwinter in communal dens located in rocky ledges. Mating takes place after they emerge from their winter dens in spring. Females bear 5 to 17 live young in the fall, but probably do not breed again for another year or two. Adults remain camouflaged among the leaf litter, waiting to ambush small rodents or birds. The remaining populations in New York are monitored regularly by biologists and the NYS DEC is working actively to protect their habitat.

SOURCES AND ADDITIONAL READING

Behler, J. L., and F. W. King. 1985. *The Audubon Society Field Guide to North American Reptiles and Amphibians.* New York: Alfred A. Knopf.

Conant, R. 1986. *A Field Guide to Reptiles and Amphibians, Eastern and Central North America.* The Peterson Field Guide Series. Boston: Houghton Mifflin.

DeGraaf, R. M., and M. Yamasaki. 2000. *New England Wildlife: Habitat, Natural History, and Distribution.* Hanover, NH: University Press of New England.

Gibbs, J. P., A. R. Breisch, P. K. Ducey, G. Johnson, J. Behler, and R. Bothner. 2007. *The Amphibians and Reptiles of New York State: Identification, Natural History, and Conservation.* New York: Oxford University Press.

7 Birds

Birds are among the most commonly observed of all Adirondack wild-life. Their vibrant colors (at least in males) and beautifully varied songs readily draw our attention. Roughly 810 bird species are known from the United States and Canada. Of these, only 220 species inhabit or migrate through the Adirondacks. Some species, like the chickadee and blue jay, are year-round residents. Others migrate northward in the spring to breed in the Adirondack Park, but spend winters in warmer southern habitats. A few species, including many warbler species, spend only a few weeks in the Adirondacks as they pass through on their annual migrations.

The fossil evidence indicates that birds evolved from theropod dinosaurs some time in the early Cretaceous, roughly 140 million years ago. Modern birds share a number of features that unite them as a group. Perhaps the most obvious feature is the presence of feathers. Feathers are made of keratin, the same protein that comprises reptilian scales. Feathers, however, are structurally complex, light in weight, and may contain pigments or three-dimensional structures that produce vivid colors. In combination, feathers (as plumage) provide considerable insulation. The flight feathers of the wing and tail are long, stiff, and light in weight; they provide a large increase in surface area for the wing with almost no increase in weight.

Another important feature is the beak. Flight is energetically costly and in order to reduce weight in the head region, birds have lost the relatively heavy teeth of their ancestors, and, instead, evolved a horny beak for grasping and manipulating food. Beaks come in myriad sizes and shapes; this diversity is very useful in identifying a bird's diet. Hawks and owls, for example, have sharp, hooked beaks used to tear flesh from their prey. Insect-eating birds, such as warblers, have short, thin beaks that are useful for probing among the leaves for insects.

Birds also exhibit many interesting behaviors such as parental care, complex mating systems, and long-distance migrations. Many species use complex songs to establish breeding territories and attract mates. Many birds construct elaborate nests in tree-holes, on the ground, or among tree branches. Some species use celestial and magnetic cues to navigate during their seasonal migrations, which may cover thousands of miles in a single year. Complete coverage of bird behavior is well beyond the scope of this book. However, birds are truly fascinating creatures and any time spent observing them in the wild will be re-warded amply.

Of the 220 bird species known to occur in the Adirondack Park, some are seen rarely and others are found only at lower elevations around the margins of the park. The 118 species accounts that follow describe the more-common bird species and those that breed within the park. Brief introductions are provided for confusing groups, such as warblers and birds of prey.

LOONS, GREBES, AND HERONS

Loons, grebes, and herons belong to the families Gaviidae, Podicipe-didae, and Ardeidae, respectively. They are grouped together here out of convenience, not because they are closely related. Loons are rel-atively large birds with legs positioned toward the rear of the body. Only one species in common on Adirondack waters. Loons are excel-lent divers, able to swim underwater for considerable distances while hunting fish. In contrast, grebes are small birds with generally short bills. Like loons, their feet are located will back on the body. There are 22 species of grebes, but only the pied-billed grebe is locally abundant. Herons and bitterns are wading birds with stilt-like legs and long, pointed beaks. They frequent wetlands and shallows where they hunt for fish and frogs. Black-crowned night herons, green herons, and least bitterns frequent the margins of the Adirondacks, but only great blue herons and American bitterns are common throughout the Park.

Common Loon (Family Gaviidae, *Gavia immer*)

Description: The common loon is a large bird with a wingspan of 47 to 58 inches (120 to 148 cm) and an average weight of 8 to 9 pounds (4 kilo-

grams). Breeding adults have a black head and thick, black bill, red eyes, white breast, and a checkered black-and-white back.

Behavior: Loons are long-bodied and sit low in the water. They feed on fish, which they catch underwater after dives of up to 200 feet (60 m). Their distinctive tremolo call and the wailing *hooo-lii* frequently are heard on Adirondack lakes. Females lay two spotted eggs on nests of mounded vegetation near water. Both parents care for the young. Loons migrate to the Atlantic coast in winter.

Pied-billed Grebe (Family Podicipedidae, *Podilymbus podiceps*)

Description: Pied-billed grebes are small, stocky birds. They average 1 pound (450 grams) and have a wingspan of only 16 inches (40 cm). Breeding adults are brown or gray in color. They have a short, blunt bill, with a prominent black band near the tip.

Behavior: Pied-billed grebes breed on remote ponds, marshes, and slow-moving streams. They are poor flyers, preferring to dive when danger approaches. They feed on fish, insects, and tadpoles or small frogs. Females lay four to seven pale blue eggs in a nest built from matted vegetation. The young are cared for by both parents and often ride on a parent's back.

Great Blue Heron (Family Ardeidae, *Ardea herodias*)

Description: Standing up to 4 feet tall with a wingspan of nearly 6 feet, their long necks, stilt-like legs, and dagger-like bills distinguish great blue herons from other wading birds. Body plumage is blue-gray. The face is white with a prominent black plume of feathers over the eyes.

Behavior: Great blue herons are common in marshes, swamps, and along the margins of ponds, lakes, and slow-moving stretches of many rivers. They feed on fish, frogs, insects, and other aquatic life. In flight, the neck is bent into an S-shaped curve and the legs trail behind the tail. The call is a series of hoarse croaks. Great blue herons nest in colonies. They lay three to six greenish blue eggs in a nest platform of sticks in tall trees.

American Bittern (Family Ardeidae, *Botaurus lentiginosus*)

Description: American bitterns are medium-sized herons with a stocky brown body. The throat and chest are streaked with patches of dark brown or black. In flight, the outer margins of the wing appear dark and contrast with the lighter brown of the inner wings and back. Adults have a black stripe down the side of the neck and a thin white stripe just above the eye.

Behavior: When approached, bitterns freeze and stretch their bills skyward in an attempt to blend in with the reeds. Only if the intruder persists will they take flight. During courtship, pairs exhibit complex aerial displays. Courtship calls, a booming "*oon-ka-lunk*," can be heard for over a quarter mile. After courtship, they build a simple platform of reeds and lay two to six olive-brown eggs. American bitterns do not form breeding colonies.

DUCKS AND GEESE (Family Anatidae)

Ducks, geese, and swans comprise the family Anatidae. Wild swans are uncommon in Adirondack waters, and Canada geese are the only goose species to regularly breed in the Adirondack Park. Ducks are generally divided into two simple categories, diving ducks and dabbling ducks. Diving ducks are completely submerged as they forage, while dabbling ducks tend to submerge only the head, neck and chest, leaving their posteriors above the surface. Northern shovelers, lesser scaup, and several other ducks can be seen in the Adirondacks during spring and fall migrations. However, only a handful of duck species breed in the Adirondacks. Gadwalls, common goldeneye, northern pintail, hooded merganser, blue-winged teal, and green-winged teal occasionally breed within the Park borders, but they are not common and are not described here.

Canada Goose (*Branta canadensis*)

Description: Canada geese have black necks and heads with white throats and cheeks. Their backs are grayish brown giving way to a paler breast plumage. They have a wing-span of over 1½ yards and weigh 8 to 14 pounds (3 to 6 kilograms).

Behavior: Flocks of these birds often feed on submerged aquatic vegeta-tion or the remains of cultivated crops. Adult Canada geese pair for life, but if one dies the other finds a new mate. Females lay four to eight eggs and both parents help incubate the eggs for 25 to 28 days. Dur-ing nesting, adults lose their flight feathers and cannot fly until after their eggs hatch. They are highly ag-gressive when protecting their young.

Wood Duck (*Aix sponsa*)   PLATE 19

Description: Wood ducks are medium-sized ducks with wingspans of about 30 inches. Adult males have colorful, iridescent plumage. The

head crest is green, black, and white, the breast is reddish, and the back is a colorful combination of greens, blacks, and blue. Males have a red eye. Females are a drab brown with a white eye-ring and a whitish breast. Wood ducks frequently perch in trees and bob their heads when swimming.

Behavior: Wood ducks prefer wooded swamps, shallow lakes, or ponds where suitable nest cavities can be found in trees near the shoreline. Females lay between nine and fourteen eggs. When the nestlings hatch, they jump from the nest tree to the ground or into the water.

American Black Duck (*Anas rubripes*)

Description: Black ducks are medium-sized ducks that often are confused with female mallards. Males have a yellow bill, lighter head and neck, dark body, orange feet, and dark eyes. Females are similar to males, and both have a purple-blue wing patch, which lacks the adjacent white patches found in mallards.

Behavior: These ducks feed on aquatic plants and invertebrates in shallow water. Breeding and nesting takes place in lakes, ponds, rivers, marshes, and other aquatic habitats. Black ducks interbreed regularly with mallard ducks. Females lay between six and fourteen greenish eggs, which hatch after about a month.

Mallard (*Anas platyrhynchos*)   PLATE 20

Description: Mallards are medium-sized dabbling ducks with a wingspan of 32 to 35 inches (80 to 90 cm) and a weight of just under 2.2 pounds (1 kilogram). Breeding males have green heads, yellow bills with black tips, and narrow white rings that separate the green neck from the reddish breast. Males also have a black rear end. Females have a dark brown bill and a light brown body. Both sexes have orange legs and blue wing bars trimmed with white bands.

Behavior: Mallards are migratory and winter farther south. They prefer wetlands, small ponds, and rivers. Mallards form temporary pairs during the breeding season. Clutches of nine to thirteen eggs are incubated by females for about a month. The ducklings are able to swim and feed themselves immediately after hatching.

Ring-necked Duck (*Aythya collaris*)

Description: Ring-necked ducks are small diving ducks with a wingspan of about 25 inches and a weight of about 1½ pounds (700 grams). Adult males have a gray bill trimmed with white, a shiny dark purple head, a white breast, and a dark grey back. Females have a pale brown head and body with a dark brown back, a dark gray bill, and brown eyes. The neck ring is dark and difficult to observe.

Behavior: These ducks dive for aquatic plants, molluscs, aquatic insects, and small fish. They prefer wooded lakes or ponds where they build nests of aquatic vegetation lined with down feathers. Females lay eight to ten eggs.

Common Merganser (*Mergus merganser*)

Description: The common merganser is a medium-sized duck with a wingspan of 34 inches and an average weight of 3 pounds (1.5 kilograms). Males have a dark green head, a pointed orange bill, and a largely white body. Females have a reddish brown head, a small white throat patch, and a gray body.

Behavior: Mergansers are common on Adirondack lakes and rivers. They consume mostly fish, which they capture using their serrated bills. They nest in tree holes or among the tangled roots along the bank. Females lay eight to eleven eggs, which hatch after 30 to 35 days.

UPLAND GAME BIRDS (Order Galliformes)

The Adirondacks are home to four species in the order Galliformes. These birds are referred to as upland game birds because they are hunted for food and (unlike ducks and geese, which are also hunted) inhabit sites well away from water. Ruffed grouse are probably the most commonly encountered, but turkeys are becoming increasingly abundant in areas outside the high peaks region. Spruce grouse are present in small numbers in several northern Adirondack counties. Ring-neck pheasant prefer farmlands around the margins of the Adirondack Park and are not described here.

Spruce Grouse (*Falcipennis canadensis*)
and Ruffed Grouse (*Bonasa umbellus*)

Description: Both species of Adirondack grouse are chicken-sized birds. They weigh approximately 1 pound and have wingspans of about 22 inches. The ruffed grouse occurs in a gray phase and a red phase. Both phases have a small crest on the back of the head, a thick black bar near the tip of the tail, distinct dark bars on the breast, and a band of dark feathers that form a neck ruff. Spruce grouse have a black tail with a brown band at the tip. Males are gray with a black throat and a distinct red patch above the eye. Females are brown with white bars on the breast and lack the red eye-patch.

Behavior: Grouse forage on the ground for berries, leaf buds, seeds, and insects. The winter diet of the spruce grouse is primarily evergreen needles. Both species prefer to run for dense cover or remain still

Ruffed grouse

when danger approaches. When flushed, they fly only short distances. Males establish territories in the spring by drumming their wings on a fallen log.

Wild Turkey (*Meleagris gallopavo*)   PLATE 21

Description: The largest terrestrial birds in the Adirondacks, turkeys average 16 pounds (7 kilograms) and have wingspans of 4 to 5 feet.

Adults have a thick, dark body perched on long orange legs. They have a long neck and naked head; males have a bluish head and red throat wattles. Turkeys have a long tail and dark, iridescent bronze wings, especially in males.

Behavior: Wild turkeys forage primarily on the ground for nuts, seeds, berries, and insects. Mating occurs in the spring, when males gobble and spread their fan-shaped tails to attract females. After mating, females lay ten to twelve eggs in simple nests on the ground. The eggs hatch after about 1 month.

DIURNAL BIRDS OF PREY (Order Falconiformes)

Birds of prey (or raptors) have powerful, hooked beaks and sharp talons for hunting reptiles, birds, and mammals. Some are active only during the day (diurnal) and others hunt almost exclusively at night (nocturnal). Diurnal species rely on their excellent vision to locate prey, while the nocturnal owls use their superb hearing. Ornithologists (those who study birds) divide diurnal raptors into three major groups: Accipitridae, Falconidae, and Cathartidae. The Accipitridae include eagles, the osprey, and hawks. Eagles, hawks, and the osprey are large birds with broad wings that tend to hunt living prey, while vultures (Family Cathartidae) have fleshy heads and feed on carrion (dead animals). The Falconidae include several species of smaller birds (called falcons) with pointed wings. The American kestral, merlin, and peregrine falcon are all members of the Falconidae. The Order Strigiformes include the nocturnal owls. Owls have large heads, forward-facing eyes, and acute hearing.

Turkey Vulture (*Cathartes aura*)

Description: Turkey vultures are large, black-bodied birds with fleshy, red heads. They have a 5- to 6-foot wingspan, with two-toned un-

derwings. As they soar, the wings typically are held in a slight V-shape called a dihedral.

Behavior: Turkey vultures are scavengers, feeding mainly on dead animals, which they locate by sight and odor. Turkey vultures have weakly curved talons and beaks unlike other diurnal raptors. They are most commonly observed soaring over open country or woodlands, and feeding at roadkills. Turkey vultures lay two eggs in a minimal nest located in a protected area such as a cliff ledge. Both parents incubate the eggs for 40 days and care for the newly hatched young until they take flight after around 10 weeks.

Osprey (*Pandion haliaetus*)

Description: Ospreys are large raptors that feed on fish. Sometimes called fish hawks, ospreys stand just under 2 feet tall and have wingspans of 5 feet. Ospreys are white underneath with dark brown wings and a dark eye stripe.

Behavior: Ospreys cruise slowly over lakes and large rivers searching for fish. An osprey may hover momentarily before plummeting feet first into the water to seize its prey. Powerful wingbeats help the osprey regain flight, and the fish is pointed head first as the bird flies

back to its nest or perch. Ospreys build huge stick nests atop trees, electrical poles, or other suitable platforms. These nests are never far from water. In late April or early May, females lay up to four light brown eggs. The eggs hatch after a five week incubation period and the young are fledged in another eight weeks.

Bald Eagle (*Haliaeetus leucocephalus*)

Description: The bald eagle is the largest bird of prey in the Adirondacks, with a wingspan of nearly 7 feet. Adults have conspicuous white heads and tails. Immature eagles have speckled brown plumage covering the head, body, and tail. The beak and feet are yellow in adults.

Behavior: Bald eagles often are found near water, as their diet consists largely of fish. They also will scavenge carrion when it is available. Bald eagles are powerful fliers and may be seen soaring on thermal updrafts. They hunt from perches high in the treetops and, having spotted a fish or other suitable prey, swoop down and grab it in their powerful talons. Bald eagles are long-lived birds that can survive for 30 years. They are believed to mate for life after reaching adulthood at around five years of age. Bald eagles construct massive stick nests in treetops or cliff faces where the pair incubates up to three eggs. The eggs hatch after 36 days and it may take another 10 to 12 weeks before the young are fledged.

Sharp-shinned Hawk (*Accipiter striatus*)

Description: The sharp-shinned hawk is the smallest of the three species of accipiters, or bird-hawks, in the Adirondacks. Adults are about 1 foot from beak to tail and have wingspans under 2 feet. The wings are short and broad for maneuvering in dense forest. Mature birds have dark gray caps, gray back and wings, and reddish chests. The tail is short and square in flight. Adults have red eyes and yellow legs.

Behavior: Sharp-shinned hawks migrate seasonally and spend their winters in the southern United States or Central America. In the summer, they inhabit boreal forests where they prey on small birds and the occasional rodent or frog. As breeding season approaches, they build a stick nest high in a large conifer or well-concealed deciduous tree. Four to five bluish eggs are incubated for just over a month. The young are cared for by both parents until they are ready to leave the nest after six weeks.

Cooper's Hawk (*Accipiter cooperii*)

Description: The Cooper's hawk is larger than the sharp-shinned hawk, with which it is often confused. Mature birds have dark gray caps, grayish back and wings, and reddish underparts. In flight, the tail of the Cooper's hawk is longer and more rounded. Adults are approximately 17 inches from beak to tail and have a wingspan of 30 inches.

Behavior: Cooper's hawks winter in the southern United States. During the summer months, they are found throughout the Adirondacks. They feed primarily on small and medium-sized birds, which they surprise as they cruise through the forests. They also eat small mammals, frogs, and reptiles. Like other accipiters, they build stick nest in tall trees where they lay three to five eggs. The eggs are incubated for 36 days. Both parents contribute to feeding the young. Fledging occurs after five weeks in the nest.

Northern Goshawk (*Accipiter gentilis*)

Description: Northern goshawks are large hawks with short, broad wings and long tails that allow them to maneuver through dense for-

ests. Adults are slate-grey on the back and wings and have fine gray bars on the underparts. They have a dark gray cap with a prominent white band just above the eye. The eyes are red and the feet are yellow. Females are larger than males. Wingspans reach 41 inches and they stand approximately 20 inches tall.

Behavior: Goshawks hunt medium-sized birds, squirrels, rabbits, and the occasional reptile. Prey are captured after a short, rapid burst of speed. Stick nests are constructed in tall trees, primarily by the female, while the male provides the food for the pair. After the female lays two to four eggs, she incubates them for 38 days. The young leave the nest after six weeks.

Red-shouldered Hawk (*Buteo lineatus*)

Description: Adults have a reddish-brown head, a reddish-orange breast, and dark brown and white bands on the tail. A reddish band on the "shoulder" is visible when the bird is perched. Adults have a wingspan of roughly 40 inches.

Behavior: Red-shouldered hawks are present in the Adirondacks during the summer months, but they migrate to more southern states in the fall. They nest and hunt in forested areas, usually near water. These hawks hunt mainly small mammals, but will take small birds and reptiles when available. They return to the same area each season and often rebuild the same nest. Territorial boundaries are maintained by repeating a loud high-pitched "*keeyuur*" call that drops in pitch at the end. The female incubates two to five eggs for roughly 33 days while the male brings food to the nest for its mate. The young remain at the nest for five to seven weeks and stay with the parents for another two to three weeks before striking out on their own.

Broad-winged Hawk (*Buteo platypterus*)

Description: The broad-winged hawk is a small forest hawk with a wingspan of roughly 34 inches. Adults have short, broad wings, with a dark border around the wing when viewed in flight. The short tail has a thick white band bordered by darker bands. There are two color morphs. The light morph has reddish bars on the chest and pale underwings. The rare, dark morph is almost entirely dark brown.

Behavior: Broad-winged hawks migrate from their tropical wintering grounds to their breeding ground in the United States. They migrate northward in groups of up to a thousand to reach their summer nesting areas. They hunt from perches and prey on mice, voles, and other small mammals as well as frogs, snakes, and small birds. They nest lower in the tree than many hawks and may convert old squirrel or crow nests by adding sticks and other material. They lay up to four spotted eggs, which the female incubates for about one month. The young are fledged after another five or six weeks.

Red-tailed Hawk (*Buteo jamaicensis*)

Description: With a wingspan of nearly 50 inches, the red-tailed hawk is the largest hawk in the Adirondacks. Adults have characteristic red tails. There is wide variation in body coloration. Most adults have

brown heads and upperwings. The chest may be light with dark bars or almost entirely dark brown. Immature birds have yellowish irises, while adults have reddish brown irises.

Behavior: Red-tailed hawks frequently are seen along road-sides, as they prefer hunting in more open country. They prey on rabbits, squirrels, voles, and other small mammals, but they also will take grouse, pheasants, and other birds. Red-tailed hawks construct stick nests high in the tallest

tree in the area. Females incubate two to four eggs for approximately 35 days. During this time, the male hunts for and feeds his partner. After hatching, the male continues to bring food to the nest, which the female feeds to the young. Fledging occurs after seven to nine weeks.

American Kestrel (*Falco sparverius*)   PLATE 22

Description: The kestrel is the smallest Adirondack falcon; it stands less than 9 inches tall and has a wingspan of 22 inches. Kestrels have long, pointed wings and long, thin tails. Males have blue-grey wings, a reddish back, a light orange chest speckled with black spots, and a brownish cap on the head. Females lack the brown cap and are reddish over most of the body with dark bars on the back and wings. Females also have red bars on a white chest and thin dark bars on the top of the tail.

Color Plates

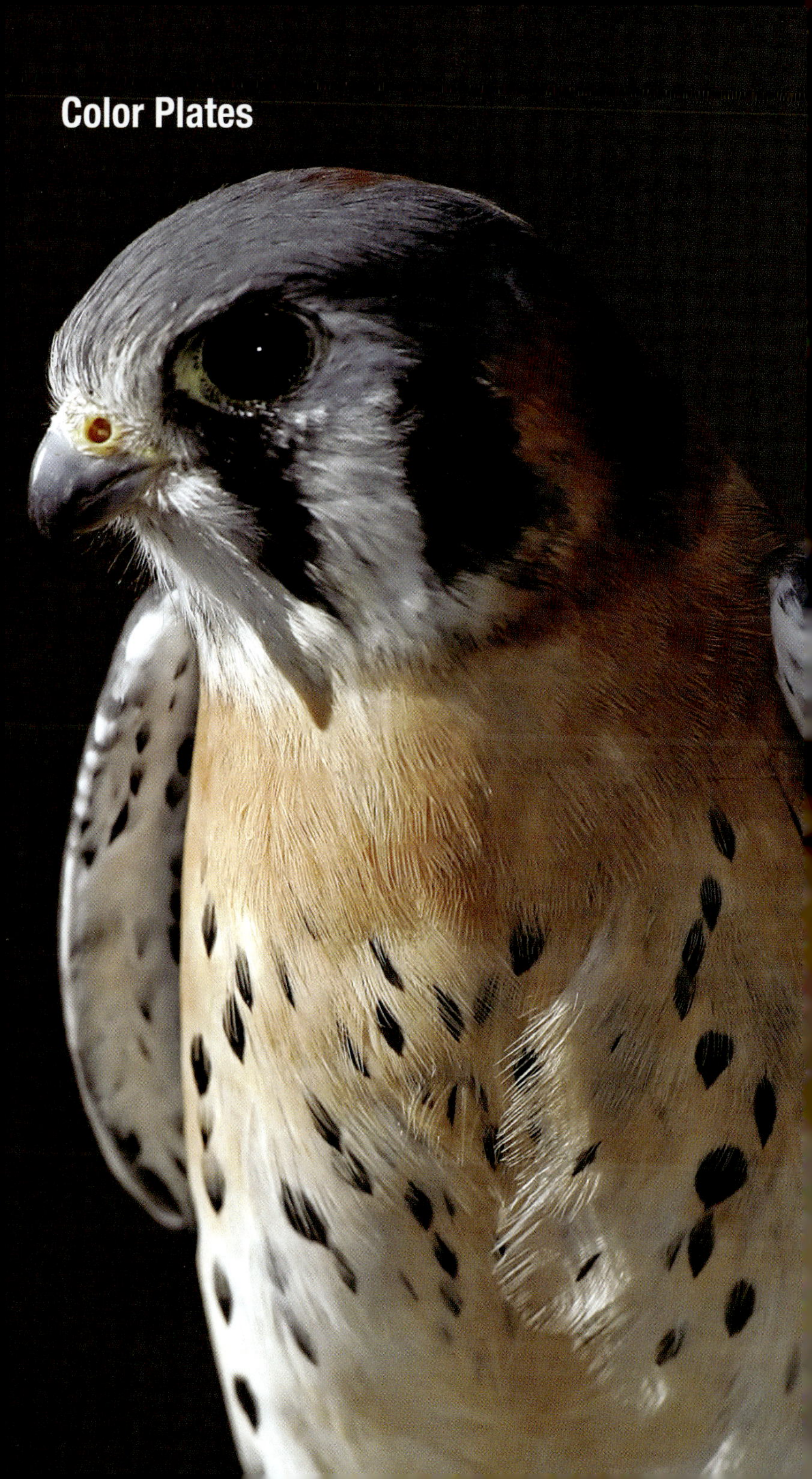

PLATE 1 *Hover fly*

PLATE 2 *Eastern Yellowjacket*

PLATE 3 *Ladybug*

PLATE 4A *Tiger swallowtail*

PLATE 4B *Tiger swallowtail caterpillar*

PLATE 5 *Black swallowtail caterpillar*

PLATE 6A *Monarch butterfly*

PLATE 6B *Monarch caterpillar, chrysalis, and butterfly*

PLATE 7 *American Painted Lady*

PLATE 8 *Red Admiral*

PLATE 9 *Isabella tiger moth caterpillar (woolly bear)*

PLATE 10 *Creek Chub*

PLATE 11 *Common Shiner*

PLATE 12 *Brown Trout*

PLATE 13 *Brook Trout*

PLATE 14 *Pumpkinseed*

PLATE 15 *Red-backed Salamander*

PLATE 16 *Eastern Red-spotted Newt*

PLATE 17 *Spotted Salamander*

PLATE 18 *Ringneck Snake*

PLATE 19 *Wood Duck*

PLATE 20 *Mallard*

PLATE 21 *Wild Turkey*

PLATE 22 *American Kestral*

PLATE 23 *American Woodcock*

PLATE 24 *Ruby-throated Hummingbird*

PLATE 25 *Yellow-bellied Sapsucker*

PLATE 26 *Northern Flicker*

PLATE 27 *Blue Jay*

PLATE 28 *Barn Swallow*

PLATE 29 *Eastern Bluebird*

PLATE 30 *American Robin*

PLATE 31 *European Starling*

PLATE 32 *Cedar Waxwing*

PLATE 33 *Yellow Warbler*

PLATE 34 *Chestnut-sided Warbler*

PLATE 35 *Magnolia Warbler*

PLATE 36 *Black-throated Green Warbler*

PLATE 37 *Black-throated Blue Warbler*

PLATE 38 *Blackburnian Warbler*

PLATE 39 *American Redstart*

PLATE 40 *Mourning Warbler*

PLATE 41 *Common Yellowthroat*

PLATE 42 *Eastern Towhee*

PLATE 43 *Rose-breasted Grosbeak*

PLATE 44 *Indigo Bunting*

PLATE 45 *Red-winged Blackbird*

PLATE 46 *Baltimore Oriole*

PLATE 47 *Pine Siskin*

PLATE 48 *American Goldfinch*

Behavior: Kestrels hunt in open country and commonly are seen along roads perched on telephone wires. They prefer farmland and open clearings. They eat mainly grasshoppers, dragonflies, and other large insects, but will take mice, voles, frogs, and other small vertebrates. They sometimes hover over fields searching for prey. Nests are often in tree holes where females lay between four and six eggs. Both parents incubate the eggs for roughly 30 days. The young are fully fledged after five weeks.

Merlin (*Falco columbarius*) and Peregrine Falcon (*Falco peregrinus*)

Description: Two other falcons occasionally are seen in the Adirondacks: the merlin and the peregrine falcon. The smaller merlin formerly was called the pigeon hawk and the peregrine falcon was called the duck hawk, after their favorite prey. However, they are falcons, not hawks. The male merlin has a blue-grey back and light orange chest and belly. Female and juvenile merlins are dark brown above and speckled brown below. Merlins are slightly larger than kestrels, with wingspans of approximately 24 inches. The peregrine falcon is larger, with a wingspan of about 40 inches. Male peregrines have a blue-gray helmet and blue-gray back, wings, and tail. The throat region is white and the chest has dark bars. Females are larger than males and have dark brown plumage.

Peregrine Falcon

Behavior: Both merlins and peregrines rely on speed to capture birds in flight. The peregrine falcon is the fastest animal on Earth; it can reach speeds of 185 mph during dives to capture prey. Merlins breed in more open country, while peregrines nest on cliff faces in more mountainous areas. Both species lay two to five eggs, which they incubate for approximately one month. Young merlins are fledged in 30 days and young peregrines require 40 to 50 days before they are able to fly. Both species migrate northward from the southern United States in the summer months.

OWLS (Order Strigiformes)

Only three owl species are common in the Adirondack Park. Although, when weather is exceedingly poor in Canada, snowy owls and great grey owls may move south into the Adirondacks in search of prey. Owls hunt at night using their acute sense of hearing to pinpoint the rustle of leaves that signal the presence of a mouse or vole. Unlike hawks and falcons, owls swallow their prey whole, digest the meat and entrails, and regurgitate the fur, feathers, and bones as a solid pellet. These pellets collect beneath roosts and are used by naturalists to determine the owl's diet. Although rarely seen, one of the most distinctive night sounds in the Adirondacks is the call of the barred owl.

Great Horned Owl (*Bubo virginianus*)

Description: Great horned owls are large, mottled brown birds with a

stocky body and a wingspan of over 40 inches. They have large ear-tufts and a light orange face with large yellow eyes. Great horned owls are much larger and stockier than the long-eared owl (*Asio otus*), which also has ear-tufts.

Behavior: Great horned owls are found in habitats ranging from dense forests to abandoned pastures. They are primarily dawn and dusk hunters. Great horned owls sit patiently on perches before swooping down to prey on rabbits, mice, voles, ruffed grouse, and other small birds. These owls take over heron or hawk nests in late January and lay two to three eggs shortly thereafter. Incubation last roughly 30 days. Both parents provide food for the young for several months. Great horned owls have a distinctive call consisting of a low-pitched series of "*hoo hoodoo hooo hoo*" that can be heard over considerable distances. These calls are used to maintain territories of up to 5 square miles from other pairs.

Barred Owl (*Strix varia*)

Description: Barred owls stand roughly 20 inches tall and have a wingspan of 40 inches. These large forest owls have round heads and lack the ear-tufts of the great horned owl. They have dark eyes and a yellow bill. The belly is creamy white with dark brown vertical streaks.

Behavior: Barred owls prefer dense woodlands, especially wet woods and swampy forests. As nocturnal hunters, they are rarely seen, but their "*hoo hoo ho-ho*" or *hoo hoo ho-hooooaw*" call (translated as "who cooks for you") is often heard during the late-winter breeding season. They prey on mice, voles, and other small vertebrates. On occasion, they may even take small fish or crayfish from streamside shallows. Nesting begins in late March, when pairs build nests in hollow trees and lay up to four eggs, which they incubate for roughly one month. The young remain in the nest for five weeks, but the parents continue to feed the young for several more months before the young leave their parents' territory for good.

Northern Saw-whet Owl (*Aegolius acadicus*)

Description: Saw-whet owls are the smallest of Adirondack owls, at only 8 inches tall. They lack ear-tufts and have large round facial disks and yellow eyes. Adults have white on the forehead and between the eyes. The body is brown with white spots on the upper wings and light brown streaks on the chest and belly.

Behavior: These diminutive owls prefer dense forests and forest edges. They also inhabit cedar swamps, alder thickets, and tamarack bogs. Their primary prey are deer mice, but they will take other small mammals, small birds, and insects. Saw-whet owls nest in tree holes such as abandoned woodpecker cavities. Here they lay four to seven eggs, which they incubate for roughly 27 days. Males bring food to the nest, but it is the female who feeds it to the young. The young owls leave the nest after four weeks, but do not hunt on their own for another month.

SHOREBIRDS AND GULLS (Order Charadriiformes)

Shorebirds and gulls are members of the order Charadriiformes. Both groups inhabit coastal and freshwater environments. However, the term shorebird is a bit misleading because killdeer and woodcock, both members of the shorebird family Scolopacidae, are not restricted to shoreline or wetland habitats. Shorebirds typically probe the mud or sand with their sensitive bills looking for tiny prey. Spotted sandpipers, killdeer, and American woodcock are relatively common in the Adirondacks. Upland sandpipers and Wilson's snipe (not described) are less common. Gulls (family Laridae) are larger, more aggressive birds. Their plumage is usually some combination of black, gray, and white. Gulls have long, sturdy beaks used for capturing fish, scavenging, or stealing food from other birds. Great black-backed gulls and ring-billed gulls are occasionally seen in the Adirondacks, but only the herring gull regularly breeds within the Park.

Killdeer (Family Charadriidae, *Charadrius vociferus*)

Description: The killdeer is the only upland plover to inhabit the Adirondacks. Killdeer have long legs, slender wings, and a long tail. They

have a brown back and wings with a white chest and belly. There are two prominent black bands across the upper chest and white patches in front of and above the eye.

Behavior: Killdeer often are seen on freshly plowed fields, golf courses, and ballfields. They prefer open areas with barren ground where they lay up to four spotted eggs in shallow depressions on the ground. Their name comes from the high "*kill deeee*" calls they make when agitated. Killdeer call repeatedly and pretend to be injured in an effort to lure would-be predators away from the nest. The young leave the nest after hatching and follow their parents for roughly 25 days before they take their first flight.

Spotted Sandpiper (Family Scolopacidae, *Actitis macularia*)

Description: Spotted sandpipers are robin-sized shorebirds that have an unusual bobbing motion when they walk. Adults are brown above with a white stripe on the upper wing. The chest and belly are white with large dark spots. They have a narrow, dark eye-stripe. Non-breeding birds lack the prominent chest spots.

Behavior: Spotted sandpipers are found along the shores of lakes, ponds, and streams. They feed on aquatic insects, small crayfish, mollusks, and minnows. When disturbed, they make a rapid bursts of wingbeats followed by a short glide to a new location down the shore. Nests tend to be hidden under shrubs or near a fallen tree. Eggs are laid in shallow nests made of grasses on the ground. Females lay four camouflaged eggs, which they incubate for three weeks. The hatchlings leave the nest almost immediately and are protected by the male for another three weeks.

American Woodcock   PLATE 23
(Family Scolopacidae, *Scolopax minor*)

Description: American woodcocks are plump-bodied birds with a large head and long bill. They have pale orange plumage on the chest and belly and a cryptic pattern of brown, black, and tan above. They have large dark eyes and short legs.

Behavior: Woodcock inhabit brushy woodlands and damp thickets. They feed on earthworms and insect larvae by probing the soft soil with their long, flexible bills. They remain motionless until nearly stepped upon, then burst into a zigzagging flight. Modified wing feathers create a whistling sound as they fly. During the spring breeding season, males perform a remarkable aerial "dance" characterized by spiraling upward and then tumbling to the ground accompanied by twittering calls. Females lay one to four eggs in a nest on the ground and incubate them for three weeks. The young are precocial — downy and mobile immediately upon hatching — and forage with their mother for up to five weeks before fledging.

Herring Gull (Family Laridae, *Larus argentatus*)

Description: Adult herring gulls have a white body with light gray back and wings. The tips of the wings are black with white spots. They have pink legs and feet and a yellow bill with a prominent red spot near the tip of the lower mandible. Immature birds are brownish and don't acquire adult coloration for several years.

Behavior: Herring gulls nest in colonies near large lakes and commonly are seen on recently plowed fields or at landfills. Herring gulls are scav-

engers that feed on fish, crustaceans, carrion, and refuse. Females lay two to four spotted, olive-brown eggs in grass-lined depression on the ground. Both parents share in incubating the eggs for roughly one month. Both parents return regularly to the nest site to regurgitate food to the young. The young begin to fly 45 days after hatching, but often remain with their parents for another month.

DOVES AND CUCKOOS

Pigeons and doves are members of the family Columbidae. The term pigeon generally refers to larger species, but there is no consistent rule for applying the terms dove and pigeon. Both pigeons and doves produce "crop milk," a milky liquid that they feed to their young. Rock pigeons are familiar urban birds, which can be found in the larger cities and towns around the edges of the Adirondack Park. Cuckoos (family Cuculidae) have slender bodies with relatively long tails. Two of their toes point forward and two point to the rear (zygodactyl).

Mourning Dove (Family Columbidae, *Zenaida macroura*)

Description: Mourning doves are small, streamlined birds with long, pointed tails. The body plumage is gray-brown with black spots on the wings. They have relatively small heads, delicate black bills, and a pale blue ring around the eye. Males may have a light blue crown. The legs and feet are reddish. In flight, the long tail is diamond-shaped with a black and white border.

Behavior: Mourning doves are common in open areas and around homes where their "*coo-ah, coo, coo, coo*" calls are easily recognizable.

They feed almost exclusively on seeds. Females choose a suitable nest site from several options presented by the male. Nests are frequently in trees or on house ledges. The male delivers building materials to the female, who constructs the nest over several days. Both parents share the incubation of two eggs for 14 days. After hatching, young are fed "milk" rich in fat and protein that is secreted from the crop, a specialized region of the esophagus. The young leave the nest after 15 days but remain nearby for another week. Mourning doves are prolific breeders and can have several broods per year.

Black-billed Cuckoo (*Coccyzus erythropthalmus*)
and **Yellow-billed Cuckoo** (*Coccyzus americanus*)
Description: Cuckoos are jay-sized birds with long, slender tails. They are brown or olive above and white on the chest and belly. Yellow-billed cuckoos have reddish-brown wings and large white and black spots on the tail. Their bill is slightly curved at the tip with a yellow lower mandible. The black-billed cuckoo lacks the reddish color on the wings and has small white tail spots and a black or gray bill. Black-billed cuckoos also have a narrow red eye ring as adults.
Behavior: Cuckoos prefer woodlands, streamside thickets, abandoned pastures, and orchards. They feed on caterpillars, including gypsy moths and tent caterpillars, and a wide range of other insects and small berries. They construct flimsy nests in dense foliage 5 to 10 feet above the ground. Females incubate two to four blue-green eggs for 10 to 14 days. The young are capable of flight after roughly three weeks. These secretive birds are more commonly heard than seen.

SWIFTS AND HUMMINGBIRDS (Order Apodiformes)
Swifts resemble swallows, but are more closely related to humming-birds, and they are placed together in the Order Apodiformes. Swifts

have a forked tail and long wings. In flight, swifts alternate short glides with several quick wingbeats. They are extremely fast aerialists. Hummingbirds (family Trochilidae) are also known for their aerial abilities; they can hover and even fly backwards. Their wings beat in a figure eight pattern at speeds up to 80 beats per second. As a result they are the only birds able to generate enough lift to hover in place as they sip nectar from flowers.

Chimney Swift (Family Apodidae, *Chaetura pelagica*)

Description: Chimney swifts are small, swallow-like birds roughly 5 inches in length with long pointed wings and very short tails. Coloration is a dirty olive-brown above with a slightly paler gray underneath. The tail is very short and rounded; the very tips of the tail feathers are reduced to stiff spines that help support the body when the bird is clinging to a vertical surface.

Behavior: Chimney swifts prefer residential or urban areas where chimneys and other structures provide suitable nesting and roosting sites. Foraging for insects takes place in flight over open areas such as agricultural lands or lakes and ponds. Swifts are fast flyers and remain in flight for most of the day. They return to their roost at dusk each night. Swifts build nests of small twigs and glue them with sticky saliva to the interior face of a chimney or other protected surface. Four or five eggs are incubated for 20 to 21 days. Nineteen days after hatching, the young leave the nest and cling to a nearby wall, where they are attended by the parents. They take their first flights after roughly one month.

Ruby-throated Hummingbird   PLATE 24
(Family Trochilidae, *Archilochus colubris*)

Description: The smallest bird in the Adirondacks, the tiny ruby-throated hummingbird has a wingspan of only 4½ inches and weighs only ¹⁄₁₀ of an ounce. They are readily distinguished by their long, thin beaks. Both sexes are green on the head and back, with white on the throat and belly. Males have a remarkable iridescent red throat.

Behavior: Hummingbirds prefer open habitats including clearings, meadows, gardens, and village parks. Their wings beat at an amazing 50 to 80

beats per second, which produces the familiar humming sound as they hover. Hummingbirds not only hover, but are the only birds capable of flying backwards. They feed on nectar by hovering in front of a flower and probing the flower base with their long bill and tongue. Hummingbirds are territorial and defend their flower patches vigorously. Nests are usually on a horizontal branch and consist of plant fibers and spider silk camouflaged with lichens. Females lay two tiny eggs, which they incubate for roughly two weeks. Females feed the hatchlings until they are ready to fly approximately three weeks later.

KINGFISHERS (Family Cerylidae)

The belted kingfisher is the only member of the Cerylidae in eastern North America. Kingfishers dive head first into the water in an effort to capture fish in their long dagger-like bills.

Belted Kingfisher (*Megaceryle alcyon*)

Description: Belted kingfishers are roughly 12 inches in length and have a wingspan of 20 inches. They have a large head and a heavy, dagger-like bill. They have a jagged crest of feathers on the head. They are bluish gray on the head, back, and upper portions of the wings. Both sexes also have a white throat and belly. Males have a single blue-gray chest band, while females have a bluish chest band in addition to patches of orange on the sides of the chest and a second rufous band on the lower chest.

Behavior: Belted kingfishers inhabit almost any habitat near water.

They usually are seen perched on a branch overhanging a river or pond. They give a loud rattling call as they fly between perches. They feed on small fish, which they take by diving into the water and grabbing the prey in their stout bills. They return to a nearby perch to swallow the fish whole. Other prey include crayfish, frogs, salamanders, and insects. Kingfishers excavate earthen tunnels, up to 6 feet long, in sand banks. Here they lay five to eight eggs. Both parents take turns incubating the eggs for roughly 24 days. The young leave the tunnels approximately 28 days after hatching and both parents continue to feed them for a few more weeks.

WOODPECKERS (Family Picidae)

Woodpeckers derive their name from their habit of using their bills to hammer on trees. The hammering serves to maintain territorial boundaries, attract potential mates, extract insects from under tree bark, and in some species to excavate nest cavities. Woodpeckers have long bristled tongues for extracting insects from their woody tunnels. Woodpeckers also have zygodactylous feet, with one pair of toes facing forward and the other pair facing backward. This arrangement, along with their stiff tail feathers, allows them to securely grasp the tree trunk. The American three-toed woodpecker and the black-backed woodpecker breed in the Adirondacks but are rarely seen. Red-bellied woodpeckers and Red-headed woodpeckers (not described) are occasionally seen at lower elevations around the margins of the Park.

Yellow-bellied Sapsucker (*Sphyrapicus varius*)   PLATE 25

Description: A medium-sized woodpecker, the yellow-bellied sapsucker is roughly 8 inches in length. The crown and forehead are red bordered by black stripes. They have a black eye stripe bordered above by a white band that continues around the back of the head. Below the eye stripe is a narrow white band that runs onto the chest. There is a large white wing patch. The body is whitish with extensive black barring. Males have a red throat bordered by black. Females and juveniles have a white or yellowish throat.

Behavior: These woodpeckers are called sapsuckers because of their unusual habit of boring small rows of holes in trees and feeding on the sap that seeps out. They also feed on insects and berries. These secretive birds drill nest cavities in deciduous trees and may use the same nest for several years. Both parents help incubate five to six eggs for roughly 13 days. The parents bring insects and sap to the young until they are ready to leave the nest approximately 28 days after hatching. The young remain with the parents for another week to 10 days.

Hairy Woodpecker (*Picoides villosus*)
and Downy Woodpecker (*Picoides pubescens*)

Description: The downy and hairy woodpeckers are nearly indistinguishable except by size. The downy woodpecker is the smallest woodpecker at only 6 inches in length. The hairy woodpecker is roughly 9 inches in length. Both species are black and white with white backs. Males of both species have small red patches on the back of the head. Downy woodpeckers have a shorter bill than hairy woodpeckers.

Behavior: Both downy and hairy woodpeckers are common in the Adirondacks, but the smaller downy woodpecker is more likely to visit bird feeders in winter. Hairy woodpeckers prefer to remain in more-forested areas. They feed primarily on insects, which they pry from under tree bark or extract from holes they drill with their pointed bills. They also eat berries and seeds on occasion. In late winter, males and females take turns drumming on dead trees to establish pair bonds prior to mating. Nesting takes place in tree holes excavated by both sexes. Between three and six eggs are incubated by both parents for roughly 14 days. Parents take turns bringing insects to the nest to feed the young. Young downy woodpeckers leave the nest at roughly 24 days; the larger hairy woodpeckers do not leave the nest for 28 to 30 days.

Downy woodpecker

Black-backed Woodpecker (*Picoides arcticus*)
and Three-toed Woodpecker (*Picoides tridactylus*)

Description: These two uncommon and inconspicuous woodpeckers are reported occasionally in the Adirondacks. Both species are roughly robin-sized at 9 inches in length. Both have a largely black back with barred underwings and belly. Males of both species have a yellow crown whereas females have a black crown. Adult three-toed woodpeckers have small, white bars on the back; black-backed woodpeckers have solid black backs. Both species have only three toes instead of the usual four.

Behavior: These woodpeckers inhabit northern boreal forests; they prefer conifer forests with stands of dead trees. They feed by prying flakes of bark off dead conifers in an effort to capture insects, including wood-boring beetles. Nest cavities are located in dead conifers, often 5 to 15 feet from the ground. Three to six eggs are incubated by both sexes for approximately 14 days. The young leave the nest between 22 and 26 days after hatching.

Northern Flicker (*Colaptes auratus*) PLATE 26

Description: Formerly called the yellow-shafted flicker, the northern flicker is a large, brownish-yellow woodpecker. Adults have a brownish back with black bars and spots. The

belly is buff with black spots and a conspicuous black crescent on the upper chest. In flight, they have a white rump and yellow underwings. Both sexes have a red patch on the back of the neck, but only males have a black band below the eye.

Behavior: Northern flickers prefer open forests, forest edges, and fields. They feed primarily on insects, but will eat berries and seeds. They often forage on the ground. Males defend nest cavities in trees with loud calls and displays. Females lay five to eight eggs and both parents share the incubation for up to 16 days. Fledging occurs after four to five weeks.

Pileated Woodpecker (*Dryocopus pileatus*)

Description: The pileated woodpecker is the largest woodpecker in the

Adirondacks with a length of nearly 17 inches and a wingspan of almost 30 inches. They have black bodies, white stripes on the neck, white underwings, and a conspicuous red crest. Males have a longer red crest and a red cheek stripe.

Behavior: Pileated woodpeckers prefer mature coniferous and deciduous forests. They excavate large rectangular holes in dead trees to get at ants and other insects. They also eat fruits and nuts. They roost in tree cavities at night. Breeding pairs are thought to mate for life and they vigorously defend their territories. Nests are in tree cavities created by both parents. Typically, four eggs are laid and incubated for roughly 17 days. Young may leave the nest cavity after 26 days but will remain with their parents for several months.

FLYCATCHERS (Family Tyrannidae)

Adirondack flycatchers (Family Tyrannidae) are a diverse group of insectivorous birds, including several species of flycatcher, the eastern wood-pewee, the eastern phoebe, and the eastern kingbird. Five species of flycatcher breed in the Adirondack Park; the willow flycatcher breeds at lower elevations around the periphery of the park.

Great Crested Flycatcher (*Myiarchus crinitus*)

Description: The largest of the Adirondack flycatchers, great crested flycatchers are roughly 9 inches in length, with a wingspan of 13 inches. They have a distinctive yellow belly, gray throat, and dark olive-brown back. The tail and upper wing tips are a cinnamon brown. The bill is large and there is a slight crest at the back of the head.

Behavior: These large flycatchers prefer open deciduous forests and abandoned orchards. They prey on butterflies, beetles, moths, crickets, and other large insects. Great crested flycatchers are more often heard than seen; they utter a loud "*wheeep*" call along with an excited "*whit-whit-whit-whit*." Although noisy and aggressive, they tend to remain hidden in the canopy. They nest in tree cavities, often using abandoned woodpecker holes. They build large nests that may include unusual items such as snake skins, string, and clear plastic. Females incubate four to six eggs for up to 15 days. The young leave the nest cavity after 15 days but remain with the parents for another week.

Olive-sided Flycatcher (*Contopus cooperi*)

Description: One of the larger flycatchers, olive-sided flycatchers are olive-gray or olive-brown birds with a large head. The breast is darker on the sides, forming a dark "vest" with white in the center. The wings are dark and lack wing bars. The upper bill is darker than the lower bill.

Behavior: Olive-sided flycatchers prefer boreal conifer forests near ponds, swamps, or clearcuts, where they often are found perched high in the tops of trees. Typical calls are "*beer beer beer*" given in rapid succession or a rapid and sharp "*piw piw piw*." Their beaks are broad and flat at the base, which aids in capturing flying insects. This species prefers to nest in conifers. Females build a well-concealed nest of grasses, twigs, and mosses, where they lay three eggs. Females incubate the eggs for roughly 16 days, but both parents feed the young after hatching. The young leave the nest after three weeks.

Yellow-bellied Flycatcher (*Empidonax flaviventris*)

Description: This small flycatcher is olive-green above and more yellowish on the throat and belly. There are two white or lemon-colored bars on the otherwise dark wings. The eye is surrounded by a pale yellow eye-ring. The upper bill is dark and the lower bill is pinkish.

Behavior: This reclusive flycatcher is rarely seen outside of boreal coniferous forest, where they prefer bogs, tamarack swamps, and other wet areas. They feed on mosquitoes, gnats, and other small insects. On the breeding territory, males repeatedly sing a hoarse "*killink*" or "*che-bunk*" song. Nests are constructed of moss on or near ground level and may be hidden among roots of fallen trees. Females incubate three or four eggs for two weeks. Both parents feed the young, being very quiet and secretive around the nest site. Young take flight after two weeks.

Alder Flycatcher (*Empidonax alnorum*)

Description: This small flycatcher is a pale gray-green on the head and back. The underparts are cream colored. It has two white wing bars and a faint white eye ring. Until the 1970s, the willow and alder flycatchers were considered one species. They are best identified by differences in songs.

Behavior: Alder flycatchers prefer alder thickets, usually near streams or swamps. They dart out from their perch to capture a variety of flying insects, including flies, bees, and moths. The song is a coarse, "*fee-BEE-o*" with a strongly accented second syllable. Alder flycatchers nest in low shrubs, often only a couple feet off the ground. Females incubate three or four eggs for a period of 14 days. The young take their first flight after roughly two weeks in the nest.

Least Flycatcher (*Empidonax minimus*)

Description: The least flycatcher is a small bird with a wingspan under 8 inches. The body is grayish to olive-gray on the head and back, and whitish on the undersides. They have a prominent eye-ring and two whitish wing bars.

Behavior: Least flycatchers prefer open woodlands, orchards, and deciduous forest edges. Like other flycatchers, they capture insects on the wing and return to a nearby perch to eat their prey. Their song is a "*che-BEC*" given in staccato and repeated roughly 40 to 50 times a minute. A female typically builds her nests in the crotch of a deciduous tree. Here she lays three to five eggs and incubates them for two weeks. The young are fed by both parents, and typically fledge 15 to 17 days after hatching.

Eastern Wood-Pewee (*Contopus virens*)

Description: This small flycatcher is olive-gray above and paler below. They have two whitish wing bars and a faint eye-ring. Wood-pewees do not flick their tails when perched.

Behavior: Wood-pewees prefer deciduous or mixed forests near openings such as ponds, clearings, and roadsides. They are difficult to see in the mid-canopy, but a mournful "*pee-ah-weee*" signals their presence. They feed on flying insects captured by making short flights from their perch. Nests are typically in deciduous trees and positioned well out from the trunk. Females incubate three to four eggs for roughly 12 days. The young are fledged after another 16 days or so.

Eastern Phoebe (*Sayornis phoebe*)

Description: Eastern phoebes are 7 inches long and have few characteristic markings. They are dark olive-green above, have a dark head and face, and lack wing bars and eye-rings. The belly is a creamy white. This species flicks its tail when perched.

Behavior: Phoebes prefer open or semi-open habitats near water. The summer diet consists primarily of insects, but they eat berries and small fruits in early spring or late fall. Their name is derived from the distinctive "*phoe-bee*" song that is repeated over and over. They are tolerant birds and often nest around buildings and bridges where they build nest of grass, mud, and moss on a ledge. Four or five eggs are incubated for roughly 16 days. The young leave the nest after another 16 days. Phoebes arrive early in spring and depart late in fall and typically raise two clutches per year.

Eastern Kingbird (*Tyrannus tyrannus*)

Description: The eastern kingbird is easily distinguished by its black head, dark gray back, and contrasting white throat and belly. They have black tail feathers with white tips.

Behavior: Eastern kingbirds require open habitat for foraging and often are seen around clearings, roadsides, and farmlands. They capture insects in mid-air, but also take berries and small fruits. Kingbirds are extremely aggressive in defense of nests and mates, and drive other birds away from the breeding territory. Nests are large piles of grass and twigs, usually positioned on a tree limb near water. Females lay three to four eggs, which they incubate for up to 18 days. Hatchlings are fed by both parents, for another 18 days before they fledge.

VIREOS (Family Vireonidae)

Vireos (Family Vireonidae) are small insectivorous birds that resemble warblers. Two species are common in the Adirondacks. Three additional vireos, the Philadelphia vireo, warbling vireo, and yellow-throated vireo are less common (not described).

Blue-headed Vireo (*Vireo solitarius*)

Description: Formerly called the solitary vireo, the blue-headed vireo is a small bird with a blue-gray head and face, a white throat and belly, and an olive-green back. They also have a bright white eye-ring and a white stripe from the eye to the base of the bill. The flanks are yellowish and there are two white wing bars.

Behavior: This species prefers moist conifer forests and mixed conifer-deciduous forests. The blue-headed vireo methodically explores the vegetation for small insects, cocking its head from side to side as it searches. Nests are suspended from forked branches and constructed of grass, bark strips, and plant fibers. Both parents take turns incubating up to five eggs for roughly 12 days. The young are fledged two weeks later.

Red-eyed Vireo (*Vireo olivaceus*)

Description: Red-eyed vireos are sparrow-sized birds with olive-green above and white below. They have a gray crown, red eyes, a gray eye-band, and a bright white band above the eye.

Behavior: Red-eyed vireos breed in deciduous or mixed forests with abundant undergrowth. They forage among the leaves for a wide array of insects and berries. Nests constructed from pine needles, grasses, spider webs, and other materials hang below a forked branch. Females incubate up to five eggs for approximately 14 days. The young leave the nest 12 days after hatching. Vireo nests are sometimes parasitized by cowbirds.

JAYS, CROWS, AND RAVENS (Family Corvidae)

Adirondack members of the family Corvidae include the New World jays, crows, and ravens. They are medium to large birds with stout beaks. Crows and ravens are both jet black and difficult to tell apart in the field. Blue jays are abundant throughout New York State, but gray jays prefer the deep, forested regions in the Adirondack high peaks.

Gray Jay (*Perisoreus canadensis*)

Description: As their name implies, these birds are dark gray above and light gray on the belly. The throat, cheek, and forehead areas are white. There is a dark eye-stripe that continues as a dark gray cap on the back of the head. The bill is black and quite short.

Behavior: Gray jays are found in dense co-niferous forests and swamps. Their diet includes berries, insects, seeds, small animals, and carrion. These omnivorous birds are well known for their habit of raiding campsites for food scraps. Pairs nest in dense conifer forests. Three to five eggs are incubated for roughly 21 days. The young leave the nest after another three weeks.

Blue Jay (*Cyanocitta cristata*)   PLATE 27

Description: One of the most conspicuous and common of Adirondack birds, the blue jay is bright blue on the head, back, and tail. The throat and belly regions are light gray to white. There are distinctive white and black bands on the wings and tail. Adults have a prominent blue crest on the head, a black eye-stripe, and a black band across the throat.

Behavior: Blue jays are found in a wide array of habitats, from oak forests to town parks and suburban backyards. They regularly visit bird feeders, where they often chase away smaller birds. Their diet con-

sists of acorns, other nuts, grains, berries, insects, frogs, birds' eggs or baby birds, and carrion. They announce their presence with a short series of harsh "*jaaay jaaay*" calls. Nests, built from twigs, grass, and mud, often are located in the crotch of a tree trunk. Parents take turns incubating four or five eggs for up to 18 days. The young jays leave the nest three weeks after hatching.

American Crow (*Corvus brachyrhynchos*)

Description: American crows are large, solid black birds roughly 18 inches in length with a wingspan of nearly 40 inches. They have a long, robust bill and black feet. In flight, American crows have a fan-shaped tail.

Behavior: Crows live in woodlands, farm country, lake shores, and other semi-open habitats. They are extremely intelligent birds and often highly social, forming large roosting flocks in winter. Crows have a distinctive call consisting of a hoarse "*caaw*." They eat a wide variety of foods, including insects, frogs, carrion, eggs, young birds, garbage, and roadkills. They build large stick nests in the fork of a tall tree. Here, females incubate four to six eggs for 18 days. Roughly five weeks after hatching, the young crows leave the nest.

Common Raven (*Corvus corax*)

Description: Larger than the American crow, the common raven is over 2 feet in length and has a wingspan over 50 inches. Ravens are distinguished from crows by having more shaggy throat feathers and a wedge-shaped tail when in flight.

Behavior: Boreal forests and rocky cliffs are the preferred habitat for common ravens. Their calls include a bell-like "*brrronnk*" and a hoarse "*kaaaaw*." Ravens scavenge garbage and carrion from roadkills. They also raid birds' nests for eggs and hatchlings. Nests tend to be perched on cliff ledges or in tall trees. Females incubate three to seven eggs for roughly three weeks. Both parents feed the nestlings after hatching. The young ravens leave the nest after six weeks.

SWALLOWS (Family Hirundinidae)

Swallows (Family Hirundinidae) are small streamlined birds with long pointed wings, which make them fast and maneuverable fliers. Swallows have short, broad bills, which they use to capture insects during flight. Three species are common in the Adirondacks; two additional species, cliff swallows, and rough-winged swallows (not described), are uncommon within the park.

Barn Swallow (*Hirundo rustica*)   PLATE 28

Description: The barn swallow is probably the most common swallow in the Adirondacks. They have dark blue or blue-black plumage on the back and head, a rust-colored throat and forehead, light orange belly, and a long, forked tail. Both sexes are similar, but males have a darker orange on the belly than females.

Behavior: Barn swallows inhabit farmland, towns, and other semi-open country. They prefer to nest near water, where they are often seen swooping low over the surface to capture fly-ing insects. Nests are made of grass and other plant materials glued with mud to the side of a building or under a bridge. Females lay up to six eggs, which they incubate for 15 days; the hatchlings leave

the nest after another three weeks. Barn swallows are graceful and ef-ficient fliers. They winter as far south as Argentina.

Tree Swallow (*Tachycineta bicolor*)

Description: Tree swallows are small birds with iridescent blue or blue-green plumage on the back and head in males. Females and juveniles are a dark gray above. The throat and belly of both sexes are bright white and the tail is dark gray.

Behavior: Marshes, lakeshores, and wet meadows are typical habitats for tree swallows. They feed primarily on flying insects, which they cap-ture on the wing. They also eat small berries. They nest in tree holes or bluebird boxes, usually close to water. The nest is made of grasses and pine needles and lined with feathers. Females incubate up to seven eggs for 14 days. Both parents feed the young until they are ready to leave the nest after roughly three weeks.

Bank Swallow (*Riparia riparia*)

Description: The smallest and least colorful of Adirondack swallows, the bank swallow is gray-brown above with white on the throat and belly. It has a distinct dark band across the chest.

Behavior: Bank swallows nest in small colonies in steep riverbanks or abandoned excavation sites. Here they dig a horizontal burrow several feet long. Females lay four to six eggs in a flimsy nest at the end of the tunnel. Both parents take turns incubating the eggs for up to 16 days. The young leave the nest approximately 22 days after hatching.

CHICKADEES (Family Paridae)

The family Paridae includes chickadees and the tufted titmouse. The black-capped chickadee is one of the Adirondack's most abundant year round residents. Boreal chickadees also breed in the more remote interior of the Adirondacks. The tufted titmouse (not described) is uncommon in the Adirondack Mountains, but frequents bird feeders in lower elevation areas around the park borders.

Black-capped Chickadee (*Poecile atricapilla*)

Description: The black-capped chickadee is one of the most common and popular birds in the Adirondacks. They are small birds with a prominent black cap and throat patch. The side of the head is white, the back is greenish gray, and the flanks are beige.

Behavior: Chickadees prefer deciduous or mixed forests with open areas or forest edges. They hop from branch to branch, probing cracks in the

bark for insects. They also eat berries and seeds, especially in the winter when insects are absent. They are curious and often form mixed species flocks that visit feeders in winter. Their "*chick-a-dee-dee-dee*" call is one of the most commonly heard bird calls in the region. Chickadees nest in tree holes or rotten stumps. Females incubate between 6 and 8 eggs for 12 days. The young leave the nest roughly 16 days after hatching.

Boreal Chickadee (*Poecile hudsonica*)

Description: The boreal chickadee is distinguished from the black-capped chickadee by its brown cap and back and more cinnamon-colored flanks.

Behavior: Boreal chickadees are restricted to spruce-fir forests and are most often seen at higher elevations. They are reclusive, spending most of the time foraging near the trunks of spruce trees. They eat a variety of insects and seeds, which they often store wedged under bark. They nest in tree holes, where they lay five or six eggs in a small nest made of lichens, plant down, and other soft materials. The incubation period lasts 12 to 16 days and the young remain in the nest for another 18 days.

NUTHATCHES AND CREEPERS

Nuthatches (Family Sittidae) and brown creepers (Family Certhiidae) are forest birds that search for insects on tree trunks and branches. Nuthatches descend trees head first, while brown creepers alight near the bottom of the tree and ascend the trunk in search of prey.

White-breasted Nuthatch (Family Sittidae, *Sitta carolinensis*)

Description: Larger of the two Adirondack nuthatches, white-breasted nuthatches are nearly 6 inches in length. They are blue-gray above, but are bright white on the cheek, throat, and belly. The crown of the head is black. They have rusty-colored plumage on the lower belly.

Behavior: White-breasted nuthatches live in deciduous and mixed forests, where they are often seen inching headfirst down tree trunks in search of food. They eat insects and seeds; the seeds are often stored, wedged under loose bark, for use in winter.

They are common visitors to bird feeders. Between five and nine eggs are laid in an old woodpecker hole or other cavity. After roughly two weeks, the eggs hatch. Both parents feed young nuthatches, until they leave the nest.

Red-breasted Nuthatch (Family Sittidae, *Sitta canadensis*)

Description: Red-breasted nuthatches are only 4 to 5 inches in length. They are blue-gray above and pale orange below. They have a distinctive black eye-band and cap, but the rest of the cheek is white. Females have a gray cap.

Behavior: Red-breasted nuthatches prefer stands of spruce, fir, and hemlock, but mature deciduous forests are also used for foraging. They feed primarily on insects during the summer and conifer seeds during the winter months. They build nests inside tree holes or in decaying snags. Females lay five or six eggs, which they incubate for roughly 12 days. Both parents take turns feeding the young until they leave the nest two to three weeks later.

Brown Creeper (Family Certhiidae, *Certhia americana*)

Description: Brown creepers are tiny birds with long tails and long curved bills. The body is mottled brown above, white on the throat and belly, and buff or tan on the flanks. They prop their long, stiff tail feathers against the tree trunk for support.

Behavior: Brown creepers have a habit of landing near the base of a tree and slowly inching their way upward as they probe the bark for insects. They inhabit both coniferous and deciduous forests wherever there are numerous mature trees. They feed on insects and their larvae, but will take seeds. Nests containing five or six eggs often are hidden behind large chunks of loose bark or in a tree cavity. The incubation period lasts just over two weeks. The young leave the nest after another two weeks.

WRENS (Family Troglodytidae)

Wrens (Family Troglodytidae), with their loud, complex songs, are usually heard before they are seen. They have long, slightly downward pointing bills and upright tails. Carolina wrens, marsh wrens, and sedge wrens are uncommon in the Adirondacks.

House Wren (*Troglodytes aedon*)

Description: House wrens are tiny birds with slender bodies, short tails, and long thin beaks. They are darker brown above and paler brown below. There is a weak fan of brown feathers below and behind the eye.

Behavior: As their name implies, house wrens live around houses, gardens, parks, hedgerows, streamside thickets, and other semi-open habitats. They are energetic little birds; they bounce rapidly from branch to branch while foraging for insects. During the breeding season, males sing a variety of gurgling songs. Nests are built in any handy cavity including such odd places as drainpipes, old boots, and rusty pails. House wrens are aggressive  in defending nest sites. Clutches of five to eight eggs are typical and incubation last roughly 12 days. The young are fledged 18 days later. There may be two broods per year.

Winter Wren (*Troglodytes troglodytes*)

Description: Winter wrens are smaller and darker than house wrens. They are dark brown birds, with a series of dark bars on the belly and flanks. The beak is short and dark. There is a pale eyebrow stripe. The tail is very short and held at a sharp upward angle relative to the body.

Behavior: Winter wrens are found in wet thickets and dense woods. These secretive birds forage near the ground for insects and berries. Nests are well concealed and often on or within a few feet of the ground. Females incubate five to seven speckled eggs over a period of two weeks. After hatching, the young are fed by both parents and leave after roughly 18 days.

KINGLETS (Family Regulidae)

Kinglets (Family Regulidae) are small, inconspicuous birds. Kinglets get their name from their crown of brightly colored feathers.

Golden-crowned Kinglet (*Regulus satrapa*)
and Ruby-crowned Kinglet (*Regulus calendula*)

Description: Both golden-crowned and ruby-crowned kinglets are roughly 4 inches in length. These tiny birds are similar in appearance; both species are pale olive-green or gray-green on the body with white bars on the wings. The golden-crowned kinglet has a black and white striped cheek and a yellow-orange crown bordered by a black stripe. The ruby-crowned kinglet lacks the facial markings and males have a bright red crown that may be difficult to see.

Behavior: Both kinglet species live in dense conifer forests in summer. The golden-crowned kinglet may winter in the Adirondacks, but the ruby-crowned kinglet spends the winter in the southern United States. Both species feed on small insects and insect eggs. Nests are suspended below a forked conifer branch. Females incubate six to nine eggs for two weeks. The young leave the nest after another two weeks. Kinglets often feed in mixed species flocks, along with chickadees and other small birds.

THRUSHES AND THEIR ALLIES (Family Turdidae)

In addition to several species of thrush, the family Turdidae includes the eastern bluebird and the American robin. Thrushes are small- to medium-sized birds that tend to forage for insects and other invertebrates on or near the ground.

Eastern Bluebird (*Sialia sialis*) PLATE 29

Description: Male eastern bluebirds are bright blue on the head, back, and upper wings. The throat and upper chest are a rusty orange color; the lower belly and underside of the wings are white. Females are gray-blue above.

Behavior: Bluebirds prefer open areas such as farmlands, meadows, and fields. They feed on insects and berries. Bluebirds take advantage

of nest boxes placed along the margins of fields or roadsides. They also will nest in natural tree holes. Females lay four to seven eggs, which they incubate for up to 16 days. The young bluebirds leave the nest after 18 days and the parents often raise a second clutch before migrating south in the fall.

Hermit Thrush (*Catharus guttatus*)
Description: The hermit thrush is smaller than a robin. They are dull brown with a reddish tail. The chest is prominently spotted and they have a white eye-ring. They have a habit of flicking their tail.

Behavior: Hermit thrushes arrive in the Adirondacks earlier and leave later than other thrushes. They signal their presence with a series of beautiful songs. Hermit thrushes prefer coniferous or mixed forests, where they forage for a variety of insects, earthworms, and berries. Nests are well-concealed, located on or near the ground, and usually contain four eggs. The eggs hatch after 12 days, and the young are fledged in another two weeks time.

Veery (*Catharus fuscescens*)
Description: Slightly smaller than a robin, the veery is a cinnamon to olive-brown color above, with pale brown spots on the upper chest. The lower belly is white and there is a faint eye-ring.
Behavior: Veerys prefer wet deciduous forest and streamside thickets with a dense understory. They are secretive birds and difficult to see in the dense understory. They forage close to the ground for insects and berries. Leaves, moss, and other plant material are used to build nests

that are placed on or near the ground. Females incubate three to five eggs for 10 to 12 days and often have two clutches per summer. They migrate to tropical forests in winter.

Swainson's Thrush (*Catharus ustulatus*)

Description: Swainson's thrushes are pale olive-brown on the back, head, and tail. The upper chest has dark spots on a faint buff background. There is a buff-colored eye-ring and beige patch on the lower cheek.

Behavior: Swainson's thrushes prefer dense coniferous forests with thick understory vegetation. They are shy birds, remaining hidden in the undergrowth much of the time. They sing a beautiful series of upwardly spiraling notes. They feed on insects, berries, and fruits. They typically build their nests in conifer trees within 10 feet of the ground. They incubate three to four eggs for roughly two weeks; after hatching, the young remain in the nest for another two weeks.

Wood Thrush (*Hylocichla mustelina*)

Description: Wood thrushes are bright cinnamon brown on the head and back. The chest is white and covered with large black spots. The lower cheek has a series of thin, dark stripes.

Behavior: Damp deciduous or mixed forests with dense understory vegetation are preferred habitats for the wood thrush. They are probably the most common thrush in the Adirondacks. They have a beautiful, flute-like song. Like other thrushes, they feed on insects and berries. They build nests in the fork of a tree branch roughly 10 to 20 feet above the ground. Females incubate three to four eggs for 14 days. The young leave the nest after 12 days, and pairs often have two clutches per year.

American Robin (*Turdus migratorius*) PLATE 30

Description: The American robin is 9 to 10 inches in length, gray-black above, and bright orange on the chest and belly. Females are similar but much paler in color, and juveniles have spotted chests.

Behavior: Robins are common in deciduous forests, open farmland, and village yards. They feed on a variety of insects and berries, but appear to prefer earthworms. It was once believed that robins located earthworms by sensing vibrations made by the worms digging close to the surface, but more recent evidence indicates that they locate earthworms by sight. Mud and vegetation are used to build nests in trees or on building ledges. Females incubate three to five blue-green eggs for roughly 13 days. The young robins are fledged in another two weeks,

but stay with the parents for a few more days. American robins often have two or three clutches per year.

MOCKINGBIRDS AND THRASHERS (Family Mimidae)

The family Mimidae includes thrashers, mockingbirds, and catbirds. All are famous for their diverse vocalizations, including the ability to mimic other birds. Northern mockingbirds (not described) prefer farmlands and thickets; they rarely venture far into the Adirondack Mountains.

Gray Catbird (*Dumetella carolinensis*)

Description: Gray catbirds are robin-sized birds with blue-gray plumage. They have a black cap on the head and orange brown under the tail.

Behavior: Gray catbirds prefer dense thickets, such as those found

along streams, hedgerows, and forest edges. They forage for insects on the ground by flipping over leaves with their beaks. They also feed on berries when available. They get their name from the cat-like mewing calls they make. Nests are built within 10 feet of the ground; they are often hidden among dense shrubs. Females incubate three or four eggs for two weeks. The young leave the nest after another 10 days.

Brown Thrasher (*Toxostoma rufum*)

Description: Longer and leaner than American robins, brown thrashers are bright reddish brown above with dark brown streaks on an otherwise cream-colored chest and belly. The tail is long and the bill is relatively long and thin. They have a yellow eye with a dark pupil.

Behavior: Brown thrashers prefer thick vegetation, including hedgerows, thickets, and woodland edges. Their diet consists mainly of insects, nuts, and berries, but they occasionally will eat frogs and crayfish. They build their nests low to the ground in dense foliage. Typically, females lay four eggs and both parents share the incubation for up to 14 days. The young leave the nest as early as nine days after hatching. Brown thrashers often have two, and sometimes three, broods per year.

STARLINGS AND WAXWINGS

Starlings (Family Sturnidae) are noisy, gregarious birds. It is believed that they were brought to North America by a member of an obscure society that attempted to bring to this continent every bird described in the writings of William Shakespeare. Approximately 100 starlings were introduced in New York City. Today there are an estimated 200 million across North America. Cedar waxwings (Family Bombycillidae) are not closely related to starlings. They prefer northern forests, where they feed on insects and berries.

European Starling (Family Sturnidae, *Sturnus vulgaris*)   PLATE 31

Description: Slightly smaller than a robin, European starlings have a stocky body with a short tail. The plumage is iridescent purple on the head and throat and greenish black on the remainder of the body. The bill is yellow during the breeding season.

Behavior: European starlings were introduced to North America in 1890. They tolerate people, cars, and the noise of urban areas. Con-

sequently, they are now one of the most widespread and abundant birds on the continent. These highly sociable birds form large flocks in the non-breeding season. They feed on seeds, berries, and insects. Starlings are cavity nesters and compete with other birds for available sites. Four to six eggs are incubated by both parents of roughly 12 days. The young are ready to leave the nest after 21 days.

Cedar Waxwing (*Bombycilla cedrorum*)   PLATE 32

Description: Cedar waxwings have sleek plumage; they are brown over most of the body, but the wings and tail are gray. They have a prominent

crest on the head and a black mask bordered by white on the face. The tail feathers are tipped with bright yellow. They have waxy red tips on the secondary wing feathers that form a distinct red band when the wing is folded.

Behavior: Flocks of cedar waxwings forage for berries and insects in residential areas, orchards, and fallow fields. They nest in midsummer to ensure an abundant crop of berries for the young. Typically, four to six eggs are incubated for 12 days. Both parents take turns regurgitating berries to feed to the young nestlings. After 18 days, the young are strong enough to leave the nest.

WARBLERS (Family Parulidae)

Warblers are small, slender birds usually less than 5 inches in length. Most are brightly colored in their spring breeding plumage, but as the fall migration approaches, they moult into far less conspicuous colors. Warblers may be difficult to identify because plumage patterns vary with sex, age, and season; many birders rely on their distinct songs to help tell the species apart.

Warblers feed on insects and other small invertebrates. Nest sites vary, but usually are in trees or shrubs. Most species lay three to five eggs and incubate those eggs for ten to fourteen days. Fledging occurs roughly two weeks later.

Roughly 50 warbler species breed in the Unites States or migrate through on their way to breeding grounds in Canada. Thirty-six species occur regularly in New York State, but only the 18 relatively common Adirondack species are described here.

Nashville Warbler (*Vermivora ruficapilla*)

Description: Breeding males have a gray head, olive-green back and wings, yellow breast and belly except for a small patch of white near the legs, and a prominent white eye-ring. Females are more uniformly olive-green with a dull gray head. They arrive in the Adirondacks in early May and leave by the middle of August.

Northern Parula (*Parula americana*)

Description: Males are blue on the head, wings, and upper tail. They have an olive-green patch on the back. The throat and breast are yellow grading to white on the belly. There are two white wing bars, an orange band across the chest, and small white semi-circles above and below the eyes. Females are similar except gray instead of blue. Northern parulas are present in the Adirondacks from early May to late August.

Yellow Warbler (*Dendroica petechia*)   PLATE 33

Description: Both males and females have yellow bodies that appear a light olive-green on the back. The undertail feathers are also yellow. Males have streaks of orange on the breast. They typically arrive in early May and depart by late July.

Chestnut-sided Warbler (*Dendroica pensylvanica*)   PLATE 34
  Description: Males and females are similar; they have chestnut-brown
  patches on either side of the white breast and belly. The crown of the
  head is yellow-green and they have pale yellow wing-bars. The cheek
  is white and the back is streaked with black. Chestnut-sided warblers
  arrive in early May and depart by late August.

Magnolia Warbler (*Dendroica magnolia*)   PLATE 35
  Description: Males have thick black streaks on the otherwise bright yellow chest and belly. The crown and back are gray. They have a large

black face patch with a white stripe above and behind the eye. Females have less black on the chest and both sexes have a single white wing-bar. Magnolia warblers arrive by the second week in May and begin the fall migration southward by late August.

Black-throated Green Warbler (*Dendroica virens*)   PLATE 36
Description: These warblers have a bright yellow face with a small olive patch just behind the eye. The back is olive-green and the throat and

sides of the breast are black. There are two white wing-bars. Females are duller than males. These warblers arrive in the Adirondacks in late April and depart in early August.

Black-throated Blue Warbler (*Dendroica caerulescens*)   PLATE 37
Description: Males and females are distinctly colored. Males are blue above, white on the belly, and have black faces and throats. A black band extends from the face down the flanks. Females are pale olive-green with a thin white eyebrow line and a small white wing-bar. Arrival in the Adirondacks is in early May and departure is at the end of August.

Yellow-rumped Warbler (*Dendroica coronata*)

Description: Also known as myrtle warblers, male yellow-rumped warblers are blue-gray on the back. The breast and flanks are streaked with black. They have bright yellow patches on the crown, chest, and rump. The face is black and the throat is white. Females are gray-brown with black streaks on the chest. Females retain the yellow patches on the flanks and rump. Yellow-rumped warblers arrive in late April and remain until early September.

Blackburnian Warbler (*Dendroica fusca*)   PLATE 38

Description: Breeding males have bright orange head and throat regions; there is a Y-shaped black patch behind the eye and a black stripe on the crown. The back and wings are black and white; there is a large white wing-bar. Females are paler orange or yellow, but otherwise similar to males. Arrival of Blackburnian warblers begins in early May, and they begin their southward migration around the second week in August.

Pine Warbler (*Dendroica pinus*)

Description: Pine warblers are yellowish olive over most of the body with two white wing-bars. Females and immature birds are similar but duller. Pine warblers arrive in mid- to late April and remain until early September.

Blackpoll Warbler (*Dendroica striata*)

Description: Breeding males are largely black and white with a prominent black cap and white cheeks. The legs are yellowish pink. Females and non-breeding males are olive-green or yellowish with faint streaking. They arrive in coniferous forests in late May and depart for South America in late August.

Black-and-White Warbler (*Mniotilta varia*)

Description: Both sexes are streaked with black and white stripes over the entire body. The crown has a white stripe down the midline. The throat is predominantly white in females, but heavily streaked in males. Like nuthatches, they creep along the trunks of trees. Arrival in the spring generally occurs around May 1, and the fall departure begins around August 10.

American Redstart (*Setophaga ruticilla*)   PLATE 39

Description: Breeding males are black with large patches of bright or-

ange on the wings, flanks, and tail. The belly is white. Females are gray on the head and olive green on the back and wings, with yellow patches instead of orange. Redstarts arrive in early May and depart in early August.

Canada Warbler (*Wilsonia canadensis*)

Description: Both sexes are gray above and yellow below. Males have a collar of small black specks on the lower throat and a conspicuous eye-ring. Females have very faint specks on the throat. Both sexes lack wing-bars. Canada warblers arrive in the Adirondacks around the second week in May and begin the fall migration by the second week in August.

Mourning Warbler (*Oporornis philadelphia*)   PLATE 40

Description: Males have a gray head, olive-green back and wings, and a bright yellow belly. A black patch on the chest separates the gray

throat from the yellow belly. Females are duller and lack the black "bib" on the chest. Mourning warblers arrive in late May and depart during the middle of August.

Ovenbird (*Seiurus aurocapillus*)

Description: Ovenbirds look like a small thrush. They are olive-green on the back and wings. The chest and belly are white with dark black

streaks. The crown is orange with black stripes on either side. The legs are pink and there is a white eye-ring. Ovenbirds are most often seen foraging on the ground, from early May until late August.

Northern Waterthrush (*Seiurus noveboracensis*)

Description: Both sexes of the northern waterthrush are olive-brown above and white to pale yellow below. The throat, chest, and belly are streaked with black. There is a thin white or pale yellow line above the eye. These mostly terrestrial warblers arrive in early May and depart for the Caribbean and South America in early August.

Common Yellowthroat (*Geothlypis trichas*)　　　　PLATE 41

Description: Breeding males have a black face mask, bright yellow throat, and a gray band on the forehead. The back, wings, and tail are olive-brown. Females and immature birds lack the face mask. They arrive in early May and depart in mid- to late August.

TANAGERS (Family Thraupidae)

Tanagers (family Thraupidae) are largely tropical or subtropical species. Only the scarlet tanager makes it far enough northward to breed in the Adirondacks.

Scarlet Tanager (*Piranga olivacea*)

Description: Adult male scarlet tanagers are unmistakable; they have scarlet red bodies with black wings and tail feathers. However, during the non-breeding season, females and males have yellow-green body plumage with black wings.

Behavior: Scarlet tanagers prefer mature oak forests or other deciduous forests. They feed mainly on insects, which they capture within the canopy foliage. Scarlet tanagers winter in tropical forests, but spend the summer breeding season in the northern woodlands. They construct their nests high in deciduous trees. Here the female lays between two and five eggs, which she incubates for up to 14 days. The young may leave the nest as early as nine days after hatching, but they remain in the vicinity and are fed by the parents for another two weeks.

SPARROWS, TOWHEES, AND JUNCOS (Family Emberizidae)

The family Emberizidae includes a number of seed-eating birds with short conical beaks. Among them are the American sparrows (which are unrelated to Old World sparrows), towhees, and juncos. Six species of sparrow are common in the Adirondacks. Lincoln's sparrow and the savannah sparrows also breed in the Adirondacks, but are less common.

American Tree Sparrow (*Spizella arborea*)

Description: This sparrow is roughly 6 inches in length. The head and neck are gray. The crown of the head is rusty brown and there is a rufous stripe behind the eye. The beak is distinctly bicolored (dark above and yellow below). The wings are brownish with two white wing bars. There is also an isolated patch of gray on the chest.

Behavior: American tree sparrows are most likely to be observed in the Adirondacks during the winter months. This sparrow breeds in the arctic and summers in the northern United States. Their preferred summer habitats are marshes and brushy areas along roadways. They feed on seeds and berries in winter, and include insects in their summer diets. Nests are placed in grassy clumps on the ground. Four to six eggs are incubated for roughly 12 days.

Chipping Sparrow (*Spizella passerina*)

Description: This small sparrow is distinguished by its pinkish bill, rusty brown crown on the head, prominent white stripe above the eye, and a thin black eye stripe at eye level. The body is gray and there are two white wing bars.

Behavior: Chipping sparrows are common in open areas including gardens, orchards, and parks. They forage close to the ground, searching for insects and small seeds. They prefer to build nests in conifers, but will even nest on the ground. The nest is often lined with animal hairs. Females incubate three to five eggs for up to two weeks. The young leave the nest after 10 to 12 days.

Song Sparrow (*Melospiza melodia*)

Description: The song sparrow is one of the most common sparrows in the northeast. They have coarse dark streaks on an otherwise white chest and belly. The central streaks form a dark breast spot. The sides of the throat are brown and surround a white throat patch just below the bill. The back and wings are brown with coarse streaks. They have a habit of flicking their tail when they fly.

Behavior: Song sparrows are among the most familiar birds because they frequent village parks, gardens, and other semi-open areas with abundant low bushes. They are also easily recognized for their many beautiful songs. Like other sparrows, they feed on insects and seeds and are easily attracted to bird feeders. Well-concealed nests are usually placed near or on the ground. Females incubate three to five eggs for 12 days and the young leave the nest 12 days after hatching. In a good year, a single female may have three clutches.

Swamp Sparrow (*Melospiza georgiana*)

Description: Swamp sparrows are stocky little birds with brown on the back, wings, and tail. They have gray breasts with just a hint of streaking. The crown is rufous brown, there is a black triangle behind the eye, and the lower cheek has a streak of buff surrounding a bright white throat.

Behavior: Swamp sparrows frequent wet, marshy areas with abundant grasses, cattails, and nearby thickets. They feed heavily on insects and also eat seeds from grasses and sedges. Grass and other marsh vegetation is used to build a nest that usually is placed over water. Females lay four to five eggs in the nest, which they incubate for roughly 12 days. Both parents feed the nestlings for another 12 to 13 days.

White-throated Sparrow (*Zonotrichia albicollis*)

Description: The white-throated sparrow is brown on the body and dull gray on the chest and sides of the face. There is a bright white throat patch and black and white stripes on the top of the head. There is also a small patch of yellow between the eye and the bill.

Behavior: These sparrows live in areas with dense cover, including mixed conifer forests and stream or pond-side thickets. They feed on small seeds during the winter, but switch to insects during the summer months. Nests are located on or near the ground and are hidden

among the grasses and shrubs. Females incubate four or five eggs for roughly 12 days and the young remain in the nest for another 9 days after hatching. In the winter, white-throated sparrows roost together in small flocks in the underbrush.

House Sparrow (*Passer domesticus*)

Description: Male house sparrows have a bold black chest patch, black throat, and stout black bill. The crown of the head is gray. The cheeks are white and the back of the head is a chestnut brown. There is a single white bar on the otherwise brown wings. Females are duller and have a yellowish bill.

Behavior: House sparrows were introduced to the United States in 1850s. They are tough, aggressive, and readily associate with human habitation. Consequently, they spread rapidly across North America and are now considered a nuisance in some areas. In rural areas, they feed primarily on seeds, but in urban areas they scavenge crumbs from sidewalks and are also frequent visitors to bird feeders. They nest in enclosed areas such as rain gutters, birdhouses, and tree holes. Both parents take turns incubating three to six eggs for up to 14 days. The young leave the nest after another two weeks. House sparrows may have two or three clutches per year.

Eastern Towhee (*Pipilo erythrophthalmus*)   PLATE 42

Description: Eastern towhees are robin-sized birds with black plumage on the back, black heads and throats, white on the belly, and red on the flanks. The tail feathers are white on the tips. Females are brown above, but otherwise similar to males.

Behavior: Towhees are fond of brushy woodlands and forest thickets. They also favor residential gardens and hedgerows. They forage on the ground for insects, seeds, and berries. Males defend nesting territories by giving a familiar "*to-wheeeee*" song from which they get their name. Nests are located on, or close to, the ground. Females incubate two to four eggs for roughly 13 days. Both parents help to feed the young nestlings for another 12 days. Towhees often have two broods per summer.

Dark-eyed Junco (*Junco hyemalis*)

Description: Dark-eyed juncos have dark gray heads, backs, and wings. The upper breast is gray and the lower breast is white. The region around the eye is black and the bill is pink. The white outer tail feathers are visible during flight.

Behavior: Juncos prefer mixed coniferous forests, but in the winter they often are found in more open areas. They forage close to the ground looking for seeds and fallen berries. They nest on the ground. Females lay three to five eggs in a well-concealed nest and incubate the eggs for roughly 12 days. The young leave the nest after another 13 days. Two clutches per year are common in many areas.

GROSBEAKS AND BUNTINGS

Grosbeaks get their name from their large conical beaks, which they use to crack open seeds. Rose-breasted grosbeaks and indigo buntings are related to cardinals (Family Cardinalidae). Cardinals (not included) are common in areas around the margins of the Adirondack Park, but rarely breed in the interior. Evening grosbeak are actually finches (Family Fringillidae), but are treated here because of their shared common name.

Rose-breasted Grosbeak   PLATE 43
(Family Cardinalidae, *Pheucticus ludovicianus*)

Description: Named for their thick bills, grosbeaks are roughly 8 inches in length and have a wingspan of 12 inches. Male rose-breasted grosbeaks have a black head and back, bright red breast, a white belly, and a pink bill. They have white wing bars and a patch of white on the rump. Females are largely brown with brown streaks on a white breast; the underside of their wings is yellowish.

Behavior: These birds prefer deciduous forest, orchards, pastures, and other areas with abundant shrubs and saplings. They feed on insects, seeds, and berries. Rose-breasted grosbeaks build a flimsy nest in which they lay three to five eggs. Both parents incubate the eggs for 14 days. The young leave the nest after 10 days, but stay in the care of the male for several more days while the female prepares a new nest for a second brood.

Evening Grosbeak (Family Fringillidae, *Coccothraustes vespertinus*)
Description: Evening grosbeaks are stocky finches with large heads and thick, pale yellow bills. Males are dark greenish brown on the head fading to olive-green or yellow on the back and breast. The lower breast is

bright yellow. There is a bright yellow eyebrow patch and large white wing patches. Females are a duller gray.
Behavior: Evening grosbeaks live in conifer forests and mixed conifer-deciduous forests. They forage in flocks, feeding primarily on seeds, and are frequent visitors to winter bird feeders. Females lay three or four eggs in loosely built nests and incubate them for roughly two weeks. Once common winter residents in the Adirondacks, their populations are now in decline.

Indigo Bunting (Family Cardinalidae, *Passerina cyanea*)   PLATE 44

Description: Indigo buntings are sparrow-sized birds. Males are bright indigo blue to turquoise in color. The wings and tail are almost black. Females are pale brown.

Behavior: These beautiful birds prefer brushy areas such as roadsides, abandoned pastures, and power-line right-of-ways. They feed on insects and seeds. Nests are usually within a few feet of the ground and constructed of woven grasses. Females incubate two to four eggs for up to 14 days. Indigo buntings typically have two broods per year.

BLACKBIRDS AND ORIOLES (Family Icteridae)

Adirondack members of the family Icteridae include blackbirds, grackles, and orioles. Bobolinks (not described) are present around the periphery of the Adirondack Park, but rarely breed in the interior.

Red-winged Blackbird (*Agelaius phoeniceus*)   PLATE 45

Description: Male red-winged blackbirds have black bodies with conspicuous red over yellow or solid red wing bars. Females are streaked with brown and white.

Behavior: Red-winged blackbirds inhabit wet areas, marshes, swamps, and moist meadows. They feed on seeds and insects; in the non-breeding season, vast flocks can be seen foraging together over fields. Nests are woven among the cattails and other marsh grasses. Females incubate three to five eggs for roughly 12 days. The nestlings leave the nest after two weeks and the female begins construction of a new nest for a second brood.

Rusty Blackbird (*Euphagus carolinus*)

Description: Adult males are an iridescent bluish green grading to purple on the head. Females are dark brown. Both sexes have pale yellow eyes.

Behavior: Rusty blackbirds prefer wooded swamps and coniferous bogs. Their diet consists of insects and seeds. They sometimes wade into shallow pools to capture aquatic insects. Nests are hidden in dense vegetation close to the ground or over water. There are usually four to six eggs per brood; the incubation period lasts 14 days.

Common Grackle (*Quiscalus quiscula*)

Description: Grackles are roughly the size of a blue jay. They have bright yellow eyes and an iridescent bronze body with a dark purple to dark blue head and shoulders. Grackles have long tail feathers that may be oriented perpendicular to the ground during flight.

Behavior: Common grackles favor open farmland, parks, lawns, and semi-open woodlands. They feed on a wide range of insects, earthworms, and other invertebrates as well as acorns, seeds, berries, and grains. Grackles are social birds; they tend to forage in small flocks and nest is colonies of roughly 20 pairs. Nests are hidden in dense foliage or in tree cavities. Females lay four to six eggs and incubate them for roughly two weeks. The nestlings are able to leave the nest after 20 days.

Baltimore Oriole (*Icterus galbula*)   PLATE 46

Description: The male Baltimore oriole is an unmistakable orange and black bird. Males are black on the head, back, and wings with bright orange on the breast, rump, and tail. They also have a single orange bar on the wings. Females are similar to males except they are olive-brown on the head and back.

Behavior: Deciduous forests and open woodlands with large shade trees are the preferred habitat of the Baltimore oriole. In the summer, they feed on caterpillars and other insects as well as berries, small fruits, and occasionally nectar. The nest is woven from plant fibers and hangs

below the branch. Females incubate three to six eggs for 14 days. The young are fledged after another two weeks or so.

FINCHES (Family Fringillidae)

Finches (Family Fringillidae) are small to medium sized seed eating birds with stout beaks. The Adirondacks are home to breeding populations of purple finch, pine siskin, and American goldfinch. House finches (not described) typically breed at the lower elevations surrounding the park. Evening grosbeaks are also technically finches, but are included with grosbeaks above.

Purple Finch (*Carpodacus purpureus*)

Description: Male purple finches are raspberry red on the head, back, and upper breast. They are off-white on the lower flanks, vent, and under the tail. The wings are a dull reddish brown. Females are brown above and white with brown streaks on the breast.

Behavior: Purple finches inhabit conifer and mixed conifer forests and may visit suburban bird feeders in winter. They eat seeds, buds, and berries in winter and add caterpillars and other insects to their diet in summer. Nests are located high in trees, usually on the outer branches. Females tend three to five eggs for up to 13 days. After hatching, both parents feed the nestlings until they are ready to leave the nest.

Pine Siskin (*Carduelis pinus*)   PLATE 47

Description: Pine siskins look like a sparrow but are closely related to the American goldfinch. Pine siskins are streaked with brown. Males

have patches of yellow on the wings and a slightly forked tail. The bill is small and pointed.

Behavior: Siskins prefer conifer forests or mixed forests with dense understory shrubs. They forage in small flocks and specialize on the seeds of spruce, alder, and other trees and shrubs. When available, they will also eat buds, nectar, and insects. In the winter, they often flock to roadsides to eat salt. Females lay three to five eggs in a shallow nest made of twigs, grasses and moss, usually in a conifer tree. The eggs hatch after a 13-day incubation period, and the young leave the nest after another 15 days.

American Goldfinch (*Carduelis tristis*) PLATE 48

Description: American goldfinches are small birds with distinctive yellow plumage. Breeding males have bright yellow bodies with black foreheads and black wings. The upper rump is white and the tail feathers are black. Non-breeding males and females are a drab tan over most of the body with smaller patches of yellow on the head and wings.

Behavior: American goldfinches feed primarily on seeds from thistles, grasses, and small trees. Therefore, they frequent roadsides, abandoned pastures, and open woodlands. Nesting begins in mid-summer when seed supplies become abundant. Females build dense, compact

nests using a variety of plant materials. Here they incubate up to six eggs for roughly 14 days. The male brings food to the female while she remains on the nest and both parents feed the nestlings after hatching. Fledging occurs after 17 days in the nest. Only a single brood is possible in most areas.

SOURCES AND ADDITIONAL READING

DeGraaf, R. M., and M. Yamasaki. 2000. *New England Wildlife: Habitat, Natural History, and Distribution*. Hanover, NH: University Press of New England.

Kaufman, K. 1996. *Lives of North American Birds*. Boston: Houghton Mifflin.

Sibley, D. A. 2000. *National Audubon Society: The Sibley Guide to Birds*. New York: Alfred A. Knopf.

———. 2001. *Sibley Guide to Bird Life and Behaviour*. London: Christopher Helm Publishers.

8 Mammals

From the tiny pygmy shrew to the massive blue whale, all mammals, including humans, share three characteristics that are unique among animals: hair as a body covering, the production of milk for the young, and three middle-ear bones for transmitting sounds.

All mammals have hair at some phase of their lives. Hair acts as insulation to slow the loss of body heat to the environment. Hair patterns and colors serve to warn predators, camouflage prey, or communicate status to members of the same species. As the quills of the porcupine aptly demonstrate, hairs sometimes are modified to provide a measure of protection. Finally, specialized facial hairs called whiskers or "vibrissae" provide additional information about touch on dark nights or in underground burrows.

Modified sweat glands, called mammary glands, produce milk rich in protein and fats for the developing young. Indeed, the lengthy period of lactation and suckling is in large part responsible for the close social bonds that often develop among mammals. Other important characteristics, including specialized teeth, a highly developed brain, and the ability to maintain a relatively constant body temperature, further separate mammals from their reptilian and avian ancestors. Mammals are incredibly successful, inhabiting every continent and all the world's seas. Of the approximately 4,600 living mammalian species, only 54 species are found within the Adirondack Park. The species accounts that follow should allow you to identify the common mammals of the park.

MARSUPIALS

The Virginia opossum (Family Didelphidae) is the only marsupial in New York State. Marsupials have a specialized reproductive strategy in which the young are born at a very early stage of development, and must crawl over the mother's fur and into the marsupium, (a specialized pouch on the abdomen). Here they attach firmly to a nipple and continue their development in the pouch. This strategy results in short gestation periods and long lactation times. By contrast, placental mammals (including all of the remaining species in New York State) evolved a strategy that includes a relatively long gestation period (supported by the placenta), resulting in more fully developed newborns.

Virginia Opossum (*Didelphis virginiana*)
Description: Adult opossums are distinguished by their coarse, gray fur and naked tails. The tail is scaly and prehensile (capable of grasping). The thin, black ears are also naked and often tattered. Both the ears and tip of the tail often show signs of frostbite. The head is conical and the eyes are small. Females have a fur-lined, abdominal pouch (marsupium) for carrying newborns. Adults average about 30 inches (74 cm) in total length and weigh 2 to 13 pounds (1 to 6 kilograms).
Behavior: The opossum has been expanding its range steadily northward in the last century. It is common in the southern Adirondacks and around the periphery but is rare in the interior of the park. Opossums prefer wooded habitats near water and woodlots bordering farmland. Almost entirely nocturnal, opossums eat a wide variety of foods, including insects, fruits, vegetables, bird eggs, and the flesh of dead animals. They have a slow, ambling gait and seek safety in trees, where they are good climbers. If safety cannot be reached in time, they "play possum" by entering a brief state of catatonia (a period of stupor). They also freeze under bright lights, a response that undoubtedly leads to high roadside mortality. The opossum is North America's only living marsupial. Opossums breed from January through May. The young are born after only 12 days of gestation, and the dime-sized young must crawl across the mother's fur and into the safety of the pouch and attach to one of thirteen nipples. After about 70 days, the young opossums leave the pouch, yet continue to travel with the mother by clinging to her fur. Opossums are prolific breeders, with up to thirteen young at a time and sometimes two litters per year.

Table 8.1 Comparative body size information on six species of Adirondack shrews

Common name	Total length (mm)	Tail length (mm)	Weight (g)
Masked shrew (*Sorex cinereus*)	80–110	30–50	3–6
Water shrew (*Sorex palustris*)	130–170	60–90	8–18
Smoky shrew (*Sorex fumeus*)	110–127	38–50	6–11
Long-tailed shrew (*Sorex dispar*)	103–135	45–67	3–8
Pygmy shrew (*Sorex hoyi*)	62–107	20–40	2–6
Short-tailed shrew (*Blarina brevicauda*)	95–140	17–30	18–30

Source: *Kays and Wilson 2002; Saunders 1989; Wilson and Ruff 1999.*

SHREWS (Family Soricidae)

Shrews are active day and night, yet are seldom seen except when dropped at the doorstep by the family cat. In some areas, shrews may even be the most abundant small mammals. In spite of their superficial resemblance to mice, shrews are more closely related to moles. Shrews are small, with long, pointed snouts and small eyes and ears.

Six shrew species breed in the Adirondack Park, but only the masked shrew, water shrew, and short-tailed shrew are common. Positive identification of shrews in the field is difficult even for experts because our glimpses of shrews and moles are fleeting at best. Table 8.1 provides body size ranges for all six species, but only the masked shrew, water shrew, and the short-tailed shrew are described in detail.

Masked Shrew (*Sorex cinereus*)

Description: Masked shrews resemble a tiny, thin mouse with a long nose and tiny eyes. The fur is a velvety brown on the back and grayish on the sides and belly. The tail is sparsely furred and has a dark tip. The head is long and tapered, and the ears are nearly hidden in the fur. Limbs are short and delicate.

Behavior: Masked shrews are common in coniferous and northern deciduous forests. In addition to forests, they inhabit marshes, bogs, fields, and clear-cuts. Like other shrews, they are confined to the forest floor, where they follow runways through the leaf litter, using logs

and other large debris for cover. Because of their small body size and high metabolic rates (over 800 heartbeats per minute), shrews spend most of their days and nights foraging for food. They feed on insects and invertebrates of all types. They are also known to eat the flesh of dead animals and plant material including fungi. They are active all winter long under an insulating blanket of snow. They probably begin breeding in April and continue throughout the summer months. Litter size varies from four to ten. Young are born naked and blind. They are weaned after approximately 20 days.

Water Shrew (*Sorex palustris*)

Description: Water shrews are adapted for a semi-aquatic life. They are large, with long tails and large hind feet. The fur is dark gray to black above and the belly is a silvery gray. The broad hind feet have a fringe of stiff hairs along the toes and are slightly webbed to provide greater thrust when swimming.

Behavior: These shrews are found throughout the central and eastern Adirondacks along rivers and streams, at the edge of marshes or bogs, and along the shores of ponds and lakes. They are excellent swimmers and forage under water for aquatic invertebrates. They also take fish eggs and the occasional tadpole. Their fur traps a layer of air next to the skin, making them exceptionally buoyant; without the constant paddling of the large hind feet, they pop to the surface like a cork. They remain submerged for only 15 to 20 seconds while their sensitive whiskers detect prey. Water shrews begin breeding as early as February and continue through August. They have two or three litters per year, averaging about 6 young per litter.

Short-tailed Shrew (*Blarina brevicauda*)

Description: Short-tailed shrews are easy to tell apart from other shrews because of their blunt snout, large size, short tail, and nearly naked feet. The eyes and concealed ears are tiny. The fur is dark gray to black. As the name implies, these shrews have tails less than 25 percent of their total length.

Behavior: Virtually all habitats, from boreal forests to grassy fields, are home to short-tailed shrews. They prefer areas with adequate soil moisture to allow the construction of elaborate burrow systems near the surface. Short-tailed shrews have poor eyesight and instead rely on a rudimentary type of echolocation to locate burrow openings and prey. They feed principally on invertebrates, especially earthworms, but are also known to cache seeds and tiny subterranean fungi, and to kill small mice on occasion. They are unique among Adirondack mammals in producing a neurotoxin in their salivary glands. The toxin is used to paralyze prey so that it can be stored in the burrow for later consumption. The toxin is not dangerous to humans, but a bite may swell and be painful for several days. The strong odor from scent glands may be one reason that few predators will eat short-tailed shrews. Like all shrews, they are active year-round. Females have four to eight young per litter and have up to three litters per year. Breeding begins in early spring and continues through the fall. The young are born the size of a bee and completely naked. They develop rapidly and are weaned after only a month. Two months after birth, females are ready to breed.

MOLES (Family Talpidae)

Moles are small, insectivorous mammals with thick bodies, tiny eyes, short fur, and powerfully built forelimbs. Their hands are spade-like, oriented laterally, and tipped with long claws. Moles are subterranean, spending most of their time burrowing through soft soils in search of earthworms, grubs, and other invertebrates.

Hairy-tailed Mole (*Parascalops breweri*)

Description: The only eastern moles with a hairy tail, these large, burrowing animals have soft velvety fur and a cylindrical body. The fur is typically black. They lack external ears and have highly reduced eyes and a long tapering snout. Total length is roughly 6 inches (150 to 157 mm), of which 1 inch is the coarsely furred tail. Males weigh more than females; weights of 2 ounces (40 to 60 grams) are common.

Behavior: Hairy-tailed moles prefer light, well-drained soils. They construct elaborate tunnel systems with one or more nest chambers up to 8 inches (20 cm) in diameter. They use their powerful, shovel-like front feet to dig through the soil looking for earthworms, insect larvae, ants, and other arthropods. The familiar ridges and mounds are created when the moles are foraging near the surface. In the winter, they remain active in tunnels below the frostline. Breeding begins in March or April, and after a gestation period of about six weeks, a litter of four or five young is born. Blind, naked, and helpless at birth, they grow rapidly, and after only a month they are nearly adult size and ready to care for themselves.

Star-nosed Mole (*Condylura cristata*)

Description: There is no mistaking the star-nosed mole. It has 22 fleshy nasal tentacles on the tip of its snout. The fur is black and the tail is long and scaly. Large forelegs are spade-like and adapted for digging. Star-nosed moles are 6 to 8 inches in total length (152 to 211 mm), have tails of 2 to 3 inches (53 to 84 mm), and weigh between 1½ and 3 ounces (30 to 75 grams).

Behavior: Star-nosed moles usually are found in wet meadows, damp woodlands, and swampy areas where the water table is close to the surface. They are good swimmers; their tunnels often exit into streams, lakes, and ponds. Drier sections of tunnels, often lined with grasses, serve as nesting chambers. These moles use their powerful forelegs to tunnel through moist soil looking for invertebrates. The conspicuous fleshly tentacles on the nose have up to 25,000 touch receptors (more than the human hand) and are used to locate prey. Females usually have a single litter per year consisting of four to seven young born in an underground nest. Litters are born in April or May and occasionally as late as August after a 45-day gestation period. The young develop rapidly, and by three weeks old leave the nest.

BATS (Order Chiroptera)

Bats are often the subject of fear, misunderstanding, and superstition. We tend to associate bats with evil, witchcraft, vampires, and the underworld. The unique behaviors of bats no doubt have contributed to our fears and to their persecution. They roam the night, often roost in caves, and one Central American species, the vampire bat, feeds on blood. Bats are also widely believed to transmit a host of diseases and parasites to humans. In reality, bats carry few parasites and only two diseases that are transmitted to humans: rabies and histoplasmosis. Of the hundreds of cases of animal rabies reported to the New York State Department of Health each year, only a few dozen cases are found in bats. We have as much to fear from rabid raccoons, foxes, and dogs. Far from being harmful, most bats are beneficial to humans. The bats that frequent the Adirondacks consume hundreds of insects per hour. Large colonies can reduce the local insect populations by millions each season. Perhaps the Chinese were right to consider bats an omen of good fortune.

The Adirondacks are home to nine bat species. Four species of mouse-eared bats (*Myotis*) spend at least part of the year in the Adirondacks. All are very similar in appearance, but only the little brown bat is common in the Park (see Table 8.2).

Little Brown Bat (*Myotis lucifugus*)

Description: As their name implies, these are small bats with glossy brown or olive-brown fur. Total wingspan is only about 8 inches (20 cm).

Behavior: Little brown bats inhabit buildings, caves, hollow trees, and cracks in concrete bridges. All four *Myotis* species hibernate in caves and abandoned mines, where temperatures remain relatively constant throughout the winter months. The little brown bat is well known for its seasonal migrations from summer maternity colonies to winter hibernation caves. Maternity colonies

Table 8.2   Body size dimensions of the four Adirondack species of mouse-eared bats

Species	Weight (g)	Total length (mm)	Forearm length (mm)	Tail length (mm)
Little brown bat (*Myotis lucifugus*)	5–13	60–98	35–40	31–40
Northern long-eared bat (*Myotis leibii*)	3–7	72–82	30–35	30–35
Indiana bat (*Myotis sodalis*)	4–11	70–96	32–40	27–42
Eastern small-footed bat (*Myotis septentrionalis*)	4–11	80–89	35–39	36–43

Source: Kays and Wilson 2002; Saunders 1989; Wilson and Ruff 1999.

often are located in barns and attics, which tend to be warmer sites that are ideal for raising young. All four Adirondack *Myotis* species emerge from roosts at dusk to forage for small insects. Foraging often occurs near or over water or near outdoor lights where insects such as mosquitoes and midges are abundant. They are voracious feeders, often eating half of their body weight in food each night. They can see, but use echolocation — high-frequency sounds well above the human range of hearing — to find insects. In the summer, females and their young are found in maternity colonies, while males roost separately. In the late summer, males and females congregate to mate.

Females mate with more than one male and store their sperm in the uterus during the long winter hibernation. In the early spring, as the bats leave the hibernation site, the females ovulate and fertilization takes place. Additional mating may take place in the spring. In June or July, a single young is born. Young remain at the maternity colony while the mother forages each night. Three weeks or so after birth, the young bat is ready to join the adults on nightly foraging trips.

Eastern Pipistrelle   (*Pipistrellus subflavus*)

Description: The fur is lighter than most *Myotis* species; it is yellowish brown to reddish brown above with a slightly lighter shade underneath. The upper surface of the tail membrane is lightly furred. Pipistrelle adults weigh between ⅛ and ⅓ of an ounce (4 to 10 grams). Overall length is between 3 and 3½ inches (75 to 90 mm), with a tail length of about 1½ inches (33 to 45 mm). The average wingspan is 9 inches (245 mm).

Behavior: During the winter months, both sexes roost in small clusters in caves or mines. In spring, they arouse from hibernation and migrate to their summer colonies in hollow trees, attics, and barns; females form maternity colonies and males roost separately. Pipistrelles emerge at twilight to race over fields and ponds searching for small insects. Summer months are spent putting on enough fat to sustain themselves during the long winter hibernation. Hibernating pipistrelles may lose 30 percent or more of their weight over the winter. Despite these physiological stresses, pipistrelles are known to live up to 15 years in the wild. Pipistrelles mate in the fall, and females store sperm in their uterus until spring, when fertilization occurs. Females give birth to two offspring, which together weigh up to a third of the mother's weight. Young pipistrelles begin foraging flights with their mothers after only three weeks.

Big Brown Bat (*Eptesicus fuscus*)

Description: The big brown bat is easily distinguished from other Adirondack bats by a combination of its large size and overall brown color. There is no fur on the wing or tail membranes. Females are slightly larger than males; body weights range from less than ½ ounce to nearly ⁹⁄₁₀ of an ounce (12 to 25 grams). They are 4 to 5½ inches (105 to 135 mm) in total length, with a 1½- to 2-inch (38 to 52 mm) tail length, and an average forearm length of 2 inches (47 mm). Their wingspan reaches 13 inches (330 mm).

Behavior: Small colonies occur mainly in buildings and hollow trees during the summer. As winter approaches, big brown bats migrate short distances to their winter roosts in caves, mines, and increasingly in walls or attics. Females and males may inhabit the same building but usually do not roost together. Big brown bats feed on moths, beetles, and a variety of flies. During the summer months, a female may eat the equivalent of her own body weight in insects each night. Big brown bats are known to live up to 20 years. Mating normally takes  place in the fall, but additional mating sometimes occurs in the hibernation roosts well into spring. Sperm from the males is stored in the female's uterus until early spring, when fertilization occurs. Females congregate at the same maternity colonies each year starting in March. Two young are born in June.

Silver-haired Bat (*Lasionycteris noctivagans*)

Description: The fur is blackish brown with a frosting of silver at the tips. The upper surface of the tail membrane is furred near the body. The short, rounded ears have a short projection (a tragus) that is curved forward. Adults are large: between 3 and 4½ inches (84 to 115 mm) in total length and 1 to 2 inches (27 to 47 mm) in tail length, with an average forearm length of 1½ inches (42 mm), and a weight of between 0.3 and 0.5 ounces (8 to 15 grams).

Behavior: Summers are spent in New York and New England, but silver-haired bats migrate to southern states in winter. They roost in tree holes (often old woodpecker holes) or under loose bark and prefer forested or semi-wooded areas. They tend to be solitary, yet they will form very small colonies. They emerge to feed just before dusk and spend most of their time hunting in the vegetation along streams or lakes. They eat all sorts of flying insects, including moths and midges. Mating takes place during the fall migration; females store sperm until they ovulate in the spring. In April or May, females migrate north to their summer roosts. After their arrival at their summer roosts females give birth to twins in late June or early July.

Red Bat (*Lasiurus borealis*)

Description: Red bats are one of North America's most beautiful small mammals. They have reddish fur that even covers the upper surface of the tail membrane. Female red bats are more of a chestnut color, frosted with white. On the front of the shoulder, there is a white patch (epaulet). The ears are short and broad. Red bats weigh between ¼ and ½ ounce (7 to 16 grams), have a total length between 4 and 5 inches (96 to 126 mm), a tail length of about 2 inches (49 mm), and forearms roughly 1½ inches (37 to 42 mm) long. The wings are narrow and pointed with a span of nearly 13 inches (330 mm).

Behavior: Red bats are common during the summer, but migrate in the fall to spend the winter in southern states. They are largely solitary and roost almost exclusively in trees. The short ears and densely furred tail membrane, which forms a blanket around roosting animals, help to reduce heat loss. Moths and beetles are the main prey, but red bats will eat a wide variety of insects, often foraging around streetlights in rural and urban areas. Red bats mate in the fall, and copulation occurs in flight. Sperm is stored in the female's uterus until the spring. Up to four young are born in June, each young weighing only half a gram. When the mother returns from foraging, the young nurse and rapidly gain weight. About six weeks after birth, they are able to fly.

Hoary Bat (*Lasiurus cinereus*)

Description: The hoary bat gets its name from the frosting of silver on its dark brown underfur. The tail membrane is furred and provides needed insulation when wrapped around the roosting bat. The fur over the throat and face is yellowish in color, and there are white shoulder patches. The short, rounded ears have prominent black rims. Females are larger than males. Adults are between 4 and 6 inches (102 to 152 mm) in total length, have tails between 2 and 2½ inches (49 to 65 mm) in length, forearms of about 1½ to 2 inches (42 to 59 mm), and weigh between 0.6 and 1.3 ounces (18 to 38 grams).

Behavior: Females and males are seldom found together, except during the fall migrations when mating occurs. Females spend their summers in boreal regions, while males apparently spend summers in the western and southwestern United States. Hoary bats roost in foliage and prefer wooded areas near streams and ponds. The hoary bat feeds largely on moths and beetles. Mating occurs during the fall migration, and fertilization is delayed until the spring. One to four young are born in May or June. Young cling to the mother to nurse during the day but remain at the roost during her nightly foraging trips. They take their first flights about a month after birth and are weaned shortly afterwards.

RABBITS AND HARES (Family Leporidae)

Adirondack members of the family Leporidae include the eastern cottontail rabbit and the snowshoe hare. Rabbits and hares have two pairs of upper incisors, unlike the single pair found in rodents. Both rabbits and hares have long hind feet, which provide the quick acceleration and powerful leaps needed to escape predators. They also have excellent hearing as evidenced by their long ears. Snowshoe hares molt into their white winter pelage in late fall, while cottontails remain brown throughout the year.

Eastern Cottontail (*Sylvilagus floridanus*)

Description: The eastern cottontail has long ears and large hindlegs. The tail is very short (1 to 2 inches) and covered with long, fluffy fur; brown above and white underneath. The body fur is brown or grayish brown above, becoming gray or grayish white on the belly. There is often a reddish brown patch on the back of the neck and a light patch on the forehead. Eastern cottontails are much smaller than snowshoe hares and do not change to a white pelage in winter. In New York, cottontails average 16 inches (414 mm) in total length and 4 inches (101 mm) in hind foot length. They have ears roughly 3 inches (60 to 75 mm) in length, and weigh about 3 pounds (1.2 kilograms).

Behavior: Eastern cottontails prefer brushy areas, old fields, swamps, cultivated areas, and sometimes residential neighborhoods. They generally are restricted to open areas at lower elevations around the borders of the Adirondack Park. Cottontails are primarily nocturnal. Several cottontails may share a common 4- to 5-acre home range. When foraging, they usually move about using a series of short hops, but they can leap 10 to 15 feet when pursued. Cottontails feed mainly on herbaceous plants in summer and woody varieties in winter. Eastern cottontails feed rapidly, then retreat to the safety of a brush pile or other shelter and defecate soft green pellets. They eat these pellets as they are produced in order to extract the important vitamins and undigested plant material that remain. After the second trip through the digestive system, cottontails deposit a firm, brown pellet. The unusual practice of re-ingesting fecal pellets is called coprophagy. Cottontails

are prolific breeders. During the spring breeding season, males perform courtship displays before the females, in which they face off, box
with the forefeet, and make short dashes at the females. The dominant male in the area usually mates with most of the females. Three to
five young are born naked, blind, and nearly helpless in April to June.
Within hours after giving birth, the female mates again. The result is
that females can have between three and seven litters and up to 35
young per year.

Snowshoe Hare (*Lepus americanus*)

Description: In summer, the snowshoe hare, sometimes called the vary-
ing hare, is rusty brown with a grayish throat and belly. The winter
pelage is almost pure white, except for the black-tipped, moderately
long ears. In fall and spring, when the fur molts over a period of two
months, snowshoe hares are mottled brown and white. They have large
hind feet with densely furred soles that act like snowshoes. Snowshoe
hares are the only rabbits found in much of the central Adirondack
Park. Females are larger than males; both sexes weigh between 2 and 5
pounds (0.9 to 2.2 kilograms). The total length is 15 to 20 inches (382 to
520 mm), with large hind feet measuring 4 to 6 inches (100 to 150 mm).
The ears are about 3 inches (66 to 79 mm) in length.

Behavior: Snowshoe hares are never found far from dense conifer forests, swamps, and brushy areas of second growth. They rest by day
under the branches of a conifer tree or beside a log. If disturbed, they
may run at speeds of up to 30 mph (50 km/h), with bounds of 10 feet
or more. In summer, they feed on grasses, green vegetation, willow,

and berries; in winter, snowshoes resort to twigs and buds of a variety of conifer species. Like all rabbits, snowshoe hares ingest their fecal pellets to extract valuable vitamins and proteins. As days grow shorter in autumn, the hare begins to grow a white winter coat that provides excellent camouflage against the snow. In spring, as the days lengthen, the winter coat is gradually shed and replaced with brown. Mating begins in March or April after brief bouts of chasing and jumping. Females produce litters of one to six young. Young are precocious and can run within hours of birth. Several litters may be produced per year.

SMALL RODENTS

Approximately 2,003 species of rodents have been identified worldwide, ranging in size from 5 grams to over 50 kilograms. All rodents share a pair of long, beveled incisors in the upper and lower jaws. The chisel-like incisors are ever-growing and because only the front surface of the tooth is coated with hard enamel, they are also self-sharpening. The evolution of gnawing was probably the most important adaptation leading to the great diversity of rodents we see today.

To simplify identification, the rodent species are ordered by size and type of rodent, beginning with a section on smaller mice and voles, then one of squirrels, and followed by the larger rodents. Many rodents are difficult to identify because they are mainly nocturnal and small, and they retreat quickly to cover when disturbed. It may not be possible to identify the animal to species, but in most cases one can determine if a small rodent is a mouse, a vole, or a lemming. In general, mice have larger ears and longer tails, whereas voles and lemmings tend to have tiny ears, short tails, and small, dark brown eyes. Slight differences in tooth structure and genetic structure serve to differentiate voles from lemmings.

Deer Mouse (Family Cricetidae, *Peromyscus maniculatus*) and **White-footed Mouse** (*Peromyscus leucopus*)
Description: Deer mice closely resemble white-footed mice. Deer mice have a tail equal to or longer than the head and body length. The tail is darkly furred above and white underneath with a tip of short, stiff hairs. The white-footed mouse has a tail less than half of the total length of the animal and the tail is not bicolored and lacks the stiff hairs at the tip. The fur of the deer mouse is soft and brownish with a faint dorsal stripe down the middle of the back, while the body fur of the white-footed mouse is more orange-brown and its fur is not as soft. Both

White-footed mouse

mice have large, dark eyes and white feet. Juveniles have gray pelage, and a seasonal moult occurs in fall and spring. Adirondack deer mice and white-footed mice have a total length of between 6 and 8½ inches (150 to 220 mm), a tail length of 2½ to 4⅓ inches (65 to 110 mm), and a weight of between 0.6 and 1.0 ounces (16 to 30 grams). White-footed mice tend to be slightly smaller and have shorter tails than deer mice.

Behavior: Deer mice inhabit all forest types in the Adirondacks, especially mixed deciduous forests. They often take shelter in houses or outbuildings as temperatures drop in autumn. White-footed mice are abundant along the edges of the Adirondack Park in brushy areas or in drier woodlands. In the interior of the park, they co-occur with the deer mouse but are usually less abundant. Deer mice are nocturnal, spending the day in nests under logs or in tree holes. In the winter, several individuals will share a communal nest for added warmth. When active, they scamper about collecting seeds, berries, fungi, and insects. Deer mice do not hibernate, and therefore must cache a large supply of food to supplement what they can find during the winter months. Unlike deer mice, white-footed mice undergo energy-saving torpor, a condition similar to hibernation where the body temperature drops to half of normal and the rate of breathing slows drastically. Both species of mice breed from early spring into the fall. Females give birth to a litter of up to eight pups, but four to six pups is the norm. The young are born blind, naked, and helpless, but grow rapidly on a supply of rich milk and are weaned within three weeks of birth. After only seven weeks, they are capable of breeding. Deer mice and white-footed mice can have several litters per year.

Meadow Jumping Mouse (Family Dipodidae, *Zapus hudsonius*) and **Woodland Jumping Mouse** (*Napaeozapus insignis*)

Description: Jumping mice are easily distinguished from other Adirondack mice by their large hind feet and long, sparsely haired tail. The pelage of the meadow jumping mouse is a coarse brown on the back, yellowish on the sides, and white on the belly. The woodland jumping mouse is more colorful; it has coarse brown to black fur on its back, reddish orange fur on the sides, and white fur on the belly. The tail is long in both mice, but only the meadow jumping mouse has a white tip on the tail. Both jumping mice have large hind feet. Woodland jumping mice are slightly larger than meadow jumping mice. Adult woodland jumping mice are between 8 and 10 inches (210 to 250 mm) in total length with a tail length of about 5½ inches (140 mm). Meadow jumping mice average about 8 inches (210 mm) in total length, and 4½ inches (120 mm) in tail length. Adult woodland jumping mice weigh 0.5 to 1.0 ounces (15 to 30 grams), while meadow jumping mice weigh slightly less.

Behavior: Meadow jumping mice are common in fields, marshes, brushy areas along streams, and woods with thick understory vegetation. Woodland jumping mice are restricted to cool, moist woodlands with dense vegetation, such as spruce-fir and hemlock-hardwood forests or woodland bogs and swamps and along streams. When startled from a hiding place, they may jump 2 to 3 feet, but generally try to remain motionless in an effort to elude predators. In September or October, in preparation for hibernation, both species build nests of shredded grass in a protected place. Their body temperature plummets to within a few degrees of freezing, and the heart beats only a few times per minute during the hibernation. When they emerge from hibernation in May, they eat caterpillars, beetles, and other insects, along with fungi, berries, the seeds of grasses, and many other green plants. The breeding season lasts from May to September, with a peak in June and August. Although females have one or two litters per year, a single litter is more common in the northern areas. Litters range in size from two to seven young. The young, born naked and blind, are weaned after one month.

Southern Red-backed Vole (Family Cricetidae, *Myodes gapperi*)

Description: The red-backed vole is easily distinguished from other Adirondack voles by its beautiful coloration; it has a broad, reddish band from its head to its tail. The face and the sides of the body are gray or yellowish gray in color, and the belly is white or cream colored. The tail is short and bicolored; it is brown above and whitish underneath. Red-backed voles are small, averaging 5½ inches (140 mm) in total length and weighing between 1 and 2 ounces (20 to 30 grams). Their short tails are only 1 to 2 inches (30 to 50 mm) long.

Behavior: These hearty voles live in a wide variety of habitats, from above treeline to mossy bogs. They are most common in moist coniferous-deciduous forests where shelter, in the form of logs, stumps, and rocks, is abundant. They are nocturnal, with reduced activity at dawn and dusk. In the warmer months, they scamper across the leaf litter, sticking close to the cover of fallen logs. They feed on seeds, berries, nuts, roots, and fungi. These voles are known to store large quantities of plant material underground to be used as a winter pantry. Red-backed voles do not hibernate in the winter but remain active under the snowpack. They begin breeding in March and continue through November. After an 18-day gestation period, two to eight young are born. Females can have two or three litters per year.

Meadow Vole (Family Cricetidae, *Microtus pennsylvanicus*), **Rock Vole** (*Microtus chrotorrhinus*), and **Woodland Vole** (*Microtus pinetorum*)

Description: The pelage of meadow voles is usually brown with a slight tinge of yellowish or reddish brown above. They are usually gray on the belly. The winter pelage is darker gray. Rock voles are rare in the Adirondack Park. They are grayish brown on the back and dull to silvery gray on the belly, but they have a characteristic orange or yellowish face and nose. The tail is sparsely haired and of average length for a vole. The woodland vole has short, silky fur that is a reddish brown above and grayish below. The eyes are small and the ears are often hidden in the fur. Meadow voles have relatively long tails for voles at 1⅓ to 2⅓ inches (33 to 60 mm). Adults are between 5½ and 7½ inches (140 to 195 mm) in total length and weigh 0.7 to 2.5 ounces (20 to 70 grams). Rock voles are 5½ to 7¼ inches (140 to 185 mm) in total length and weigh 1.0 to 1.6 ounces (30 to 46 grams). Woodland voles are between 4 and 6 inches (105 to 145 mm) in total length and weigh 0.7 to 1.4 ounces (19 to 39 grams). The tail is only ½ to 1 inch (12 to 29 mm) long.

Behavior: Meadow voles usually are associated with grassy fields, marshes, and woodland meadows where grasses and sedges are present. In the Adirondacks, meadow voles have been captured on the treeless summit of Mount Marcy, the state's highest peak. Rock voles are habitat specialists, occupying the cooler, moister hardwoods and mixed deciduous-coniferous forests where rocky, moss-covered

Woodland vole

boulder fields are present. Woodland voles, in contrast, only live in the southeastern edge of the Adirondack Park. They prefer deciduous woodlands with loose soils and thick leaf litter or herbaceous groundcover.

Meadow voles can be active at any time, but peak activity occurs at night, at dawn, and at dusk. They construct numerous surface runways and occasional underground burrows. Grass nests are located at the end of the runways or under a tussock of grass. Meadow voles are almost entirely herbivorous, eating tubers, many grasses, clover, and, in the winter months, even bark. They are capable of eating their own body weight in vegetation each day. Meadow vole populations can increase rapidly, only to crash a few years later. The population crashes are due in part to heavy mortality from their many predators; they are a mainstay in the diet of many carnivores. Meadow voles have two to eight litters per year depending on availability of food. Litters of up to eleven young (average of 4 to 6) are produced from early spring through late fall in northern regions. Although naked and helpless at birth, they are weaned by the end of their third week. Young females are ready to breed only 28 days after they are born. Rock voles and woodland voles seldom have litters of more than six young.

Southern Bog Lemming (Family Cricetidae, *Synaptomys cooperi*) and **Northern Bog Lemming** (*Synaptomys borealis*)

Description: Bog lemmings are vole-like in appearance. They are small, stocky animals with short legs and a relatively large head. The pelage is a long, shaggy brown above and gray below. The northern bog lemming may occur in the northeastern Adirondack Park. This species can be distinguished from the southern bog lemming only by details of its tooth structure. Adults are between 4½ and 5⅓ inches (115 to 135 mm) in total length and weigh 0.7 to 1.7 ounces (21 to 50 grams). The tail is very short (½ to 1 inch).

Behavior: Northern bog lemmings are rare below the United States–Canada border; they have been collected on Whiteface Mountain in the Adirondacks. Southern bog lemmings are also uncommon; they live in meadows, brushy areas, and dense woodlands wherever grasses and sedges are abundant. In other parts of their range, they also inhabit bogs, but this does not appear to be the case in the Adirondacks. Grasses, sedges, and clover are the mainstay of their diet; fungi and mosses are also eaten on occasion. Southern bog lemmings usually live in a complex of subsurface runways just below the ground. Southern bog lemmings are capable of year-round breeding, but few litters are born during Adirondack winters. Litters of three or four young are typical, but litters of up to eight are possible. Young are weaned by the end of their third week.

CHIPMUNKS AND SQUIRRELS (Family Sciuridae)

Chipmunks, red squirrels, and gray squirrels are active during the day, highly vocal when disturbed, and more conspicuously colored than many other rodents. Consequently, squirrels are perhaps the most commonly observed mammals in the Adirondacks. "Squirrel" is a common term used primarily for chipmunks and tree squirrels, but woodchucks, flying squirrels, and western prairie dogs are all squirrels belonging to the family Sciuridae. Squirrels have thick, busy tails and relatively large eyes. These exceedingly clever animals frequent campgrounds and residential areas, where they raid bird feeders, dig burrows under buildings, and scamper about caching nuts and seeds for use later in the year. Chipmunks and woodchucks spend most of their time on the ground and pass the winter hibernating in underground dens. In contrast, tree squirrels are highly arboreal and remain active all winter long.

Eastern Chipmunk (*Tamias striatus*)

Description: Eastern chipmunks are small, reddish brown squirrels with 5 black stripes separated by brown or white fur stripes on their backs. They also have light and dark facial stripes above and below their eyes. They have flattened, reddish brown tails that are not as bushy as tree squirrels. Adults weigh 2.8 to 3.2 ounces (80 to 90 grams) and are about 9 inches (24 cm) in total length.

Behavior: Chipmunks are partial to hardwood forests and mixed deciduous-coniferous forests with an understory where rocks, stumps, and logs provide observation perches and potential escape routes. Chipmunks eat nuts, acorns, seeds, fungi, fruits, berries, insects, and occasionally small vertebrates. They live in shallow burrows created by carrying away the dirt in their cheek pouches. These burrows can include up to 90 feet of tunnels with multiple entrances and exits. Eastern chipmunks are diurnal and solitary, defending small territories around their burrows from neighboring chipmunks. Chipmunks spend considerable time in the fall gathering food in the cheek pouches and storing it near their underground nests. Eastern chipmunks hibernate from late fall to early spring, waking every few days to eat from their food caches. Males and females use two calls: a trill of "*chip-chip-chips*" repeated at a rate of about 120 chips per minute and a lower-pitched, slower "*chuck . . . chuck . . . chuck*." These calls probably are used to enforce territorial boundaries and to warn of predators.

Unlike most squirrels, eastern chipmunks have 2 breeding seasons. The first begins in February and lasts until April; the second begins in June and ends in August. Females produce litters of four to five young with a maximum litter size of nine.

Eastern Gray Squirrel (*Sciurus carolinensis*)

Description: This tree squirrel is grayish brown above, with hints of yellow on the head and shoulders; the underparts are gray to white. The tail is bushy, slightly flattened, and gray with silver tips. In some regions, a black (melanistic) form of the gray squirrel is common in local areas. Adults are 19 inches (48 to 50 cm) in total length, with a 7- to 10-inch (18 to 25 cm) long, bushy, gray tail. Weights range from 1 to 1½ pounds (450 to 680 grams).

Behavior: Gray squirrels are rare in the central portions of the Adirondack Park but are common in deciduous forests along the eastern and southern margins of the park. They prefer hardwood or mixed forests, especially oak-hickory forests, but may be locally common in towns and small cities within the park. They are active during the day (diurnal) and active year round, even during the coldest days of winter. They feed primarily on acorns, hickory nuts, beechnuts, and walnuts. They bury nuts individually in separate locations around their home range and rely on these cached nuts during the winter months. Eastern gray squirrels are arboreal, and den in natural tree cavities or build nests of leaves and twigs in large oak, beech, and maple trees. Gray squirrels use a variety of vocalizations; when disturbed they use an aggressive bark accompanied by tail flicks. Mating occurs in January or February followed by a second round of mating in June or July. Several males may compete for a single female by repeatedly chasing each other, but only the dominant male typically mates with the female. A single litter of two or three young is born after each mating period.

Red Squirrel (*Tamiasciurus hudsonicus*)

Description: Perhaps the most commonly observed mammal in the Adirondack Park, red squirrels are reddish above, olive-gray on the sides, and white below. There is a prominent white eye-ring. The winter pelage includes a narrow black stripe between the reddish back and the white belly, as well as short ear tufts. The summer coat is a duller olive-gray. Adults average about 12 inches (27 to 38 cm) in total length, including a 5-inch (12 cm) tail. Weights range between 5 and 9 ounces (140 to 252 grams).

Behavior: Red squirrels prefer coniferous forests or mixed coniferous-deciduous forests at all elevations. They remain active all year, feeding

heavily on pine seeds. They extract the seeds from the cones, leaving large piles of cone fragments at the base of the tree. In the fall, they cut and bury green pinecones underground. During winter, they eat the terminal buds of evergreens. Various seeds, fruits, buds, fungi, and the occasional insect or bird's egg complete the diet. Red squirrels also store food in large caches in the ground, a tree cavity, or at the base of a tree. Red squirrel nests, constructed of grass and bark, typically are found in a tree cavity, fallen logs, a hole in the ground, or as a leaf nest in the branches of a conifer tree. Territorial boundaries are advertised by regular vocalizations that include a long, loud trill; this is a common sound in many Adirondack forests. Males congregate on a female's territory during the single day when she comes into heat. Females produce a litter of three to seven young in March or April. After a second round of mating, a second litter may be born in August or September.

Southern Flying Squirrel (*Glaucomys volans*)
and **Northern Flying Squirrel** (*Glaucomys sabrinus*)
  Description: Both Adirondack species are small squirrels with soft, silky fur that is grayish brown above and white below. Northern flying squirrels tend to be a richer brown, with a grayish white belly. In both species, the flattened, gray-brown tail serves as a steering rudder during gliding. Large black eyes distinguish flying squirrels from any other Adirondack species. Adult southern flying squirrels are between 8 and 10 inches (20 to 25 cm) in total length, have a tail between 3 and 5 inches (8 to 12 cm) in length, and weigh 1.6 to 3.5 ounces (45 to 100 grams). Northern flying squirrels are slightly larger at 10 to 14 inches (27 to 35 cm) in total length and at weights of 2.6 to 5.0 ounces (75 to 140 grams).

Flying squirrel

Behavior: In the Adirondack region, southern flying squirrels are found at lower elevations in deciduous forests, such as beech-maple and oak-hickory woodlands. By contrast, the northern flying squirrels prefer coniferous and mixed forests at all elevations. Flying squirrels are the only nocturnal tree squirrels and are seldom seen in the wild. The name is misleading because they are not capable of true flight; instead, they glide from one treetop down to the base of another. Long glides of over 75 yards are possible because the outstretched legs support a fold of skin between the wrists and ankles that act as a parasail to slow descent. Both species are active in all seasons, but only the southern flying squirrel will enter torpor in times of extreme cold or food scarcity. Torpor, a state of reduced metabolism, is shallower than true hibernation. In winter, several squirrels may huddle together in a single den to save body heat; as many as 50 have been found in one nest in winter. Flying squirrels eat a variety of foods, including nuts, seeds, berries, lichens, fungi, bird eggs and nestlings, some insects, and sometimes carrion. They store great quantities of seeds, nuts, and acorns for winter use at various locations on their home range. Faint, bird-like chirping at night may indicate the presence of a flying squirrel. During the day, they may be located by tapping the trunk of a dead tree. If they are present, they often will peek out or glide away. Southern flying squirrels mate in early spring, producing two to seven young. Sometimes a second litter is born in August or September. In contrast, northern flying squirrels mate in late winter. They appear to have a single litter per year consisting of two to five young.

LARGER RODENTS

Woodchuck (Family Sciuridae, *Marmota monax*)
 Description: Better known as groundhogs, woodchucks are large mar-
mots in the squirrel family. Woodchucks have short legs and a stocky
body covered in grizzled brown fur. The feet and lower legs are dark
brown or black. Adults are about the size of a cat, with a length of 16 to
32 inches (41 to 82 cm) and a weight of 4.4 to 14 pounds (2 to 6.4 kilograms). The tail is bushy and short, at 4 to 6 inches (10 to 15 cm).
 Behavior: Woodchucks are common throughout the Adirondack
Park at elevations up to 2,500 feet. Open areas with dry soils, such as
woodlands, meadows, old fields, and roadsides are typical habitats.
Woodchucks are active during the day, especially in early morning and
late afternoon. They are solitary except during the short mating season. They build large burrow systems with several escape exits. The
main entrance hole has a mound of dirt on its perimeter, but escape
holes tend to lack these conspicuous mounds. As fall approaches,
woodchucks amass a heavy layer of fat in preparation for hibernation.
During hibernation, their body temperature falls to near 40°F (4°C),
they take a single breath every 6 minutes, and their heart rate drops
from over 100 beats per minute to only 15 beats. Males emerge in early
spring, about one month before females, in order to establish a home
range and to search for mates. Grasses, clover, alfalfa, and the like,
form the diet; they also will feed heavily on corn and can damage veg-
etable gardens. Woodchucks have a single litter of four or five young
each year. The young are born in April or early May.

Muskrat (Family Cricetidae, *Ondatra zibethicus*)
 Description: Muskrats are large, semi-aquatic rodents with dense, dark
brown fur above and paler fur below. Unlike beavers, which share the
same habitats, muskrats have long, scaly black tails that are slightly
flattened (like a rudder) and taper to a point. The hind feet are only
partially webbed. Adults are 16 to 25 inches (41 to 63 cm) in total
length, with a 7½- to 12-inch (19 to 30 cm) long tail. The maximum recorded weight is 4 pounds (1.8 kilogram), but most individuals weight
about 2.2 pounds, or 1 kilogram.
 Behavior: Muskrats are most common in ponds, lakes, rivers, and
slow-moving streams. They are active at any time of day and in all
seasons; they spend much of their time in the water. Muskrats eat
many types of aquatic vegetation, including cattails, sedges, rushes,
and some terrestrial plants. Freshwater clams, crayfish, frogs, and fish
may supplement the diet in winter. They can remain submerged for

up to 17 minutes and will travel long distances underwater. Muskrat lodges are smaller than beaver lodges and are constructed of cattails and other aquatic vegetation. They are territorial and use scent posts covered with musky secretions to identify their territorial boundaries. Mating begins in late winter and runs through early September in the Adirondacks. Females frequently mate again while still nursing their current litter, resulting in up to five litters per year. Litters average six or seven young (maximum is 11 young).

Beaver (Family Castoridae, *Castor canadensis*)
Description: Their dark brown fur and large, paddle-shaped tail make this animal easy to identify. They are stocky rodents, with small, rounded ears, shorter forelimbs, and a conspicuous scaly black tail.

Beavers are highly aquatic and use their large, webbed hind feet to power them through the water. They also have a robust skull with large orange incisors that are used to slice through wood. The beaver is the largest North American rodent. Adults are roughly 3 feet (100 to 120 cm) in total length, with a tail length of 12 to 16 inches (30 to 40 cm). Mature beavers usually weigh 44 to 60 pounds (16 to 30 kg) but may reach nearly 86 pounds (40 kg) on occasion.

Behavior: Beavers occur throughout the Adirondacks wherever rivers, streams, marshes, lakes, and ponds are present, but they prefer forested areas where trees are available for lodge and dam construction. Beavers are most active at dusk and at night, when they emerge from their lodges to add to their food stores or repair leaky dams. Although rarely seen on land, the neatly beveled stumps of felled trees, along with their massive dams and lodges, reveal their presence in the area. Beavers living in small streams, lakes, and ponds usually build dams and a lodge, while those in larger rivers tend to live in burrows in the riverbank. Lodges have a large central living area above the waterline with one or two underwater entrances. Dam designs vary with stream size and topography. Poplar, aspen, willow, birch, and maple are used for construction and for food. Trees are felled by gnawing out large woodchips until the tree is deeply girdled. Small-diameter trees (2 to 6 inches) are preferred, although occasionally trees as large as 30 inches thick are felled to get at the more-nutritious branches. Branches are used for construction, eaten immediately, or stored in underwater caches for winter. Beavers are excellent swimmers; they use their webbed hind feet to swim up to 6 mph and can remain submerged for nearly 15 minutes. Only the beaver's head is visible when they are swimming (both head and back are visible in muskrats). Beavers are insulated from the chilly water by a thick layer of fat under the skin and by a luxurious coat of fur. The fur is kept waterproof by the application of castoreum, an oily secretion from glands near the anus. These anal glands are also used to mark the territorial boundaries of the colony. Beavers form long-lasting pairs; they stay together until one member of the pair dies. Mating occurs in late January or February, and four or five kits are born in April or June. The kits are capable of swimming within a week. The young remain with their parents for two years before dispersing to form colonies of their own.

Porcupine (Family Erethizontidae, *Erethizon dorsatum*)

Description: There is no mistaking the porcupine. They are large, stocky animals with an arching back, stiff quills on the back and tail, and black or brown fur tipped with white. The pelage consists of a wooly

underfur with coarse guard hairs interspersed with barbed quills. The undersurface of the tail is covered with stiff bristles that aid in climbing trees. Adults are 24 to 40 inches (63 to 100 cm) in total length, with tails of 5½ to 12 inches (14 to 30 cm) and weights between 9 and 40 pounds (4 to 18 kg).

Behavior: Deciduous, coniferous, and mixed forests are the preferred habitat of porcupines, especially large stands of hemlock, spruce, birch, and beech trees. Porcupines are primarily solitary, but are active year-round. They are nocturnal, spending their days alone in hollow trees, underground burrows, or hidden in the treetops. On the ground, they walk with a slow, waddling gait, yet they are excellent climbers. Porcupines have about 30,000 quills (modified hairs) that are attached loosely to the skin. When threatened, the porcupine erects its quills and strikes at its enemy with its tail. On contact, the quills detach easily and are driven forcefully into the predator. Each quill is tipped with a series of microscopic barbs that continue to work their way deeper and deeper into the flesh with every movement of the victim. Despite these formidable weapons, porcupines are not aggressive. Porcupines feed on a wide variety of leaves, twigs, nuts, and green plants. In winter, they strip away the outer bark of various trees to eat the inner cambium layer. Porcupines like salt and have an appetite for plywood buildings and outdoor furniture. Mating occurs in October or November. When she is ready, the female relaxes her blanket of quills and lifts her tail over her back to allow the male to mate. A single, precocious young is born in May or June. Offspring are born in a membranous sac to prevent its short, soft quills from harming the mother; the quills harden within one hour.

WEASELS AND THEIR ALLIES (Family Mustelidae)

Members of the family Mustelidae show considerable variation in size, but all are carnivorous. They all have relatively long bodies with short legs and dense fur. Most species have well-developed scent glands used to attract mates and mark territorial boundaries. Because skunks also share powerful scent glands, they were included in the family Mustelidae. Recent genetic evidence, however, suggests that they should be placed in their own family, the Mephitidae.

Short-tailed Weasel (*Mustela erminea*)

Description: The short-tailed weasel, or ermine, is a small, thin weasel with an elongated body and short legs. In the summer, they are dark brown above and whitish below. The brown tail terminates in a black tip. In winter, they are completely white, except for the black tail tip. Males average about 10 or 11 inches (27 cm) in total length, have a tail about 3 inches (7 cm) long, and weigh 3.2 to 5.0 ounces (90 to 140 grams). Females are about half the size of males.

Behavior: Short-tailed weasels occur in all terrestrial habitats throughout the Adirondack Park. They are active day or night. These small carnivores hunt on the ground, pursuing their prey under fallen logs, into burrows, and even up trees. They feed mainly on voles, mice, shrews, baby rabbits, birds, frogs, lizards, snakes, and many kinds of insects. Male territories are larger and include several female territories, but the sexes rarely interact except during the breeding season. Mating usually occurs between June and July. Shortly after mating, embryonic development stops until the following spring, a litter of four to nine young are born in April.

Long-tailed Weasel (*Mustela frenata*)

Description: Long-tailed weasels retain the short-legged, elongated body common to all weasels, but the tail is proportionately longer. The fur is a rich brown above and white or yellowish below. The feet are brownish. The winter pelage is entirely white except for the black tail tip. The long-tailed weasel is larger than *M. erminea*. Males weigh between 7 and 9½ ounces (200 to 270 grams), about twice as much as females. Adult males are 15 to 18 inches (38 to 45 cm) in total length, compared to only 12 to 14 inches (30 to 36 cm) for adult females. Tails average 5 inches (13 cm) in length for males and 4 inches (10 cm) for females.

Behavior: These weasels occupy a wide variety of habitats, including forests, brushy second-growth forests, swampy areas, and abandoned farmland.

Voles and mice are the mainstay of the long-tailed weasel diet, but they also eat young rabbits, chipmunks, shrews, some birds, and, on rare occasions, an insect or earthworm. These weasels bite their victims at the base of the skull and eat the choice parts first, caching the remainder for a later date. Long-tailed weasels have anal glands that release a powerful musky scent used to locate mates and mark their home range. The short days of fall trigger a gradual moult to a white winter coat that provides camouflage against the snow. Mating occurs in midsummer. Embryonic development ceases until the following April or May, when a single litter of four to eight young is born.

American Mink (*Mustela vison*)

Description: The semi-aquatic mink has a long, slender body with rich brown fur. Some individuals have a white patch on the throat. Mink retain their brown pelage even in winter. Males average about 21 inches (53 cm) in total length, while females average slightly smaller. For both, the weight range is between 1½ and 3½ pounds (650 to 1600 grams). The tail is about a third of their total length.

Behavior: Mink occur wherever rivers, creeks, lakes, ponds, and marshes provide sufficient food and shelter. They are excellent swimmers and spend much time hunting in ponds and streams for crayfish, frogs, fish, birds, and small mammals. The mink covers considerable distances while hunting and marks its range with scent from its anal glands. The home range of a male normally includes the ranges of several females, but both sexes are hostile to intruders, and males fight viciously when they encounter one another. Males mate with several females from January through April. Litters of four or five young are common (the range is one to ten offspring).

American Marten (*Martes americana*)

Description: Martens have a long, slender body, short limbs, and a bushy tail. Thick, dark brown fur covers the back and tail. The head is gray, and the chest is a cream or orange color. Martens have large eyes, rounded ears, and a pointed snout. Males are larger than females; males measure 21 to 27 inches (55 to 68 cm) in total length, with females measuring only 19 to 23 inches (49 to 60 cm). The tail length is between 7 and 9 inches (18 to 23 cm) in males. Martens weigh between 1.3 and 2.6 pounds (0.6 to 1.2 kilograms).

Behavior: The marten's prime habitat is the northern spruce-fir forests, where the forest floor is covered with dead trunks, branches, and litter that provide cover for its principal prey, red-backed voles. Martens are active at various times of the day and night, especially in the early morning and late afternoon. They wander about their 5- to 15-square-mile home ranges hunting for rodents, mice, and voles. Martens are also skilled climbers and move with great ease in trees, hunting squirrels and birds. The diet is not limited to meat; they also consume carrion, insects, eggs, berries, conifer seeds, and honey. Martens do not hibernate in winter. They are normally solitary animals, but during the short breeding season, from June to August, mates locate one another by following a trail of pungent scent marks. Although breeding occurs in the summer, the embryos don't develop much until February. In late March or early April, one to five blind young are born.

Fisher (*Martes pennanti*)

Description: Fishers are similar to martens but larger and darker. Their fur is a luxurious dark brown with a silvery frosting on the head and shoulders. The legs, belly, and tail are almost black and they may have light patches of fur on their chest and throat. Males are larger and heavier than females; adult males reach about 40 inches (1 meter) in total length, have a tail length of 12 to 16 inches (32 to 40 cm), and weigh between 7½ and 12 pounds (3.5 to 5.5 kg).

Behavior: Fishers prefer stands of conifer and hardwood forests where the tree canopy is continuous overhead. They eat mice, squirrels, snowshoe hares, and grouse, and are one of the few animals to attack and kill porcupines. When the opportunity arises, fishers also will con-

sume a white-tailed deer carcass. Fishers and martens are both agile climbers that often hunt squirrels. They are quite solitary; aggression between males on adjacent territories is common. Home-range size varies from 2 to 15 square miles (6 to 35 square kilometers). Fishers use scent marking to communicate and establish territories. They are active year-round. Breeding takes place in late winter and early spring. Gestation lasts almost a full year because the early embryos do not implant in the uterus for almost eleven months (termed delayed implantation). Once implanted, the embryos develop normally until litters of one to five young are born the following spring.

River Otter (*Lontra canadensis*)

Description: The river otter is the largest and most aquatic member of the weasel family in the Adirondacks. They have a long, streamlined body, a flattened, rudder-like tail, and webbed feet. The head is broad and slightly flattened, with small ears and eyes. Otters are dark brown above with a lighter belly and throat. Males are larger than females. River otters are about 40 inches (1 meter) in total body length, with a tail length between 12 and 20 inches (30 to 50 cm). Otters weigh 11 to 25 pounds (5 to 14 kg).

Behavior: Otters are relatively common in the Adirondacks and often are seen in the more secluded rivers, ponds, and lakes. Otters are active during the day. They are incredibly graceful swimmers; their flexible bodies allow rapid changes in direction while chasing fish. Otters can remain underwater for several minutes and reappear on the

surface as far as a ¼ mile (0.4 km) away. In the winter, otters alternate short bursts of running with sliding; they use their streamlined bodies to toboggan across the snow on their bellies. Otters prey mainly on fish but also eat small mammals, frogs, crayfish, and other aquatic invertebrates. They maintain a permanent den in a riverbank or an abandoned beaver lodge. Males may have home ranges 9 miles (15 km) across, while those of females are much smaller. Both sexes defend territories from other otters of the same sex. The male river otter presumably mates with one or more females that have home ranges within his territory. The female establishes the natal den shortly before giving birth. Mating takes place between December and May, just after the birth of the litter from the previous season. Implantation of the embryos is delayed, making the gestation period appear to last nine months. A litter of one to six young is born in March or April.

Striped Skunk (Family Mephitidae, *Mephitis mephitis*)
Description: There is no mistaking this Adirondack resident. Striped skunks are black with two broad, white stripes running from a white cap on the head to the tail. There is also a thin white stripe down the center of the face. The bushy black tail may have a fringe of white hairs or a white tip. Males are larger than females; both sexes are between 20 and 31 inches (50 to 80 cm) in total length. The tail is about a third of the total length and weights range from 6 to 14 pounds (1.2 to 6.3 kg).
Behavior: Striped skunks are common in woodlands, fields, brushy areas, agricultural lands, and in and around villages. Like other skunks, they advertise their presence to potential enemies by their bold, black and white coloration. Predators quickly learn that skunks are not to be bothered. The skunk's anal glands produce a foul, oily scent (butyl-

mercaptan) that can be sprayed up to 15 feet. Skunks warn intruders by elevating the tail, chattering their teeth, and stomping the ground with the front feet. If this warning is not heeded, they quickly present their backside, raise the tail straight up, and spray their scent at the intruder's face. Skunks are primarily nocturnal and active year-round. They do not hibernate, although in extremely cold weather they may become temporarily dormant. The striped skunk is an omnivore, feeding on insects and grubs, small mammals, amphibians, and the eggs of ground-nesting birds. They also eat fruits when available. Striped skunks mate between February and April. In May, the female gives birth to a litter of four to seven young. A mother skunk is fiercely protective of her young and will spray if approached by an intruder.

PROCYONIDS

Raccoons are the only members of the family Procyonidae in the Adirondack Mountains. Most procyonids, including raccoons, have prominent tails bands. Raccoons are omnivorous, nocturnal, and relatively solitary creatures.

Raccoon (*Procyon lotor*)

Description: The raccoon is easy to distinguish from other mammals by its black facial mask and bushy tail with 4 to 7 black rings. Coloration is usually grayish brown. The forepaws are highly dexterous and their naked soles are very sensitive to touch. Their total body length ranges

from 24 to 39 inches (60 to 100 cm), with the tail comprising about 40 or 50 percent of their length. Raccoons have thickset bodies and generally weigh from 13 to 15 pounds (6 to 7 kilograms).

Behavior: Raccoons are extremely adaptable but prefer forests that are close to water. Raccoons are omnivorous and opportunistic feeders, eating nuts, wild grapes, cherries, apples, berries, and acorns. In agricultural areas, corn is the mainstay of its diet. Raccoons also consume crayfish, insects, freshwater mussels, rodents, frogs, and bird eggs. Their human-like forepaws enable raccoons to manipulate difficult prey with relative ease. Raccoons have excellent hearing and night vision. They are nocturnal and mostly solitary. During extremely cold periods, raccoons remain in their dens but do not hibernate. On the ground, they usually amble along rather slowly, yet are capable of short bursts of 15 miles per hour. In trees, they are agile climbers. In the Adirondacks, the mating season is January through March. Raccoons generally have a single litter of three or four young each year. The young remain under their mother's care well into the winter, even after they are weaned, then they disperse in the spring.

CANIDS

The family Canidae comprises the dog-like carnivores, which in North America include foxes, coyotes, and wolves. Foxes are generally solitary and hunt small mammals. Larger canids form social groups called packs that allow them to chase down larger prey. Typically, a dominate alpha male and female pair lead the pack and sire most of the offspring.

Red Fox (*Vulpes vulpes*)

Description: Red foxes are reddish brown to yellowish red above and whitish below. The lower legs and the back of the ears are black. The bushy tail has a white tip. Two color phases also occur: the cross fox and the silver fox. The cross fox has reddish gray fur with a black stripe down its back. The silver fox ranges from silver to black. Both variants are uncommon (fewer than 25 percent of individuals) but occur in the same litters with normal red foxes. Red foxes average about 36 inches in total length, about one-third of which is the bushy tail. Males are slightly larger than females; typical weights for females and males are 9 and 11 pounds (4 to 5 kg), respectively.

Behaviors: Red foxes occupy a wide range of habitats, including grasslands, farmlands, and forests. The red fox is an omnivore, eating rodents, rabbits, birds, insects, fruit, and carrion. Red foxes hunt mice and voles by pouncing and pinning the rodent to the ground. Red foxes do not form packs. Adults are solitary and have home ranges that vary in size from 5 to over 50 square kilometers if the habitat is poor. An adult male shares its range with one or two adult females and their offspring. Red foxes are most active from dusk to dawn and tend to remain in the same home range for life. Female red foxes are receptive for one to six days. They typically breed between January and March. Gestation is about 52 days. The average litter size is five pups, but litters of thirteen pups are possible.

Gray Fox (*Urocyon cinereoargenteus*)

Description: Gray foxes resemble red foxes, except that they are grizzled (salt and pepper) above and on the sides. They have orange-brown fur on the back of the ears, on the neck, on the lower part of their sides, and on their legs. The tail has a dorsal stripe of long black hairs terminating in a solid black tip. Males are slightly larger than females. Adults are 31 to 39 inches (0.8 to 1.0 meters) in total length, 9 to 17 inches (23 to 44 cm) in tail length, and weigh 7 to 13 pounds (3 to 6 kg).

Behaviors: Gray foxes prefer deciduous woodlands, brushy areas, and mixed coniferous-deciduous forests, avoiding the agricultural habitats preferred by the red fox. Gray foxes are solitary hunters that seldom are seen during the day. They are omnivorous and eat a wide variety of plant and animal foods. Voles, mice, shrews, and birds all contribute to the diet, but the most important winter prey are usually cottontail rabbits. Gray foxes also will gorge themselves on apples or other fruits when the opportunity arises. The breeding season of gray foxes in the Adirondacks begins in late January and continues through May. Females give birth to a litter of three to five pups (maximum is seven pups). The young pups begin to hunt with their parents after three or four months.

Coyote (*Canis latrans*)

Description: Coyotes vary considerably in coloration, but Adirondack coyotes tend to be grayish brown or orangish gray above, with whitish underparts. The long, black-tipped guard hairs may produce a faint black stripe along the back and shoulders. The coyote's legs are long, thin, and rusty yellow in color. The bushy tail has a prominent black tip. The ears are large relative to the size of the head, and the muzzle is long and slender. Coyote have erect, pointed ears, and unlike domestic dogs, the tail typically is held below its back when they run. Coyotes are smaller than gray wolves and much larger than foxes; adult coyotes measure 22 to 26 inches (55 to 66 cm) in height, have a total length of 39 to 51 inches (1.0 to 1.3 meters), and a tail length of 12 to 15 inches (30 to 40 cm). They weigh 20 to 40 pounds (9 to 20 kg), with exceptional individuals reaching nearly 55 pounds (25 kg).

Behavior: Coytes occupy virtually any habitat, but prefer areas with a combination of brushy areas, woodlots, and open country. They are mainly active at night. Coyotes are opportunistic carnivores, eating many species of small mammals, as well as birds, reptiles, insects, and many fruits. In the Adirondacks, white-tailed deer are an important winter food source. Rabbits and other small mammals may make up the bulk of the diet in other seasons. Coyotes are solitary hunters most of the time but may combine efforts to chase down larger prey, such as white-tailed deer. They are excellent runners, cruising at 25 to 30 mph (40 to 50 km/h), with short bursts of up to 40 mph (65 km/h). Coyotes do not have permanent dens but will use temporary maternal

dens for raising the young. The coyote's distinctive call, heard at dusk, dawn, or during the night, consists of a series of yelps, followed by a long howl, and finishing with a series of short yaps. This call appears to keep the pack together and reunite them when they are separated during a hunt. The coyote may pair for many years following a courtship of approximately two to three months. Breeding occurs between late January and late March. Litters of up to nineteen pups are possible, but the average is six.

FELIDS

Cats belong to the carnivore family Felidae. Felids have relatively long limbs and short faces. Unlike canids, cats hunt using a stealthy approach followed by a rapid burst of speed to bring down their prey. Three species once roamed the Adirondacks, bobcats Canadian lynx, and mountain lions. Today only the bobcat remains.

Bobcat (*Lynx rufus*)

Description: Bobcats are medium-sized, reddish gray cats with black spots and a short stubby tail. The tail has two or three indistinct black bars and a black tip on the upper surface. The face is marked with thin black streaks radiating onto a broad cheek ruff. The pointed ears have slight tufts of black hairs and often have bold black and white patches on the back surface. Males are larger than females. Both sexes are 28 to 39 inches (0.7 to 1.0 meter) in total length, with a 4- to 7-inch (11 to 19 cm) tail. Adults weigh between 15 and 33 pounds (7 to 15 kg).

Behavior: Bobcats prefer hardwood, coniferous, or mixed forest broken by swamps, farmland, or rocky ledges. Bobcats are active in the early morning and late evening hours and spend the remainder of the day resting. Their home range varies in size depending on the sex of the animal, the time of year, and the abundance of prey. Bobcats mark their ranges with urine, feces, and anal gland secretions. Bobcats are opportunistic hunters; they prey on snowshoe hares, mice, squirrels, woodchucks, opossums, birds, and just about any other small vertebrate. Bobcats are capable of killing white-tailed deer when the snow is deep or when fawns are available. They are ambush hunters, attacking by stalking and then a quick sprint, followed by a bite to the throat or neck. Bobcats are solitary animals; males and females come together only during a short mating season. Females typically breed in February or March. During this mating season, several males may attend to a single female, but only the dominant male normally breeds with her. A litter of one to seven (usually two or three) young are born in late April or early May.

BEARS (Family Ursidae)

Bears belong to the family Ursidae. They are large carnivores with thick bodies, powerful limbs, and short, stubby tails. They walk with a deceptively awkward gait, owing to their slightly longer hind legs. However, they are fast runners and excellent climbers.

American Black Bear (*Ursus americanus*)

Description: Black bears are large mammals with coarse, shaggy fur, rounded ears, and an inconspicuous tail. Despite the name, the fur varies in color from brown to black, and there is often a white patch on the chest. The long, tapering muzzle is tan with a black nose pad. Eyes are relatively small and black. Adult males generally are larger than adult females. Adult males normally weigh 250 and 500 pounds (113 to 250 kg), while females are 100 to 450 pounds (45 to 204 kg).

Behavior: Black bears occur throughout the Adirondack Park but prefer densely wooded forests and swamplands. Black bears are active during the daytime, especially at dusk. They feed on a wide variety of food items, including meat, but most of their diet consists of insects, fruits, and other plant material. They have an excellent sense of smell, good hearing, but only average vision. Solitary by nature, they often travel many miles each night. They are good swimmers, excellent climbers, and are capable of running over 30 mph over short distances. In late fall, as temperatures drop, the bears feed heavily to put on the extra fat they will need to sustain themselves during the long winter. In October, the bears enter their winter dens, usually in cavities under stumps, in excavated holes, or under brush piles. Here the bears enter a shallow form of hibernation called "winter lethargy." Body temperature, heart rate, and other physiological processes do not decrease to the extreme levels of true hibernators. Mating generally occurs from mid-June to mid-July. In January or February, the female gives birth in her winter den. Twins are typical, but black bears can have from one to five cubs. Newborns weigh about 1 pound and are roughly 7 inches long.

UNGULATES

Ungulates are hoofed mammals that walk and run on the tips of their digits. Adirondack ungulates include white-tailed deer and moose, both in the family Cervidae. Males of both species grow a pair of antlers each summer, which are shed in the winter. Antlers grow from a bony pedicle atop the skull. Newly formed antlers are covered in velvet; a skin rich in capillaries that nourishes the growing bone underneath. In the fall breeding season, changing hormone levels trigger the shedding of the velvet and the hardening of the antler. Antlers are used to advertise a male's fitness to females and as a weapon during fights with other males.

White-tailed Deer (Family Cervidae, *Odocoileus virginianus*)
Description: White-tailed deer have a tan or reddish brown summer coat that is grayish brown in winter. The belly and throat region are

white. The tail is brown with a white fringe on the outer surface and bright white underneath. A small white band encircles the nose and the eye. Males (called bucks) have antlers with a main beam arching forward and several straight tines branching vertically from the main beam. The young (called fawns) have white spots along the flanks. Adult males weight between 150 and 310 pounds (68 to 141 kg), while females (called does) weigh only 90 to 211 pounds (41 to 96 kg).

Behavior: White-tailed deer are now common in farmlands, brushy areas, and forests up to about 2,500 feet in elevation. White-tailed deer are most active in the evening, when they move along well-worn trails to feeding areas. As dawn approaches, they move back to concealed areas and bed down for the day. White-tailed deer browse on woody vegetation, including the twigs and buds of birch, maple, and many evergreens. In the fall, they also eat large quantities of acorns, beechnuts, and other nuts or corn. The number of tines on the antlers is related to nutritional factors and not directly to age. The sexes remain separate for most of the year, but in winter bucks and does gather together in "yards" where winter forage is abundant. By yarding, the herd (as many as 150 deer) keeps foraging trails open and provides protection from predators. Loud snorts and hoof stamping alert others in the herd to danger. If the danger persists, they raise the white tail flag as they flee, signaling danger to other deer and helping a fawn to follow her mother. In the fall, the males begin to shed the velvet from the antlers. Shortly afterward, rutting season begins with sparring among males to establish their dominance. Bucks make several "rubs" and "scrapes" in the area and revisit them regularly during the rut. The glandular secretions and urine left by the male at these scrapes attract does, who visit the scrapes and also urinate in them. The buck then follows the doe's scent trail and attempts to mate with her. Courtship begins in late October or early November in the Adirondacks. In May or June, one to two fawns are born after a gestation of over six months. The fawn is able to move about within hours. Young fawns lie hidden in the vegetation while the mother forages; she returns to nurse them only once or twice each day. After several days, the fawns travel more with their mothers. Weaning occurs after one or two months, but fawns usually stay with their mothers well into the winter months.

Moose (*Alces alces*)

Description: Moose have a coat of dark brown fur, a dewlap under the chin, and a long, thick snout. They have long, slender legs and humped shoulders. Males, much larger than females, grow a massive pair of broad, flattened antlers. Calves are lighter brown but not spotted. At

700 to 1,200 pounds (300 to 600 kg), the moose is the largest member of the deer family in the world.

Behavior: Moose prefer spruce forests, swamps, and aspen and willow thickets in close proximity to wetlands. By 1870, moose had disappeared completely from the Adirondacks, but in recent years a small population has re-colonized the region. Moose are generally solitary in summer. They most often are seen feeding along streams or ponds. The summer diet consists of willows and aquatic vegetation. In winter, they browses on twigs, buds, and bark of woody plants, including willow, balsam, aspen, birch, and maple. Despite their awkward appearance, moose can run at speeds up to 35 mph (55 km/h) through the forest and swim for several hours. Male moose begin growing antlers in March. By August, the antlers reach their full size and are shed between December and February. Bulls search the forest looking for grunting cows and challenging rival bulls with bellows and mock fights. If neither bull withdraws, the fight escalates to a battle that includes antler wrestling and much pushing and shoving. The winner of these contests then mates with the cow for a day or so before moving on to find another cow. Moose are unpredictable and can be dangerous. Mating occurs from mid-September through late October. One or two calves are born in late May or early June. The newborn calf, weighing 24 to 35 pounds (11 to 16 kg) at birth, can walk along side its mother within a few days and can swim within a couple of weeks.

EXTIRPATED CARNIVORES

Large predators, including wolves and mountain lions, once roamed the Adirondack Mountains. However, increasing human settlement, loss of habitat from logging and farming, and persecution from hunters and trappers seeking cash bounties for each animal killed, inevitably led to the complete loss of three of New York State's top predators by the early 1900s. No one knows what effect this had on the Adirondack ecosystem, and debate continues today over whether to restore the ecosystem by reintroducing native predators.

By the late 1880s, extensive logging decimated the prime habitat of the lynx (*Lynx canadensis*) and its main prey, the snowshoe hare, and the lynx completely disappeared from the Adirondack Mountains. Between 1989 and 1992, biologists reintroduced 83 Canadian lynx into the central High Peaks region. All were fitted with radio collars to allow researchers to track their locations. Unfortunately, 32 were killed by vehicles or accidental shootings, or died of other causes. The others appear to have left the Adirondacks for Canada and New Hampshire. A subsequent survey of 240 square miles of prime Adirondack habitat failed to find any sign of lynx. Currently, no state or federal plans exist for releasing more lynx in the Adirondacks. Occasional sightings of "lynx" in the Adirondacks are almost certainly bobcats.

Mountain lions (*Puma concolor*), were also native to Adirondack forests, but were extirpated by the beginning of the 1900s. Mountain lions go by a variety of local names, including cougar, puma, panther, and catamount. They are large cats, weighing up to 200 pounds in large males, with a tan or gray coat and a long tail tipped in black. In the past decades, the number of alleged mountain lion sightings in the Adirondacks has increased. Since 1980, over 130 sightings have been reported. While many of the sightings are questionable, a handful of observations are credible. The majority of sightings have occurred in the High Peaks region or the northeastern areas of the Park. This unusual distribution suggests that mountain lions occasionally may enter the Adirondacks from Vermont or southern Quebec. Some wildlife biologists now believe that mountain lions are rare visitors to the Adirondacks, but that resident or breeding populations have not been re-established in the Park.

Wolves (*Canis lupus*) were also former residents of the Adirondacks. Federal bounties of up to $50 per wolf decimated wolf populations in the northeastern United States. By 1900, wolves were exterminated from New York State and most of the lower 48 states. The 1973 Endangered Species Act provided protection for wolves and their populations have recovered slowly in Minnesota and several western states. Efforts to reintroduce wolves into the Adirondack Park began in the late 1970s. Feasibility studies showed that sufficient prey (primarily white-tailed deer) and wilderness exists to support small packs of wolves in the Park. Nevertheless, the report was pessimistic about the long-term survival of wolf populations, because of the mosaic of roads, towns, and other human activities. The report suggested that wolf populations likely would last less than 100 years before becoming locally extinct again. For now, plans to reintroduce wolves into the Adirondack Park are on hold.

SOURCES AND ADDITIONAL READING

Kays, R. W., and D. E. Wilson. 2002. *Mammals of North America*. Princeton Field Guides. Princeton, NJ: Princeton University Press.

Saunders, D. A. 1989. *Adirondack Mammals*. Syracuse, NY: Syracuse University Press.

Wilson, D. E., and S. Ruff. 1999. *The Smithsonian Book of North American Mammals*. Washington, DC: Smithsonian Institution Press.

Glossary

Abdomen The third and most posterior body segment in insects, spiders, and crustaceans.

Abscisic acid A plant hormone that plays a major role in the plant's response to stress.

Abscission The process by which plants drop leaves, fruits, or flowers.

Acid deposition A more general term for acid rain or any other form of acidic precipitation. Acid deposition is caused by emissions of sulfur and nitrogen compounds released during the combustion of fossil fuels, which react in the atmosphere to produce acids.

Acid-neutralizing capacity A measure of the ability of a water sample to neutralize strong acids.

Adipose fin A small, fatty fin located between the dorsal and tail fins of some fish, including trout.

Aestivation A rare state of dormancy similar to hibernation, but in response to heat and drought instead of cold. Animals that aestivate spend the summer months inactive and insulated against heat.

Algae A large and diverse group of photosynthetic organisms that vary from small, single-celled forms to complex multicellular forms. They are distinguished from plants by the absence of true roots, stems, and leaves.

Anadromous Describing fish that migrate up rivers from the sea to breed in freshwater.

Anal fin The median, unpaired fin on the fish's belly, between the anus and the caudal fin.

Anesthesia The condition of local or general insensibility to pain. It may or may not be accompanied by a loss of consciousness.

Annelid Any segmented worm of the phylum Annelida, including the earthworms and leeches.

Annual Describing a plant that completes its entire life cycle, from germination to death, in a single growing season.

Anthocyanin Any of a group of water-soluble plant pigments that give flowers colors ranging from red to blue.

Antibacterial Destructive to or inhibiting the growth of bacteria.

Anticoagulant A substance that delays or prevents blood clotting.

Antler One of a pair of hornlike, usually branched growths, on the head of a deer, moose, or other member of the deer family. The antlers are shed each winter and a new set begins growing in the summer.

Aphids A group of tiny insects (family Aphididae) that suck sap from plant stems and leaves. Aphids are important pests of many trees and plants.

Aphotic zone The depth, in a lake, below which sunlight does not penetrate and no photosynthesis occurs. It lies just below the photic zone.

Aquifer An underground geological formation of porous earth that contains or conducts ground water.

Arachnids A group of arthropod (class Arachnida), including spiders, scorpions, mites, ticks, and daddy-longlegs. Arachnids have two body regions, the cephalothorax and the abdomen, eight legs, no antennae, no wings, and they are usually carnivorous.

Arboreal Having adaptations for moving about in trees.

Arthropods A large group of invertebrate animals (phylum Arthropoda), that includes insects, crustaceans, and arachnids. They have an exoskeleton made of chitin, a segmented body, and pairs of jointed appendages.

Auxin A class of plant compounds that regulate or modify plant growth, including root growth and leaf drop.

Attenuation The process by which light intensity decreases with increasing distance from the light source. The decreased light intensity is due to the absorption, scattering, spreading of light in three dimensions as distance increases.

Bacteria A huge group of single-celled organisms, lacking a nucleus and certain organelles. They also lack chlorophyll and reproduce by fission. Bacteria are capable of fermentation, putrefaction, nitrogen fixation, and may be pathogens.

Barbel Slender, whisker-like tactile organ extending from the head of certain fishes, such as catfish and bullhead.

Basking The process of exposing the body to the Sun's warmth.

Benthos Organisms (plants and animals) that live at or near the bottom of a lake (or ocean).

Bioaccumulation A process that takes place within an organism when the rate of intake of a substance (such as a toxic chemical) is greater than the rate of excretion or conversion of that substance, resulting in a buildup of the chemical within the body.

Bioluminescence The production of visible light by living organisms such as the firefly. Light is emitted when a pigment (usually luciferin) is converted to another form without giving off heat.

Biomonitor Any organism that provides quantitative information about the quality of the environment around it. Biomonitors typically are used to detect the presence of pollutants in aquatic environments.

Bog An area having a wet, acidic substrate composed chiefly of sphagnum moss and peat, which produces a spongy mat of vegetation including shrubs and sometimes trees.

Boreal Pertaining to the northern North Temperate Zone, dominated by coniferous trees including spruce, fir, and pine.

Boulder A large, rounded mass of rock.

Browsing The process of eating plant material including leaves, shoots, or buds.

Bulblet A small bulb arising from the leaf axil.

Butylmercaptan A volatile liquid that produces the strong odor of a skunk.

Cache A place where provisions are stored; the act of storing.

Cambium A cylindrical layer of rapidly dividing tissue between the bark and wood of the stems and roots of woody plants.

Cambrian A period of the Paleozoic Era, from 570 million to 500 million years ago, when life consisted predominantly of algae and marine invertebrates.

Camouflage Concealment that alters or obscures the appearance of an organism.

Canopy The leafy upper branches of forest trees.

Carapace The upper shell of a turtle, consisting of hard, bony outer plates. Also denotes the chitinous portion of the exoskeleton covering the head and thorax of a crustacean.

Carbohydrates Any of a group of organic compounds produced by plants that includes sugars, starches, celluloses, and gums and serves as a major energy source in the diet of herbivorous animals.

Carbonate rocks A class of sedimentary rocks including limestone and dolomite, composed of calcite and the mineral dolomite respectively.

Carcass The dead body of an animal.

Carnivore An animal that feeds on the flesh of another animal.

Carotene A group of three yellow or orange pigments in plant leaves that aid in the absorption of light energy by transferring the energy to chlorophyll and act as antioxidants protecting chlorophyll from damage.

Carrion The flesh of dead and decaying animals.

Caste One of several specialized levels in a colony of social insects, such as a queen, worker, or soldier. Each caste performs distinct, specialized behaviors within the colony.

Castoreum A bitter orange-brown substance produced in two anal sacs of the beaver, that produces a strong, penetrating odor used to mark territories.

Catatonia An abnormal condition of stupor and rigidity of the limbs used by opossums to feign death.

Caterpillar The wormlike larva of a butterfly or a moth.

Celestial Pertaining to the visible sky.

Cephalothorax The fused head and thorax of arachnids and many crustaceans.

Cerci A pair of whip-like appendages at the rear of certain insects, which serve as tactile organs.

Chelae The pincer-like front claws of crustaceans or arachnids, such as a lobster or crayfish.

Chitin A compound related to cellulose that forms a horny exoskeleton, or outer covering, of insects, crustaceans, and arachnids.

Chlorophyll Any of several green pigments found in photosynthetic plants, algae, and cyanobacteria. Chlorophyll absorbs red and blue wavelengths of light, but reflects green. When it absorbs light energy, a chlorophyll molecule ultimately is used in the synthesis of ATP, which provides chemical energy for metabolism.

Chrysalis The pupa of moths and butterflies that is enclosed in a firm case or cocoon from which the adult eventually emerges after metamorphosis.

Cirque A bowl-shaped mountain basin with steep walls carved by glaciers.

Clubmoss A group of small vascular plants (genus *Lycopodium*), resembling mosses or tiny conifers and reproducing by spores.

Clutch A group of eggs laid or incubated at one time.

Cobbles Rock fragments between 64 and 256 millimeters (2½ and 10 inches) in diameter, often naturally rounded by water.

Co-dominants Two or more species that are equally dominant in a particular community.

Competition The struggle for food, space, mates, and other vital resources, by organisms of the same or different species.

Condense The process of reducing one form to another and denser form, such as a gas forming a liquid.

Conifer Any of the evergreen, needle-leaved (or scale-leaved), cone-bearing trees or shrubs such as pines, spruces, firs, cedars, and yews.

Copepods Tiny marine or freshwater crustaceans, lacking compound eyes or a carapace and usually having six pairs of appendages on the thorax. They are abundant in plankton.

Coprophagy The behavior of feeding on dung to extract vital minerals and vitamins.

Copulation The process of sexual intercourse.

Costal grooves A set of parallel, vertical grooves on the sides of some salamanders and newts.

Cretaceous A period of the Mesozoic Era, from 140 million to 65 million years ago, distinguished by the evolution and subsequent extinction of dinosaurs and the advent of flowering plants and insects.

Crop A sac-like extension of the esophagus of many birds, used to hold food for later digestion or for regurgitation to nestlings.

Crown The leaves and living branches of a tree.

Crustacean A group of predominantly aquatic arthropods (class Crustacea), including lobsters, crabs, shrimps, and barnacles, with segmented bodies, chitinous exoskeletons, and paired, jointed limbs.

Cyanobacteria Photosynthetic bacteria (class Coccogoneae or Hormogoneae), generally capable of nitrogen fixation. Cyanobacteria once were thought to be algae (blue-green algae).

Dabbling duck One of the group of ducks, including mallards and teals, that feed in shallow water.

Decibel A unit expressing the intensity of a sound.

Deciduous Dropping off of a part that is no longer needed. Deciduous trees drop their leaves in the fall.

Decomposition The process of rotting, where tissues are returned to their basic elements.

Deforestation The removal of all or most of the trees in a forested area.

Delayed implantation A process that occurs after fertilization where the embryo does not immediately implant in the uterus, but is maintained in a state of dormancy. No development takes place as long as the embryo remains unattached to the uterine lining. As a result, the normal gestation period is extended, sometimes up to a year. Also known as embryonic diapause.

Desiccation The process of drying due to the removal of water.

Detritivore Any organism that feeds on and breaks down dead plant or animal matter, returning essential nutrients to the ecosystem.

Dewlap A fold of loose skin hanging from the neck of certain animals, such as moose.

Diatom A group of microscopic, unicellular algae (phylum Chrysophyta), with cell walls containing two interlocking silica valves.

Dihedral The angle formed by the wings of a soaring bird. Typically refers to the V-shaped wing posture of soaring vultures.

Diurnal Being active during the day.

Diving ducks Ducks that dive deep underwater to obtain much of their food. They have large webbed feet, legs located well back on the body, and wings with relatively small surface areas. These adaptations aid in swimming underwater, but make it difficult for them to burst into flight. Instead, they must run across the water to build up speed before taking off.

Dorsal fin A single median fin on the back of a fish that helps to maintain an upright position when swimming.

Dorsolateral ridge Folds of skin in frogs that begin at the eye, go around the eardrum, and run on either side of the back.

Drone A male bee whose sole function is to mate with the queen bee.

Echolocation A sonar-like system used by bats (and dolphins) to locate objects by emitting high-pitched sounds that reflect off the object and return to the animal's ears (or other sensory receptors).

Elytra The chitinous forewings of a beetle or other insect, which encase the membranous hind wings that are used in flight.

Enzyme A protein produced in living cells that accelerates or catalyzes chemical reactions within an organism's cells.

Epilimnion The warmer surface layer of a lake above the thermocline.

Episodic release Periodic or sporadic letting go or emission.

Esker A long, winding ridge of gravelly and sandy material deposited by a stream flowing in or under a melting glacial ice sheet.

Esophagus A tubular passage connecting the mouth with the stomach in animals.

Ethylene A plant hormone that aids in ripening fruit.

Euphotic zone The uppermost layer of water that receives enough sunlight for photosynthesis.

Eutrophic A term denoting a lake with an abundant accumulation of nutrients, which results in dense alga growth. The decay of these organisms eventually depletes the shallow waters of oxygen.

Evaporation The change of a liquid into a gas at a temperature below the boiling point.

Evapotranspiration The process of transferring moisture from the soil to the atmosphere by plants.

Ever-growing Capable of continued growth throughout the life of the animal.

Exoskeleton The hard outer shell of an insect or crustacean that is made of chitin and provides protection or support for an organism.

Extinct No longer in existence; leaving no living representatives.

Extirpated Locally or regionally extinct.

Extraembryonic membranes A group of membranous tissues, derived from the fertilized egg, that enclose or otherwise contribute to the support of the developing embryo. They include the yolk sac, allantois, amnion, and chorion membranes.

Falcon Bird of prey (family Falconidae) with long, pointed wings. Falcons typically dive and seize prey in mid-air.

Fault A geologic term for a fracture in the bedrock in which adjacent surfaces are displaced relative to one another, caused by a shifting of the Earth's crust.

Feeding guild A group of organisms that all feed on the same resource in a similar way.

Fertilization The physical union of male and female gametes (sperm and ova in an animal or pollen and ovule in a plant).

Filamentous algae Single algae cells that form long visible chains, threads, or filaments. These filaments intertwine forming wet mats.

First-order stream A headwater stream with no tributaries.

Fir waves Alternating bands of fir trees at different stages of development. Fir waves typically develop following wind disturbance on mountain sides.

Flank The side of an animal.

Fledge To rear young until they are ready to fly or are ready for independence; the act of leaving the nest for the first time.

Floodplain A relatively flat area along a stream or river that is periodically subject to flooding.

Food web A complex set of predator-prey and consumer-resource interactions in an ecological community.

Forest fragmentation The breakup of continuous forests into small blocks separated by roads, agricultural fields, urban areas, or other human development.

Frenum A fold of membrane that restricts the motion of another body part.

Fry A recently hatched fish.

Gestation period The time a developing embryo spends in the uterus from conception until birth (pregnancy).

Glacial erratic A large boulder made of rock that is not native to the area and that was carried to the current locations by glaciers or massive ice sheets.

Glacier A huge mass of ice, formed where snow accumulation exceeds melting, and slowly flowing over a land mass.

Gnawing The process of biting or chewing with the incisors.

Gregarious The tendency to form a group with other members of the same species.

Grenville Province A geologic term for an ancient set of rocks that extend from Labrador as far to the southwest as Mexico.

Groundwater Water from rain or melting snow that collects or flows in the porous spaces in soil, sediment, and rocks beneath the surface. It is the source of water for aquifers, springs, and wells.

Groundwater seepage To pass slowly through small openings or pores in the soil.

Haemophagic Subsisting on blood.

Hallucinogen Any psychoactive compound that induces hallucinations or altered sensory experiences.

Halteres A pair of tiny hind wings used for maintaining equilibrium during flight in flies.

Hardening In trees, the physiological and biochemical process by which a tree prepares for cold weather.

Hardwood A non-conifer tree; a deciduous tree with generally harder wood than typical confer trees.

Hatchery A facility where fish eggs are hatched under artificial conditions and later sold or distributed when they reach sufficient size.

Headwaters The source water from which a stream arises.

Heartwood The nonliving central wood of a tree or woody plant that functions to support the tree. Unlike the softer sapwood, it no longer conducts water.

Heath Any low-growing shrub having small evergreen leaves.

Hemoglobin The oxygen-carrying pigment of red blood cells.

Herbaceous Describing a flowering plant lacking a woody stem that generally dies back at the end of each growing season (such as grasses and forbs).

Herbivore An animal that feeds chiefly on plants.

Heritage strains Populations or strains of a particular species that are native to a particular locality.

Hermaphrodite An organism having both male and female reproductive organs in a single individual (such as earthworms or flowering plants).

Hibernate The ability to enter an inactive state resembling deep sleep in which certain animals pass the cold winter. In hibernation, the body temperature is lowered and breathing and heart rates slow down.

Hormone Any internally secreted compound formed in endocrine glands that are transported in the blood and affect the function of other organs or tissues.

Hybridize To cross or mate two different breeds or species of animals or plants.

Hydrologic cycle The continuous sequence by which water is circulated throughout the Earth and its atmosphere.

Hypolimnion A layer of cold water in a thermally stratified lake below the thermocline.

Igneous rock Rock formed by the cooling and solidifying of molten materials either beneath the Earth's surface or at its surface (lava).

Impermeable Not permitting the passage of fluids including water.

Inseminate To introduce or inject sperm into the female's reproductive tract.

Invertebrate An animal lacking a backbone or spinal column.

Iris The round, pigmented part of the eye, perforated by the pupil. The iris regulates the amount of light entering the eye.

Iroquois Confederacy A coalition of Native American nations that originally consisted of the Mohawk, the Oneida, the Onondaga, the Cayuga, and the Seneca. The Tuscarora joined after the original five nations were formed.

Keel A longitudinal ridge.

Keratin A group of tough, fibrous proteins that form the main structural component of hair, nails, horns, feathers, and hooves.

Kettle hole lake A small, circular lake or pond formed when a large ice block broke away from a receding glacier, became buried by glacial outwash, and later melted into a kettle-shaped depression with no inlet or outlet stream.

Killing temperature The temperature at which ice crystals form within plant cells resulting in cell death.

Krummholz Literally, "twisted wood"; a stunted forest near the timberline on a mountain.

Lactation The period during which milk is produced in mammals.

Land bridge A strip of once-submerged land that connects adjacent continents and serves, at least temporarily, as a dispersal route for plants and animals.

Lateral line A row of sensory pores along the head and sides of fish (and some amphibians), used to detect water currents, vibrations, and pressure changes.

Leeward The side sheltered from the wind.

Lichen A composite organisms formed when a fungus grows symbiotically with algae.

Lignin An organic compound that binds to cellulose and strengthens plant cell walls; a chief constituent of wood.

Luciferase An enzyme that catalyzes the oxidation of luciferin and ATP, to produce light in bioluminescent organisms such as fireflies.

Lyme disease An inflammatory disease caused by a spirochete (*Borrelia burgdorferi*) that is transmitted by ticks. The disease begins as a circular rash followed by fever, joint pain, and headache. If left untreated, the disease can result in chronic arthritis and nerve and heart problems.

Macrophyte A plant large enough to be visible to the naked eye.

Magma Molten rock originating under the Earth's crust. It forms igneous rock when cooled below the surface, or volcanic rocks when it flows out over the surface as lava.

Mammary glands One of the glands in female mammals that produces milk. It is present but undeveloped in the male.

Mandibles The pincerlike mouthparts of insects and other arthropods.

Marsupium An external pouch or fold on the abdomen of most female marsupials, containing the mammary glands and in which the young continue to develop after birth.

Maternity colony A group of animals gathered at one location to give birth and raise young.

Melanistic morph The darker of two different types or varieties in a population of the same species.

Mesic Pertaining to a habitat having moderate or balanced moisture.

Mesotrophic Pertaining to lakes with an intermediate level of productivity. These lakes are commonly clear-water lakes and ponds with beds of submerged aquatic plants and medium levels of nutrients.

Metabolic rate The measure of the amount of energy expended by an organism in a given time period.

Metalimnion The layer (also called the thermocline) of water in a lake where the temperature changes rapidly with depth.

Metamorphic rock Rock that has changed form due to extreme heat, pressure, or both without becoming molten.

Metamorphosis The change in body form from one stage to the next in the life history of an organism, as from the tadpole to a frog.

Migrate The process of moving periodically from one region or climate to another.

Molecule The smallest physical unit of an element or compound, consisting of one or more like atoms (e.g., O_2) in an element and two or more different atoms in a compound (e.g., CO_2). The fundamental components of chemical compounds and the smallest part of a compound that can participate in a chemical reaction.

Morph A physically distinct form of an organism or species.

Mortality Being subject to death, or the ratio of deaths in an area to the population of that area per year (or some other measure of time).

Moss A tiny, leafy, flowerless plant, reproducing by spores and typically growing in mats on moist ground, rocks, or trees.

Moult To shed a part or all of an outer covering (feathers, exoskeleton, or skin), which subsequently is replaced by a new growth.

Muzzle The projecting snout of an animal, including the mouth and nose.

Naiad The juvenile form of the dragonfly, damselfly, or mayfly.

Native Originating in a certain place or region.

Needle ice A form of ground ice consisting of clusters of vertical ice slivers at the ground surface.

Neurotoxin A chemical that damages or destroys nervous tissue, including the brain.

Nocturnal Active at night (e.g., owls and bats).

Nymph The larval stage of certain insects, in which the juvenile resembles a small version of the adult form, but lacking fully developed wings.

Oligotrophic A lake classification in which the lake lacks nutrients such as phosphates, nitrates, and organic matter, resulting in few plants and a large amount of dissolved oxygen.

Omnivore An animal that feeds on both animal and plant material.

Operculum A bony flap covering the gill opening in some fish.

Organic compound Any compound composed of carbon and another element or a radical.

Organic material Substance derived from living organisms.

Ovipositor An organ at the end of the abdomen in certain female insects that deposits eggs.

Ovulate To discharge mature eggs from the ovary in the female reproductive tract.

Parasitism A symbiotic relationship in which the parasite benefits and the host is generally harmed. Parasites typically gain nutrition from their host, while the host loses nutrition.

Parental care Behaviors by which adults provide food, shelter, and protection for their young as they mature.

Parotoid gland A group of skin glands forming warty masses near the ear in certain toads.

Pectoral fin A fin on the side of the body behind the head in fish.

Perennial Describing a plant that has a life cycle lasting more than two years.

Periphyton Attached organisms, including algae and small crustaceans, that project from surfaces at the bottom of a freshwater environment.

Petiole The thin stalk by which a leaf is attached to a stem.

pH A measure of the acidity or alkalinity of a solution, numerically ranging from 0 (extremely acidic) to 14 (extremely alkaline), with pH 7 for neutral solutions. Each one unit change in pH is a ten-fold change in acidity or alkalinity.

Pheromone A chemical substance released by an animal that serves to influence the behavior of other members (usually the opposite sex) of the same species.

Photosynthesis A complex process whereby organic materials, especially carbohydrates, are formed from carbon dioxide, water, and other molecules using sunlight as the source of energy.

Phytochromes A group of pigments found in the cells of green plants and some green algae that absorb red light and regulate dormancy, seed germination, and flowering.

Phytoplankton Free-floating algae, protists, and cyanobacteria capable of photosynthesis and serving as the base of the aquatic food web.

Pioneer species A species that colonizes previously barren soils.

Plastron The ventral shell of a turtle.

Pleistocene The epoch beginning about two million years ago and ending 10,000 years ago, characterized by ice ages and the advent of modern humans.

Plover Any wading bird of the family Charadriidae, having a rounded body, short tail, and short bill.

Pollinator An animal that carries pollen from one flower to another.

Precipitation Any form of water that falls to the ground, such as rain, snow, sleet, or hail.

Precocial Refers to a newborn animal that is active and able to move freely from birth or hatching, and needing little or no parental care.

Prehensile Adapted for grasping by wrapping around an object (e.g., the tail of opossums).

Primary consumer Any organism that feeds on plant material.

Primary producer Any green plant or microorganism capable of photosynthesis.

Primary succession The slow formation of plant and animal life in barren areas devoid of topsoil (e.g., the revegetation of a lava field).

Proboscis The elongate mouth parts of certain insects, adapted for sucking or piercing.

Protozoan A large group of single-celled organisms (called protists) that live in water or as parasites (including amoebas, flagellates, foraminiferans, and ciliates).

Pulpwood The soft wood of spruce or other conifers used for making paper.

Pupae A nonfeeding stage between the larva and adult in which the larva undergoes complete metamorphosis within a protective cocoon or hardened case.

Raptor Bird of prey that uses its feet to capture prey; raptors have exceptionally good vision, sharp, hooked beaks, and powerful feet with curved, sharp talons.

Ray cells A group of radial cells in wood and phloem of a plant.

Regurgitate To cast up partially digested food to feed offspring.

Resin Any substance that oozes from certain trees and plants.

Respiration The process of inhalation and exhalation of air (breathing). Alternatively, the chemical processes in an organism by which oxygen is conveyed to tissues and cells, and used to generate cellular energy.

Riffles A set of rapids in a brook or stream.

Runoff The excess water that drains off the land into streams and rivers.

Rutting season Period during the fall when adult male deer mark territories and fight with other males, in an attempt to attract females for mating.

Salivary gland A gland that secretes saliva into the mouth.

Samara A winged fruit that typically contains a single seed, such as that produced by maple trees.

Sapwood The outer wood just inside the cambium of a tree trunk that is active in transporting water.

Scavenger An animal that feeds on dead or decaying matter.

Scute A bony external plate or scale making up a turtle's shell.

Second-order stream A stream formed by the joining of two or more first-order streams.

Secondary consumer Any animal that feeds on plant-eating animals.

Sedimentary rock Rock that formed through the layered deposition of sediments that later become solidified into rock

Serrated Having an edge composed of saw-like teeth.

Sexual maturity The age (or stage) when an organism is capable of reproduction.

Shrub A low-growing, woody plant usually with several stems arising from the base instead of a single trunk.

Silt A sedimentary material consisting of very fine particles deposited by a river or other water body.

Spawn To deposit eggs or sperm directly into the water.

Spinneret An anatomical structure that spiders and certain insect larvae use to secrete the silk threads they use to build webs or cocoons.

Splake A hybrid fish resulting from the mating of a brook trout and a lake trout.

Sport fish Any fish that is prized for the sport it gives the angler.

Stocking The act of releasing into the wild fish that have been raised in a hatchery.

Substrate A surface on which an organism grows or is attached.

Suckling The process of taking milk at the breast or udder.

Surface tension A property of liquids such that their surfaces behave like a thin, elastic film because water molecules at or near the surface are more strongly attracted to each other, while water molecules not near the surface are attracted to other molecules equally in all directions. Surface tension allows a liquid to support light objects, such as water striders.

Stomate A minute pore in the surface of a leaf or stem through which gases and water vapor pass.

Stratification The formation of layers or strata.

Streamlined Having a shape with the least possible resistance to a current of air or water (e.g., a teardrop shape).

Symbiosis The process by which two dissimilar organisms live together. The relationship between the two organisms may be mutualism, commensalism, amensalism, or parasitism.

Talons The sharp, curved claws of birds of prey, used for grasping or tearing prey.

Tannin A compound, including tannic acid, that occurs naturally in the bark and fruit of various plants.

Terminal moraines An accumulation of boulders, stones, or other debris carried and deposited at the leading edge of a glacier.

Terrestrial Living on or in the ground.

Territory An area occupied by an animal or group that is defended vigorously against intruders of the same species.

Thallus A type of body found among lichens, mosses, liverworts, many algae, and fungi that is not differentiated into roots, stems, or leaves.

Thermal updraft A mass of warm air that rises because the ground surface is heated by the Sun.

Thermocline A layer of water in a lake that separates warmer surface waters from cold, deep-water regions. The water temperature across the thermocline changes dramatically.

Theropod Any carnivorous dinosaur that had short forelimbs, walked or ran on its hind legs, and was a member of the suborder Theropoda.

Thorax The region of the insect body between the head and abdomen.

Timberline The elevation on a mountain above which trees do not grow.

Topography The three-dimensional relief or surface configuration of an area.

Torpor A short-term state of decreased body temperature and reduced metabolism in an animal.

Toxin A poisonous substance produced by living cells or organisms that is capable of causing damage or disease when introduced into the body.

Tragus A tongue-like projection of skin-covered cartilage in front of the ear opening (espically prominent in bats).

Tributary A stream that flows to a larger stream or river.

Trophic Refers to the feeding habits of different organisms within a food web.

Tubercle A small, rounded projection or lump.

Tundra A treeless area of Arctic regions, having permanently frozen soil and low-growing vegetation such as lichens, mosses, and stunted shrubs.

Turbid Having sediment or other particles suspended in solution.

Tymbale A membrane stretched across an opening in certain insects that vibrates with sound waves much like an eardrum in mammals.

Tympanum The thin, semitransparent, oval-shaped membrane, also called an ear drum, that separates the middle ear from the external ear, and vibrates in response to sound waves.

Underfur The fine, soft, thick fur under the longer, coarser outer hairs in many mammals.

Understory The shrubs and plants growing beneath the main canopy of a forest.

Underwings The pair of hind wings of an insect such as a moth.

Upland An area of land lying above the zone where flooding occasionally occurs.

Uplift A geologic term describing the process of upheaval where land rises to a higher elevation. Uplift is involved in the process of mountain building.

Vapor The gaseous state of a substance.

Vegetarian An herbivore that consumes only plant material.

Vegetative A type of asexual reproduction in plants, such as fission or budding, that does not require the union of gametes.

Velvet The furry covering on the developing antlers of deer.

Venomous Having a gland for secreting venom; refers to animals able to inflict a poisoned bite or sting.

Vibrissa One of the stiff, bristly hairs (whiskers) growing adjacent to the mouth of certain mammals.

Viviparous Giving birth to living young that develop within the mother's body rather than hatching from eggs.

Vitrification Process by which a liquid such as water, through very rapid cooling or the introduction of antifreeze agents, forms ice without sharp crystals that might rupture cells.

Watershed The region enclosed by ridgelines where all surface water drains downslope into a river, river system, or other body of water.

Wattles Fleshy lobes hanging down from the throat or chin of certain birds (e.g., turkeys).

Weaning The process of substituting other food for the mother's milk in the diet of a young mammal.

Weathering A processes by which rocks exposed to weather undergo chemical decomposition and physical disintegration.

Wingspan The distance between the wing tips.

Winter drought The combination of cold temperatures and constant winds that depletes plants of moisture during the cold winter months.

Wisconsin glacial period The last ice age in the Pleistocene epoch, which ended about 10,000 years ago, when thick sheets of ice covered many areas of the Northern Hemisphere.

Yard A tract of land used as winter pasture for deer, typically in sheltered areas such as conifer swamps.

Zooplankton Microorganisms that consists of tiny animals, such as rotifers, copepods, and krill.

Species Checklist

COMMON FISH

- ☐ Bass, Largemouth
- ☐ Bass, Rock
- ☐ Bass, Smallmouth
- ☐ Bullhead, Brown
- ☐ Chub, Creek
- ☐ Chub, Lake
- ☐ Cisco
- ☐ Dace, Eastern Blacknose
- ☐ Dace. Longnose
- ☐ Dace, Northern Redbelly
- ☐ Dace, Pearl
- ☐ Darter, Tessellated
- ☐ Fallfish
- ☐ Killifish, Banded
- ☐ Minnow, Bluntnose
- ☐ Minnow, Brassy
- ☐ Minnow, Cutlips
- ☐ Minnow, Flathead
- ☐ Mudminnow, Central
- ☐ Perch, Yellow
- ☐ Pickerel, Chain
- ☐ Pike, Northern
- ☐ Pumpkinseed
- ☐ Salmon, Atlantic
- ☐ Sculpin, Slimy
- ☐ Shiner. Bridle
- ☐ Shiner, Common
- ☐ Shiner, Golden
- ☐ Smelt, Rainbow
- ☐ Sucker, Longnose
- ☐ Sucker, White
- ☐ Sunfish, Redbreast
- ☐ Trout, Brook
- ☐ Trout, Brown
- ☐ Trout, Lake
- ☐ Trout, Rainbow

☐ Walleye
☐ Whitefish, Lake
☐ Whitefish, Round

AMPHIBIANS AND REPTILES
☐ Bullfrog
☐ Frog, Gray Tree
☐ Frog, Green
☐ Frog, Leopard
☐ Frog, Mink
☐ Frog, Pickerel
☐ Frog, Wood
☐ Newt, Red-spotted
☐ Peeper, Spring
☐ Rattlesnake, Timber
☐ Salamander, Northern Dusky
☐ Salamander, Northern Two-lined
☐ Salamander, Red-backed
☐ Salamander, Spotted
☐ Salamander, Spring
☐ Snake, Brown
☐ Snake, Garter
☐ Snake, Milk
☐ Snake, Northern Water
☐ Snake, Red-bellied
☐ Snake, Ribbon
☐ Snake, Ringneck
☐ Snake, Smooth Green
☐ Toad, American
☐ Turtle, Painted
☐ Turtle, Snapping
☐ Turtle, Wood

BREEDING BIRDS
☐ Bittern, American
☐ Blackbird, Red-winged
☐ Blackbird, Rusty
☐ Bluebird, Eastern
☐ Bunting, Indigo
☐ Catbird, Gray
☐ Chickadee, Black-capped
☐ Chickadee, Boreal

- ☐ Creeper, Brown
- ☐ Crow, American
- ☐ Cuckoo, Black-billed
- ☐ Cuckoo, Yellow-billed
- ☐ Dove, Mourning
- ☐ Duck, American Black
- ☐ Duck, Ring-necked
- ☐ Duck, Wood
- ☐ Eagle, Bald
- ☐ Falcon, Peregrine
- ☐ Finch, Purple
- ☐ Flicker, Northern
- ☐ Flycatcher, Alder
- ☐ Flycatcher, Great Crested
- ☐ Flycatcher, Least
- ☐ Flycatcher, Olive-sided
- ☐ Flycatcher, Yellow-bellied
- ☐ Goldfinch, American
- ☐ Goose, Canada
- ☐ Goshawk, Northern
- ☐ Grackle, Common
- ☐ Grebe, Pied-billed
- ☐ Grosbeak, Rose-breasted
- ☐ Grosbeak, Evening
- ☐ Grouse, Ruffed
- ☐ Grouse, Spruce
- ☐ Gull, Herring
- ☐ Hawk, Broad-winged
- ☐ Hawk, Cooper's
- ☐ Hawk, Red-shouldered
- ☐ Hawk, Red-tailed
- ☐ Hawk, Sharp-shinned
- ☐ Heron, Great Blue
- ☐ Hummingbird, Ruby-throated
- ☐ Jay, Blue
- ☐ Jay, Gray
- ☐ Junco, Dark-eyed
- ☐ Kestral, American
- ☐ Killdeer
- ☐ Kingbird, Eastern
- ☐ Kingfisher, Belted
- ☐ Kinglet, Golden-crowned

- ☐ Kinglet, Ruby-crowned
- ☐ Loon, Common
- ☐ Mallard
- ☐ Merganser, Common
- ☐ Merlin
- ☐ Nuthatch, Red-breasted
- ☐ Nuthatch, White-breasted
- ☐ Oriole, Baltimore
- ☐ Osprey
- ☐ Ovenbird
- ☐ Owl, Barred
- ☐ Owl, Great Horned
- ☐ Owl, Northern Saw-whet
- ☐ Phoebe, Eastern
- ☐ Raven, Common
- ☐ Redstart, American
- ☐ Robin, American
- ☐ Sandpiper, Spotted
- ☐ Sapsucker, Yellow-bellied
- ☐ Siskin, Pine
- ☐ Sparrow, American Tree
- ☐ Sparrow, Chipping
- ☐ Sparrow, House
- ☐ Sparrow, Song
- ☐ Sparrow, Swamp
- ☐ Sparrow, White-throated
- ☐ Starling, European
- ☐ Swallow, Bank
- ☐ Swallow, Barn
- ☐ Swallow, Tree
- ☐ Swift, Chimney
- ☐ Tanager, Scarlet
- ☐ Thrasher, Brown
- ☐ Thrush, Hermit
- ☐ Thrush, Swainson's
- ☐ Thrush, Wood
- ☐ Towhee, Eastern
- ☐ Turkey, Wild
- ☐ Veery
- ☐ Vireo, Blue-headed
- ☐ Vireo, Red-eyed
- ☐ Vulture, Turkey

- ☐ Warbler, Black-and-white
- ☐ Warbler, Blackburnian
- ☐ Warbler, Blackpoll
- ☐ Warbler, Black-throated Blue
- ☐ Warbler, Black-throated Green
- ☐ Warbler, Canada
- ☐ Warbler, Chestnut-sided
- ☐ Warbler, Magnolia
- ☐ Warbler, Mourning
- ☐ Warbler, Nashville
- ☐ Warbler, Northern Parula
- ☐ Warbler, Pine
- ☐ Warbler, Yellow
- ☐ Warbler, Yellow-rumped
- ☐ Waterthrush, Northern
- ☐ Waxwing, Cedar
- ☐ Woodcock, American
- ☐ Woodpecker, Black-backed
- ☐ Woodpecker, Downy
- ☐ Woodpecker, Hairy
- ☐ Woodpecker, Pileated
- ☐ Woodpecker, Three-toed
- ☐ Wood-Pewee, Eastern
- ☐ Wren, House
- ☐ Wren, Winter
- ☐ Yellowthroat, Common

MAMMALS

- ☐ Bat, Big Brown
- ☐ Bat, Eastern Pipistrelle
- ☐ Bat, Hoary
- ☐ Bat, Little Brown
- ☐ Bat, Red
- ☐ Bat, Silver Haired
- ☐ Bear, American Black
- ☐ Beaver
- ☐ Bobcat
- ☐ Chipmunk, Eastern
- ☐ Coyote
- ☐ Deer, White-tail
- ☐ Fisher
- ☐ Fox, Red

- ☐ Fox, Gray
- ☐ Hare, Snowshoe
- ☐ Lemming, Northern Bog
- ☐ Lemming, Southern Bog
- ☐ Martin, Pine
- ☐ Mink, American
- ☐ Mole, Hairy-tailed
- ☐ Mole, Star-nosed
- ☐ Moose
- ☐ Mouse, Deer
- ☐ Mouse, Meadow Jumping
- ☐ Mouse, White-footed
- ☐ Mouse, Woodland Jumping
- ☐ Muskrat
- ☐ Opossum, Virginia
- ☐ Otter, River
- ☐ Porcupine
- ☐ Rabbit, Eastern Cottontail
- ☐ Raccoon
- ☐ Shrew, Masked
- ☐ Shrew, Short-tailed
- ☐ Shrew, Water
- ☐ Skunk, Striped
- ☐ Squirrel, Eastern Gray
- ☐ Squirrel, Northern Flying
- ☐ Squirrel, Red
- ☐ Squirrel, Southern Flying
- ☐ Vole, Meadow
- ☐ Vole, Rock
- ☐ Vole, Southern Red-backed
- ☐ Vole, Woodland
- ☐ Weasel, Long-tailed
- ☐ Weasel, Short-tailed
- ☐ Woodchuck

Index